ALEXANDER'S TOMB

ALEXANDER'S TOMB

THE TWO THOUSAND YEAR OBSESSION TO FIND THE LOST CONQUEROR

NICHOLAS J. SAUNDERS

BASIC
BOOKS

A Member of the Perseus Books Group
New York

Books published by Basic Books are available at special discounts for bulk
purchases in the United States by corporations, institutions, and other or-
ganizations. For more information, please contact the Special Markets Department at the Perseus Books Group, 11 Cambridge Center, Cambridge
MA 02142, or call (617) 252-5298 or (800) 255-1514, or e-mail spe-
cial.markets@perseusbooks.com.

Designed by Lisa Kreinbrink

Library of Congress Cataloging-in-Publication Data
Saunders, Nicholas J.
   Alexander's tomb : the two thousand year obsession to find the lost con-
queror / Nicholas J. Saunders.
        p. cm.
   Includes bibliographical references and index.
   ISBN-13: 978-0-465-07202-6 (alk. paper)
   ISBN-10: 0-465-07202-X (alk. paper)
   1. Alexander, the Great, 356-323 B.C.--Tomb. 2. Alexander, the Great,
356-323 B.C.--Death and burial. I. Title: Two thousand year obsession to
find the lost conqueror. II. Title.

   DF234.2.S28 2006
   938'.07092--dc22
                                                2006000973

06 07 08 / 10 9 8 7 6 5 4 3 2 1

For Alexander and Roxanne, naturally

CONTENTS

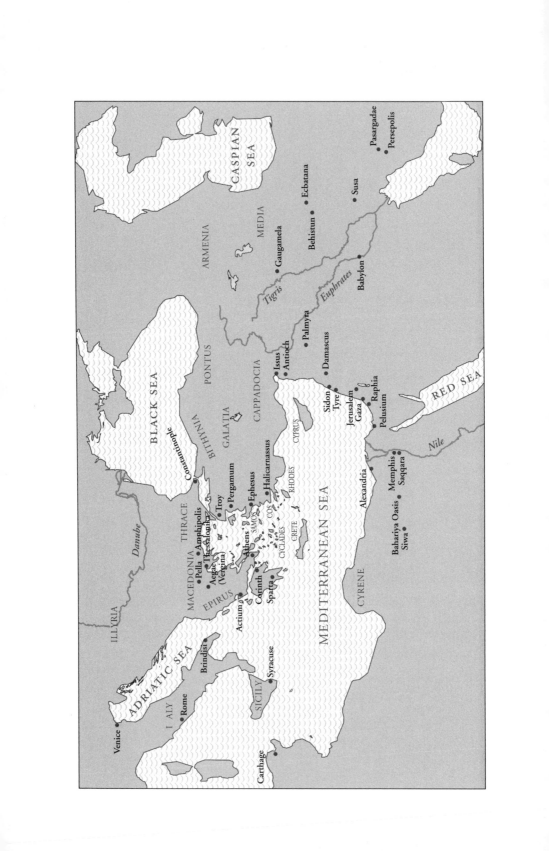

TIMELINE

July 20, 356 B.C.E. Birth of Alexander at Pella.

343–340 Alexander taught by Aristotle at Mieza.

340–339 Alexander regent at Pella in Philip's absence.

336 Philip assassinated at Aegae; Alexander becomes king as Alexander III.

336 Alexander takes command of the invasion of Persia and crosses into Asia. Alexander and Hephaestion pay respects to Achilles and Patroclus at the heroes' graves near Troy.

336 Battle of the river Granicus.

September 334 Alexander conquers Halicarnassus and sees the mausoleum.

November 333 Alexander defeats Persian king Darius at the battle of Issus.

January–March 331 Alexander visits Siwa Oasis and is welcomed as "Son of Ammon"; founds Alexandria on Egypt's Mediterranean coast.

October 1, 331 Alexander defeats Darius at the battle of Gaugamela.

October–December 331 Alexander marches south to Babylon, Susa, and Persepolis. Visits the tomb of Cyrus the Great at Pasargadae.

Spring 329 Alexander crosses the Hindu Kush to Bactra.

Spring 327 Capture of the Sogdian rock; Alexander marries Roxanne.

September–October 325 Alexander marches through the Gedrosian desert.

October 324 Alexander's close friend Hephaestion dies in Ecbatana, Alexander orders the body mummified.

April–May 323 Alexander oversees Hephaestion's funeral in Babylon.

June 10, 323 Alexander dies in Babylon at age 33.

323–321 Alexander's mummified remains lay in state in Babylon; Alexander's hearse prepared.

321 Alexander's hearse hijacked by Ptolemy near Damascus, taken to Memphis and buried.

Spring 320 Perdiccas invades Egypt to retrieve Alexander's body, is defeated by Ptolemy and murdered by his own men.

317 Olympias murders Philip III Arrhidaios.

316 Cassander has Olympias stoned to death.

309 Polyperchon murders Alexander's mistress Barsine and their illegitimate son Heracles on Cassander's advice; Cassander murders Alexander's wife Roxanne and their legitimate son, Alexander IV, at Amphipolis.

305 Ptolemy is crowned king-pharaoh of Egypt.

298–283 Likely years for Ptolemy moving Alexander's body from Memphis to Alexandria and burying it in the first tomb.

283 Ptolemy dies, and his son Ptolemy II Philadelphus is crowned king-pharaoh.

275–274 Ptolemaia festival in Alexandria in which the Grand Procession of Ptolemy Philadelphus was a part.

215 Alexander reburied in a new (second) tomb within the Soma funerary park built by Ptolemy IV Philopater.

89–90 Ptolemy X melts down Alexander's golden sarcophagus and replaces it with one of glass or crystal.

48 Julius Caesar visits Alexander's tomb.

31 Cleopatra VII takes gold from Alexander's tomb to pay for continuing fight against Octavian.

30 Alexandria conquered by Octavian, who visits Alexander's tomb.

130 C.E. Roman emperor Hadrian visits Alexandria, and probably Alexander's tomb.

199 Roman emperor Septimus Severus visits Alexandria and seals up Alexander's tomb, possibly with secret books inside.

215 Roman emperor Caracalla visits and removes items from Alexander's tomb; builds wall around the Brucheum.

297–298 Roman emperor Diocletian besieges Alexandria, causes destruction to the Brucheum district, and erects his eponymous column.

324 Roman emperor Constantine I (the Great) proclaims Christianity the official religion of the empire.

325 Bishop Ossius visits Alexandria; Council of Nicaea; Bishop Makarios discovers the tomb of Christ in Jerusalem.

360–363 Alexandria's Bishop Georgias murdered after announcing he might destroy the city's temple to the Genius (identified possibly as Alexander's tomb).

365 Earthquake and tsunami damage Alexandria.

390–391 Libanius writes letter to the emperor possibly inferring Alexander's body on display in Alexandria.

391 Christian riots in Alexandria destroy the Serapeum and possibly also Alexander's tomb.

400 John Chrysostom asks where is Alexander's tomb and does anyone know on what day Alexander died.

642 Alexandria surrendered to Muslim Arab general Amr-ibn-al-As.

870 Alexandria shrinks behind new city walls built by Sultan Ahmed-Ibn-Tulun.

1515–1517 Arab traveler Leo Africanus visits Alexandria and describes the greenstone sarcophagus in the Attarine Mosque.

1573 Map of Alexandria by G. Braun and F. Hogenberg published in Cologne.

1670–1682 Arab traveler Evliya Celebi visits Alexandria and describes the greenstone sarcophagus in the Attarine Mosque, observing its hieroglyphic decoration and hinting at its use as a basin for ritual ablutions.

1798 The French savant Dominique Vivant Denon travels to Egypt with Napoleon, finds and removes the greenstone sarcophagus from the Attarine Mosque.

1801 English scholar and traveler Edward Daniel Clarke retrieves the greenstone sarcophagus (which he identifies as Alexander's tomb) for the British. Sarcophagus taken to the British Museum in London.

1805 Clarke publishes his book, *The Tomb of Alexander*.

1822 Jean-Francois Champollion announces his decipherment of Egyptian hieroglyphs and soon afterward the Alexander Sarcophagus in the British Museum is realized to belong to the Egyptian pharaoh Nectanebo II.

1850 In Alexandria, Greek-born dragoman, Ambroise Schilizzi, announces discovery of Alexander's mummy and tomb in the depths of the Nabi Daniel Mosque.

1851 French archaeologist Auguste Mariette begins excavating at Memphis-Saqqara, and discovers the Serapeum and the Philosophers Circle of Greek statues.

1866 Mahmoud Bey el-Falaki begins excavations across Alexandria to produce a map of the ancient city for French emperor Napoleon III.

1887 Ottoman (Turkish) painter and archaeologist Osman Hamdi Bey discovers elaborate sarcophagus in the royal Phoenician cemetery at Sidon. After brief association with Alexander it is identified as belonging to king Abdalonymus.

1888 German archaeologist Heinrich Schliemann arrives in Alexandria to search for Alexander's tomb beneath the Nabi Daniel mosque. He leaves after failing to get permission to excavate.

1872 Mahmoud Bey el-Falaki publishes his investigations and map of ancient Alexandria in Copenhagen as *Mémoire sur l'antique Alexandrie*.

1893 Greek named Ioannides announces discovery of the tombs of Alexander and Cleopatra VII behind subterranean bronze doors in the Chatby district of Alexandria.

1907 Italian archaeologist, Evaristo Breccia, director of Alexandria's Graeco-Roman Museum, discovers a pile of alabaster slabs in the Latin Cemeteries area of the eastern city.

1930s Italian archaeologist, Achille Adriani, Breccia's successor, investigates and reassembles the Alabaster Tomb, thinking it might be Alexander's tomb.

1950s Greek café waiter Stelios Koumtasos begins digging throughout Alexandria in search of Alexander's tomb.

June 1961 Professor Peter Fraser of Oxford University meets Koumatsos in Alexandrian tea room to appraise the latter's "Alexander Book."

November 1977 Manolis Andronikos discovers the rich unplundered Tomb II at Vergina in Macedonia, northern Greece, and ascribes it to King Philip II.

1979 Stephan Schwartz holds a remote-viewing séance at the Alabaster Tomb.

1995 Liana Souvaltzi announces Alexander's tomb is at Siwa oasis in the western Egyptian desert.

2000 Achille Adriani's research into the Alabaster Tomb, and his identification of it as Alexander's sepulchre, is published posthumously as *La Tomba di Alessandro*.

2002 Retired Greek army general Triantafyllos Papazois launches English-language website to publicize his interpretation that Alexander, not Philip II, was buried in Tomb II at Vergina.

2002–2004 Englishman Andrew Chugg reopens the case for Nectanebo II's sarcophagus being Alexander's tomb, and suggests that Alexander may lie in St. Mark's basilica in Venice. Publishes his book, *The Lost Tomb of Alexander the Great*.

INTRODUCTION:
GHOSTS IN RUINS

THERE IS A SENSE OF HISTORY IN THIS PLACE—a feeling of standing where great events once unfolded. Wind-driven clouds chase shadows across the antique land. Below me, the ancient river Strymon flows toward the Aegean through a lush green plain splashed with springtime color. To the east, sunlight sparkles on Mount Pangaeum with its thickly wooded flanks concealing ancient gold and silver mines. The wind that blows down from Bulgaria through the Rupel gorge seems to carry the voices of those who once lived here.

This is Macedonia in northern Greece, and I am standing amid the remains of ancient Amphipolis.[1] This once thriving city belonged to Alexander the Great, and from here he launched his bid for one of history's most spectacular empires. Amphipolis is a mirror of Alexander's age and of his life. In its reflection we see dimly the splendor and tragedy of a man who changed history, a man who still fires imaginations after two thousand years.

Philip II, Alexander's father, stormed the city in 357 B.C.E., inaugurating a Macedonian tradition of siegecraft that his son later used to devastating effect, from the Mediterranean coast to beyond the Hindu Kush.[2] Amphipolis was Alexander's last glimpse of home as he set out for Asia in the late spring of 334 B.C.E.—some 2,340 years ago—never to return.[3] His wife, the Bactrian princess Roxanne, and his only legitimate child, Alexander IV, were held captive here after his death. Later, in 309 B.C.E., they were cut down by Cassander, the most spiteful of Alexander's successors. Heirs to the largest empire the world had ever seen, their bodies were quickly disposed of in tombs that have never been found.

During the heady years of Alexander's reign, as victory followed victory, vast quantities of gold and silver bullion were funneled back to Amphipolis. The royal mint here produced 13 million silver *tetradrachm* coins in eighteen years.[4] This made the city the leading banker and center of the wealthiest state of the time.[5] Yet all that surrounds me now is a carpet of billowing grass. Where did all that wealth go?

In the hills beyond the road, four hundred rock-cut tombs cluster behind bushes and trees. All are empty now, robbed of their gold and bones in antiquity. Once their inhabitants walked the streets where I am standing and talked of the great deeds of their invincible king. A glimpse of the city's former majesty is displayed in the local museum—a magnificent silver ossuary crowned with a golden wreath of olive leaves, an evocative but silent witness to the metalsmith's art and the status of one of the city's wealthier inhabitants.[6]

Yet among all these tombs there is none for Alexander. The man who changed the world, overthrew empires, spread Hellenism as far as India, and inspired loyalty and loathing in equal parts has no tomb. All that remains of Alexander is the force of his personality and the story of his astonishing deeds.

I retrace my steps down past the old city walls and cross a bridge to the western bank of the river, where I view the faded white sculpture known as the Lion of Amphipolis.[7] In 1937 archaeologists reassembled it from fragments and mounted it on a pedestal of blocks dredged from the river where they had been used in a medieval dam. The monument may have been a tomb marker or a memorial to a native son,[8] perhaps Laomedon, a naval officer in Alexander's fleet, or even Nearchus, the king's admiral and companion.[9] There is no inscription, and the one memorialized remains anonymous in this landscape of former glories.

Amphipolis, the silvered city of Alexander, is now just one more archaeological site. Since Alexander's time, empires have fallen, paganism has died, and Christianity, Islam, and modernity have reshaped the land. Two thousand years have passed, but as we walk the city's rutted streets, we feel the pull of Alexander's world.

We are drawn toward him, caught fast in the web of one of history's greatest unsolved mysteries. How did he die in Babylon? Why was his golden mummy hijacked to Egypt? How many tombs did he have and where are they now?

This is not an account of Alexander's brief, spectacular life, but of his momentous and unexplained death, his multiple burials, and the never-ending quest for a man-god's final resting place. This is the story of the search for Alexander's tomb over the course of two thousand years. Although Alexander himself has never slipped from memory or history, his mausoleum has been lost.

In the search for Alexander's tomb, we travel across the ancient world, witness extraordinary events, and encounter some of history's most famous and infamous figures. Along the way, from Macedonia to Mesopotamia, from Egypt to India and back again, we are ambushed by intrigue, deception, greed, and murder, seduced by astonishing wealth, drawn to military genius and extraordinary acts of bravery, repulsed by appalling brutality, and mystified by claims to divinity. We pick our way through contradictory accounts, intrigued and amused by the many personalities who claim to have discovered his tomb. We learn that archaeology can be hijacked to serve political ends.

In this world of history and imagination, of archaeology and fantasy, Alexander became immortal. We know of his epic marches and stunning victories, but what of the people who passed by the tomb during its time among the living? When did they come and what did they see? What legends did they hear, and what tales did they spin?

Alexander's tomb is as powerful as an idea as it ever was as a physical place. It has been a lodestone for the worlds of classical paganism, Christianity, and Islam, and a sorcerer's stone for history, archaeology, and the tortured politics of the modern world. Alexander's life was short, but the aftermath of his death—some three hundred years before Christ—is surely the longest postmortem affair in human history. The search for the tomb is an epic tale whose final chapter remains unwritten.

THE CLOAK
OF IMMORTALITY

THE SUN RISES ABOVE THE PALACE ROOMS OF PELLA, the capital of Macedonia, unfurling a carpet of pale light over the pebbled mosaics. Inside a small but luxurious room, a mother cradles her newborn son. She hears the sound of running feet and chinking armor, which stops suddenly outside the heavy oak door. A key turns, the door creaks open, the messenger places a note in the hands of an earnest attendant.

Queen Olympias strains to listen as her companion reads softly to avoid disturbing the two-week-old child. Astounding news! The great temple of Artemis in Ephesus has mysteriously caught fire and burned to the ground. When they learned of the event, the Persian magi fore-told the destruction of Asia. Olympias smiles to herself. The portentous event will forever mark the advent of her son Alexander into the world.

As her companion lights the altar, Olympias lays the baby on a pile of blankets and moves across the room to a basket. Removing the lid, she reaches carefully inside and removes a huge snake that coils and writhes as incense fills the room. It is time for Olympias to offer thanks to the gods for her newborn son.

This scene, or something like it, occurred in high summer of 356 B.C.E., according to legend. Alexander was born on July 20, and the event was embellished with rumors fanned by sycophantic courtiers; later stories emphasized Olympias's volatile, ambitious temperament and streak of mysticism.

Of Alexander's beginnings, legends and myths are mainly what we have.[1] According to one legend, Olympias on her wedding night dreamed of being penetrated by a thunderbolt. A few months later, another legend recorded that her husband, King Philip II, dreamed of sealing her vagina with wax and later spied her embracing a serpent. Another version of Alexander's supernatural origins is contained in *The Alexander Romance*, a collection of legendary tales concerning Alexander's life and adventures that began to circulate soon after his death.[2] According to the *Romance*, the Egyptian pharaoh Nectanebo II disguised himself as the ram-horned god Ammon and made love to Olympias, leaving her pregnant with Alexander.[3]

Alexander, of course, had a natural father, but throughout his life he was told of his heroic genealogy. As a princess of the royal house of Epirus, Olympias never tired of telling her son of his descent through her bloodline from Achilles. His father Philip counted Heracles and Dionysus among his ancestors.

The past stalked the present, goading Alexander to excel. In every act, dream, or wind-blown rustle of leaves, the gods could manifest their will, foretelling greatness, joy, tragedy, or disaster. Alexander's world was saturated with age-old traditions reaching back into the realms of sorcery, divination, and oracles.[4] From his earliest years, Alexander foresaw that nature and nurture were equal partners in propelling him toward a life unlike that of any man before him.

Most of the men who charged across the earth with Alexander were boyhood companions of his from the royal court at Pella. Some were Alexander's age and others were slightly older. They functioned as informal advisers to the young prince, but all became part of his charmed inner circle.[5] Most were royal pages—an institution Philip invented to educate the sons of the Macedonian nobility. A royal page was in effect a pampered hostage, guaranteeing his father's loyalty to Philip. Hephaestion, Craterus, Ptolemy, Perdiccas, Nearchus, Leonnatus, and Eumenes were part of the young Alexander's dazzling cadre of ambitious and gifted young men united by their unswerving loyalty to him.

Philip distrusted Olympias's mysticism and was eager to remove Alexander from her influence. He ordered that Alexander be schooled among the idyllic surroundings of Mieza in western Macedonia. There

Philip ensured that his son and friends were educated in Hellenic ways, courtly ritual, and war. He appointed Aristotle as their intellectual guide. In the lush foothills of Mount Bermion, Alexander was tutored in literature, religion, rhetoric, and natural history.[6]

Here Alexander first read Homer and Herodotus, Aeschylus and Sophocles. He was drawn to Euripides and learned by heart the playwright's famous *Bacchae*, an epic of Dionysus whose wild and wanton cult featured prominently in Macedonian religion.

Alexander loved to read, but he loved to hunt even more. He started hunting foxes and birds and later bears and the lions that roamed Macedonia at the time (only the king and his descendants had the right to hunt lions). Alexander's bucolic isolation was more apparent than real, for Pella was only a fast horse ride away.

From his earliest years Alexander was recognized as precocious and quick-witted, with an almost unnerving grasp of people and situations. Among the leafy paths of Mieza Alexander honed these qualities as he forged lifelong bonds with friends and advisers who would go to the ends of the earth with him and help sharpen his character.

Of all these companions, one struck an immediate rapport with Alexander that only death would end. Hephaestion was a handsome young man, the same age as Alexander. Vain, spiteful, and overbearing according to some, Hephaestion was defined by his utter devotion to his prince. He even took Alexander's opinions as his own. Alexander loved Hephaestion, and Hephaestion owed everything to Alexander. Their deep lifelong emotional attachment was formed during these early days. Reading the *Iliad*, Alexander identified with heroic Achilles and cast Hephaestion as Achilles's doomed lover Patroclus.

Whether sex, love, or some indefinable psychological interdependence, the relationship between Alexander and Hephaestion was endlessly analyzed in antiquity, as it is today. From the early days at Mieza, their affair elicited scabrous reactions. Olympias loathed Hephaestian for his hold over Alexander's affections and blamed him for her son's lack of interest in women. Philip also disapproved and even sent the courtesan Kallixeina to break his son's indifference.[7]

Alexander had other friends as well. Craterus was the son of a nobleman from the mountains of Orestis. A fierce patriot, he was loyal to

Alexander as prince and royal heir. Tough and daring, Craterus became a brilliant commander, adored by his men.[8]

At Mieza, Alexander witnessed the early signs of jealous rivalry between his beloved Hephaestion and Craterus. Alexander quickly mastered the art of dealing with those who clashed as they vied for his affections. Hephaestion and Craterus tested him sorely, even drawing swords and coming to blows on one occasion. Alexander "swore by Zeus Ammon and the rest of the gods that these were the two men he loved best in the world, but that if he ever heard them quarelling again, he would kill them both."[9] Alexander never resolved the lifelong antipathy between these two men.

Perdiccas, a scion of the Oresteian royal house, was another youthful companion. His arrogance and vaulting ambition earned him respect and suspicion in equal parts.[10] He would prove a loyal friend and effective general. After Hephaestion died, Alexander made Perdiccas grand vizier of the empire, and some said that Alexander on his deathbed gave his signet ring to Perdiccas.

At Mieza, Ptolemy son of Lagus was overshadowed by his more illustrious peers, as he hailed from a lesser branch of Macedonian royalty. But Ptolemy outlived his peers and reigned as a god-king into old age, finally dying of natural causes.

Alexander's circle included others who were lesser known. Seleucus, the son of an aristocratic officer in Philip's army, was a cavalry commander during Alexander's lifetime who achieved prominence after the king died. Nearchus (Alexander's Cretan-born admiral), Leonnatus (a gifted relative of Philip's mother), and Harpalus, whose unidentified physical ailment kept him off the battlefield but saw him appointed Alexander's treasurer—all played bit parts in the melodrama of Alexander's life.

Mieza and Pella were the twin poles of Alexander's youth. In Mieza, Alexander received rigorous intellectual training. In Pella, he was introduced to the politics of empire. Philip's court was filled with hard-drinking Macedonian warriors, Greek mercenaries, politicians, ambassadors, and royal visitors from across the ancient world.[11] Alexander moved easily between both worlds and matured quickly. He relied on his small group of allies who, combining talent and royal blood, constituted a ready-made network for a future king.

Precociously self-confident and ambitious, Alexander used his talents brilliantly on the battlefield, and Philip encouraged him. In 340, when Alexander was only sixteen, Philip appointed him regent during a temporary absence fighting at Byzantium. Alexander led the army in a lightning strike against the Maedi tribe in neighboring Thrace. Routing the enemy, Alexander gave a sign of what was to come by founding Alexandropolis on the site of the Maedi capital.[12] Two years later, in 338, Philip entrusted the eighteen-year-old Alexander with the command of the elite Macedonian cavalry against the armies of Athens and Thebes at the Battle of Chaeronea. Alexander led the decisive charge.

Alexander had come into his own. These early victories gave credence to his legendary kinship with Achilles and Heracles. His favorite line from the *Iliad* (a special edition annotated by Aristotle that he carried throughout his life) was that spoken by Achilles during the siege of Troy: "Ever to strive to be best, and outstanding above all others."[13]

This potent combination of myth and reality fired Alexander's ambition, which was described at the time (and throughout his life) as *pothos*—an all-consuming desire for greatness. He complained that his father's many victories would leave him nothing to achieve in his own right. But unlike Philip, Alexander possessed a deep mystical streak. His mother, after all, belonged to the cult of Dionysus and a snake-handling cult of Kaberoi fertility gods of the island of Samothrace. Throughout his life Alexander was propelled by a mystical sense of his own destiny.

Alexander's early military feats brought enmity into his own household. Philip resented his son's boasting about his victory at Chaeronea and may have suspected Alexander and Olympias of conspiring against him. Philip's reaction was as violent as it was unexpected. Only a few months after the victory at Chaeronea, Philip repudiated Olympias, accusing her of adultery, and married the well-connected Cleopatra in her place. Alexander and his mother fled to Epirus, Olympias's homeland.

Alexander was recalled to Pella the following year. His doting mother was divorced and exiled, and his father's new wife was already with child. Cleopatra's loyalty and kinship ties were with powerful nobles such as Parmenion and Attalus, who saw Philip's estrangement from his son as an opportunity to strengthen their political influence at court. Alexander must have sensed that the politics of succession had shifted against him.

Matters came to a head the following year, in 336. Philip was in the early stages of his long heralded invasion of the Persian empire. A Macedonian advance force had secured the Hellespont crossing to Asia Minor. As it swept down the western seaboard of what is now Turkey, geography and politics were uppermost in Philip's mind. At this critical juncture, Prince Pixodarus of Halicarnassus (modern Bodrum in southwest Turkey) offered his daughter in marriage to Alexander's retarded half brother, Philip Arrhidaios, the illegitimate offspring of Philip and a Thessalian dancer named Philinna. Their child was a year older than Alexander.

Alexander, nervous about his standing in the court, suspected that Philip was planning to make Arrhidaios his heir. Exercising questionable judgment, Alexander offered himself to Pixodarus as a marriage partner for the prince's daughter. Philip found out and exploded into Alexander's quarters in a fiery rage. He accused him of ignoble and unworthy behavior, and of going behind his back. Pixodarus, caught between father and son, changed his mind. The negotiations were dropped and Halicarnassus remained a loyal Persian city. Philip banished Alexander's companions for championing the prince's behavior. Father and son eyed each other with icy suspicion from now on.

A few months later, Alexander escorted his father to the theater at Aegae—the ancestral home of the royal Argead dynasty—for his sister Cleopatra's wedding to King Alexander of Epirus. Commanded to stay behind so that Philip could make his grand entrance alone, Alexander looked on helplessly as one of Philip's bodyguards rushed forward and then thrust a sword into the king's chest and killed him instantly.

The assassin was cut down and Alexander was acclaimed as the new king. Alexander was now undisputed ruler of Macedonia. Soon Olympias was accused of inciting the assassination, and later of honoring the body and grave of the assassin.[14] Who had the most to gain from the royal murder? Alexander. But his rapid acclamation as king rendered these suspicions as pointless as they were dangerous. Alexander ruled, and silence became loyalty, which all knew he valued above everything.

Alexander oversaw his father's burial. A great pyre was built, and Philip's body placed on it. His armor and weapons were laid by his side, together with his gold and silver ornaments. Two men, Heromenes and Arrhabaeus who were implicated in the plot, and the assassin's three sons and horses were all killed and placed on the pyre. After everything had been burned and the fire doused with wine, Philip's charred remains were placed inside a small gold box (larnax) with a wreath of golden oak leaves and acorns. This was placed inside the tomb, which was then sealed, and a tumulus of red earth piled on top.

Alexander swiftly assumed control of the forces massing for the invasion of Asia. Before leaving Macedonia, he terrified his opponents by spectacular victories over the Triballi and Illyrian tribes bordering his kingdom. If anything, the son was more formidable than the father. This lesson was impressed on the rebellious Greeks when Alexander besieged Thebes and then razed the city to the ground, selling its inhabitants into slavery.

In the spring of 334, Alexander marched east, crossed the Hellespont, and famously strode ashore through the surf to claim Asia as his own. Soon after burying his father at Aegae, Alexander was paying respects to another ancestor. In the fields before Troy, the Roman historian Arrian tells us, Alexander placed a wreath on Achilles's tomb while Hephaestion placed one on the tomb of Achilles's beloved Patroclus. Both men then stripped off their clothing and ran naked around the tombs, paying respect to the heroes in traditional Greek fashion.

In a final flourish, Alexander paid his respects at the temple of Athena, goddess of war, at nearby Ilium. He dedicated his ceremonial armor to the goddess and received ancient Trojan armor in return. By this act, Alexander petitioned Athena for success in war and invoked the past by stressing his kinship with Achilles.

A few weeks later the Macedonians joined battle with the Persians at the river Granicus. Alexander prevailed narrowly against an enemy expecting an easy victory and reinforced by well-trained Greek mercenaries commanded by the renowned general Memnon. The Macedonians charged through the river, and Alexander escaped death only by the timely help of a Macedonian nobleman named Cleitus the Black. This was interpreted later as a sign of Alexander's divine good fortune. The Persians had underestimated Alexander and were now on the defensive. The victorious army then marched south to Halicarnassus, where the Persian fleet lay at anchor. After several bitterly fought encounters, during which

Alexander was forced to request a truce so that he could retrieve his dead, the Macedonians entered the burning city. It took Ptolemy a full year to subdue the surrounding area.[15]

Alexander's stay at Halicarnassus was brief, but he saw the largest funerary monument in the ancient Greek world—the memorial tomb of King Mausolus (the origin of our term "mausoleum"). Almost two hundred feet tall, the mausoleum towered over the devastated city, eventually becoming known as one of the seven wonders of the world.[16] Mausolus had employed renowned artists to adorn it with huge freestanding sculptures—Ionic columns, lion statues, and friezes depicting clashes between humans, centaurs, and Amazons. It was capped by a pyramid on which stood a giant sculpture of the four-horse chariot known as a *quadriga* driven by Mausolus himself.[17]

The mausoleum would inspire the tombs of great men for centuries to come. Ptolemy had ample time to dwell on its magnificence, and when he built Alexander's tomb in Alexandria, he surely recalled it.

In November 333, Alexander fought and defeated the great Persian king Darius III on the gravelly plains at Issus. The royal road to Persia was now open, but Alexander marched the army south, hugging the coastal road down through what is now Lebanon, until he reached the city of Sidon. Always seeking to burnish his image, Alexander ordered new gold and silver coins depicting himself as his heroic ancestor Heracles.

From Sidon, the Macedonians continued south to the Phoenician city of Tyre. Built on an island just offshore and ringed by massive walls, Tyre was a superbly positioned naval base and thus vital to Alexander. If he controlled Tyre, he would strengthen his overstretched communication lines back to Macedonia and prevent the Persian fleet from landing an army behind his advance.

Alexander set up camp on the mainland opposite the fortified island and plotted his attack. First, he tried to draw on his ancestry. The Tyrians worshiped a god called Melkart, who was widely identified with Heracles. Alexander tried to disguise his strategic interest in the city by announcing that he wished to pay his respects to Melkart/Heracles in the god's temple, and so honor the Tyrians and his own ancestor. The Tyrians were not fooled, and refused his request, believing themselves safe behind their impregnable walls.

For seven long months in 332, Alexander besieged Tyre. He pushed a great causeway out across the sea to the island and eventually seized the city. He let his soldiers run riot, pillaging and slaughtering until the streets flowed with the blood of men, women, and children. The survivors were crucified along the shore as a warning to others.

Alexander's victory over Tyre inspired fear and respect for his indomitable will and brilliant military tactics. But what came next revealed another dimension to Alexander's ambition. In 331, the Macedonian army crossed into Persian-occupied Egypt, where Alexander was welcomed as liberator and acclaimed as pharaoh. Among the shadows cast by the greatest monumental tombs the world had ever seen, Alexander's ideas of divinity took a dramatic turn.

In early spring he rode out to the desert oasis of Siwa to consult the prestigious oracle of Zeus Ammon. Alexander insisted on being closeted alone with Ammon's chief priest, and consequently no one knows what passed between them. Most likely, he was welcomed as a living god, as the Egyptians traditionally addressed the pharaohs. It was left to Aristotles's nephew Callisthenes—Alexander's chief propagandist—to interpret the meeting. Rumors leaked out, as Alexander surely planned. According to one story, Alexander was not Philip's son but was in fact the divine offspring of Zeus Ammon. Tales of Alexander's divine parentage made powerful propaganda, burnishing the public image that he was constructing for himself. By casting himself as the son of Ammon, Alexander gave religious sanction to the idea that his conquests were a kind of divine imperialism. It was an important component of a broader image campaign.

Callisthenes kept a colorful and dramatic account of Alexander's exploits. The sculptor Lysippus was appointed to portray the young king with trademark lion's mane hair, upward-looking eyes, and neck slightly tilted to the left. Alexander's exclusive court artist, Apelles, painted him on horseback grasping Zeus's thunderbolt or accompanied by Nike, the Greek goddess of victory.[18] Alexander's image was perpetuated after his death, revitalized by his successors on gold and silver coins: wearing a spectacular lion helmet, sporting an impossible elephant tusk headdress, or with Ammon's ram horns emerging from his curly locks.

The power of Alexander's imperial image came from his unprecedented military victories. He was clearly mortal yet succeeded as if immortal and, after Siwa, claimed divine support.[19]

Alexander officially founded Alexandria on April 7 and then journeyed to Memphis on the Nile, where he was again hailed as pharaoh. The unique funerary pyramids of the Egyptian kings shimmered in their polished stone cladding. The Macedonians were also amazed by mummies, which gave the dead an appearance of life. Ptolemy was deeply impressed and may have decided at this time to claim Egypt as his share of Alexander's empire.

From Egypt the Macedonians marched north through Syria and then south, dropping down into Mesopotamia where the third and climactic victory over Darius took place on the plains of Gaugamela on October 1, 331.[20] Alexander briefly visited Babylon and then pushed south to the Persian court at Susa and then the ancestral heartland of Persia (modern Iran).

By the spring of 330, Alexander had turned the Greek dream of taking revenge on Persia into reality. He rode at the head of his army into the empire's capital, Persepolis, and put the magnificent city to the torch. Scorch marks of the conflagration can still be seen today.

Always fascinated by royal funerary monuments, Alexander visited the tomb of Cyrus the Great in a royal park at the old capital of Pasargadae. Alexander's architect Aristobulous remembered seeing an inscription written in Persian on the royal sepulchre: "I am Cyrus, who founded the empire of the Persians and was king of Asia. Begrudge me not this monument." When the royal party went inside they found a golden couch, a table set with drinking cups, and a golden coffin.

Then he fought his way across Persia and into the wild country of modern-day Afghanistan. In 329 the Macedonians crossed the snowy passes of the Hindu Kush. They spent the year 328 campaigning around the city of Maracanda (Samarkand), and in 327 Alexander's men scaled and took the heretofore impregnable Sogdian rock. Immediately afterward, Alexander announced he would marry Roxanne, the daughter of the local ruler Oxyartes. Allying the Macedonians to the local Bactrians secured his army's lengthening communication lines.

Alexander was now beyond the known world, following in the foot-steps of the god Dionysus, whose adventures in Asia were celebrated in Greek mythology. Alexander stood to excel Dionysus when he invaded India in 327. In May of the following year, Alexander fought his last great battle, against Rajah Porus. The Macedonians prevailed despite Porus's war elephants. But later that summer at the Hyphasis river, with the plains and forests of India and countless battles opening up before them, Alexander's army mutinied. After eight years of constant fighting and with no end in sight, they were exhausted.

Alexander capitulated, and in 326 the army turned back to Babylon. Craterus marched part of the army by a northern route, while Alexander led some 85,000 soldiers and camp followers on a disastrous crossing of the Gedrosian desert (in southern Iran) without enough water or food. After sixty days of appalling privation, the ragged army stumbled out of the desert and into Pura, the capital of Gedrosia, leaving a trail of corpses in its wake. Some calculations reckon that of the 85,000 who began the march, only 25,000 survived.

Alexander's route took him back through the old Persian capital of Pasargadae, where he revisited Cyrus's tomb. He was appalled to find the grand sarcophagus smashed and Cyrus's body scattered in pieces on the floor.[21] Although the tomb's Persian guardians, the magi, were unable to explain the desecration, a Macedonian commander was executed.[22] Alexander ordered Aristobulous to repair the damage and reseal the mausoleum.

Calanus was a Brahman priest, a gymnosophist (naked philosopher) who had joined the Macedonians at Taxila in the Punjab. He fell ill in Pasargadae and wished to die according to his own religious customs instead of continuing to suffer. This meant suicide by fire.

The pyre was built, and Calanus climbed up onto it. As the flames licked at his flesh, at a prearranged signal, bugles began to blast, soldiers raised their war cry, and elephants trumpeted. After Calanus's immolation, Alexander marched back to Susa, where he persuaded or coerced his senior officers into a mass wedding with Persian noblewomen. These high-status marriages were intended to create a new Macedonian–Persian elite to administer Alexander's empire. After lavish nuptials, the army moved north, bypassing Babylon and camping at Opis by the banks of the river Tigris. Here Alexander faced down the last challenge to his authority and became the undisputed master of the ancient world.

Alexander's brief life was filled with warfare, intrigue, treachery, cover-ups and murder, sex scandals, and unimaginable wealth. It was enlivened by the ideas of destiny and death, unimpeachable valor, glory, entombment, and everlasting fame. No man before him, and probably few after, had ever seen so many different ways to die—and to live on in the imaginations and memories of the living.

Alexander carried the ashes of dead Athenian warriors after Chaeronea and then observed traditional funeral rites for his father at Aegae. Within months he was paying his respects at the tombs of Achilles and Patroclus at Troy, and gazing on the splendor of the mausoleum at Halicarnassus. He stood in wonder before the pyramids of Egypt and was impressed by the embalmer's uncanny art of mummification. He wept over the maimed and dying after the slaughters at Issus, Gaugamela, and the Hydaspes river.

He knew of the great burial mounds (kurgans) of the horse-riding Scythians on Asia's steppes and watched amazed as Calanus had himself immolated. He observed the elaborate Persian funerary rites, sanctioned by the prophet Zoroaster in honor of the great creator Ahura Mazda. And he refurbished Cyrus's desecrated tomb at Pasargadae.

The prospect of dying haunted Alexander throughout his life. He watched his father die and his mother place a golden crown on the head of the assassin's corpse. What strange and complex ideas swirled through Alexander's mind at such sights, and do they explain his own mercurial character, at once gifted and cruel?

Paradoxically, Alexander achieved immortality when he died. But fate, not Alexander, was the master of his undying fame, the guardian and architect of his gilded memory. It chased him across Asia to the furthest edge of the world, and almost caught him in the desert wastes of Gedrosia. Now it waited at Opis.

DEATH AND
DYING IN BABYLON

AT OPIS IN BABYLONIA, IN THE SUMMER OF 324, Alexander vanquished the last earthly challenge to his authority and seized absolute power. Alexander announced to an army assembly that he was sending ten thousand veterans home to Macedonia under Craterus's command and replacing them with Persians trained and armed in the Macedonian fashion. In response, the soldiers insulted the Persians and ridiculed Alexander. If he held the Persians in such high regard, they shouted, then they could all be dismissed, and he could conquer the world with his father, alluding sarcastically to Alexander's claim that Zeus Ammon was his father. Alexander in turn accused them of ingratitude, haranguing them on how they owed everything to him:

> I have sword-cuts from close fight; arrows have pierced me, missiles from catapults bruised my flesh . . . for your glory and your gain. Over every land and sea, across river, mountain and plain I led you to the world's end, a victorious army. . . . Out of my sight![1]

For several days Alexander talked to high-ranking Persians and refused to see Macedonians. Finally the opposition collapsed. The Macedonians swore undying loyalty and wept in gratitude when Alexander forgave them and sealed the reconciliation with a kiss of royal favor for each man. As the last soldier stepped forward, the prospect of a full-scale mutiny disappeared.

Sending away Craterus was an astute move, though the Roman historian Arrian tells us in *The Campaigns of Alexander* that all sides had tears in their eyes. It removed a thorn from Hephaestion's side and an ultra-traditionalist from Alexander's inner circle. Unlike Craterus, the three other marshals—Perdiccas, Ptolemy, and Seleucus—were more accepting of Alexander's Persian dress and courtly affectations. Also, they acknowledged Hephaestion's special place in Alexander's affections. At ease with himself and his men, Alexander was soon on the move. Opis disappeared in the haze of dust kicked up by the departing army.

With Hephaestion at his side, Alexander led long columns of armored men away from the stifling heat of the Mesopotamian plain and up into the cool valleys of the Zagros mountains. They were heading northeast for Ecbatana (modern Hamadan), the ancient capital of Media, where the Persian kings had built a royal palace as a summer retreat.

There was no rush, and for once no enemy to confront. The king's court and the rank and file slipped into a relaxed regime, enjoying frequent stops en route as they ascended to a more temperate climate. By night, Alexander's courtiers showered him with their customary adulation and praise at wine-drenched parties.

As the ruler of an imperial superpower, he was heavily occupied with matters of state. But he still made time for the business of pleasure. He sent a long list of demands to Atropates, his satrap (provincial governor) in Media, ordering him to prepare a lavish celebration for the army's arrival at Ecbatana.

With Craterus gone, Hephaestion could focus his petty spitefulness on Eumenes, Alexander's Greek-born secretary. For example, Eumenes's lieutenants once requisitioned a billet for him and were preparing it when Hephaestion's men arrived and ejected them, installing a flute player instead. When Eumenes complained to Alexander, the king rebuked Hephaestion. But later he changed his mind and reprimanded Eumenes. For Alexander, the dilemma of Hephaestion's imperious behavior remained unresolved.

Alexander's route meandered among the foothills of the Zagros, turning the march into a grand sightseeing tour. At one point, he detoured the whole army to encamp below a towering cliff at Behistun on the route that later became the Silk Road to Samarkand. Here, in 521, Darius the

Great had carved a huge image of himself and victory inscription five hundred feet up on a sheer cliff face. Unreadable from the ground, the stony text extolled Darius's virtues for the eyes of the Persian gods in a way that probably appealed to Alexander: "According to righteousness have I walked; neither the weak nor the strong have I wronged."[2]

The army heaved into life and Alexander marched up and over the valley's rim and out onto the rolling grasslands of the Nisaean fields. Here the Persian kings once pastured 150,000 of their finest thoroughbreds, though Alexander found only 50,000 remaining after the depredations of the local horse-thieving Cossaeans. Alexander and his men lingered in the lush surroundings for a month before departing on the final leg of the journey to Ecbatana.

Autumn chilled the air as Alexander led the army onto a wide plain fed by icy waters flowing from snow-capped Mount Alvand. Ecbatana was built on rising ground and ringed by imposing walls and turrets, with the citadel and its glittering palace rising above. Darius had spared no expense in building his summer retreat. Cedar and cypress-wood columns were sheathed in gold, and the roof was plated with silver interspersed with turquoise tiles and sparkling jewels.[3] Ecbatana symbolized the empire's wealth and radiated the sacred glow of the Persian god Ahura Mazda—the Lord of Light.

To honor Dionysus, Alexander sponsored games, gymnastics, theater, and sacrifices by day, and banquets and drinking parties by night. Alexander paid for three thousand Greek performers—the artists of Dionysus—to journey overland from Greece and entertain them. In return for his largesse, Alexander received an endless flow of praise, gifts, and golden crowns in honor of his conquests. His companions and satraps were joined at court by ambassadors and envoys from across the Mediterranean world.

They dined in Ecbatana's silvered palace, where the air was thick with the aromatic fumes of smouldering myrrh. Alexander's grand entrances played to his heroic ancestry and his identification with the gods. He would arrive draped in purple and wearing the horns of Ammon, or sporting winged sandals and a broad hat to impersonate Hermes, the messenger of the gods, or sometimes carrying a lion skin and wielding an oversize club as Heracles. The atmosphere was a heady mix of opulence, excess, and exotic fancy dress, resting on the brute power of Macedonian arms.

Imported Greek wine was mixed with pure mountain water and poured into waiting cups. Reclining on couches in Greek fashion, Alexander, Hephaestion, Perdiccas, Ptolemy, and Seleucus toasted each other as the richest and most powerful men in the history of the world. They had plundered Asia, seizing tens of thousands of talents (hundreds of millions of dollars) from the Persian treasuries at Babylon, Susa, Persepolis, and Pasargadae. They sequestered vast amounts of gold, silver, and gems, and controlled the trade in spices, dyes, incense, and hardwoods. Astonishing wealth poured into the treasury daily, swelling imperial revenues almost beyond measure. At Ecbatana, a fraction of this wealth was spent on an extraordinary victory party.

Alexander was at the zenith of his power as lord of Asia. He now enjoyed great fame as an invincible conqueror, excelling even his heroic ancestors, Achilles, Heracles, and Dionysus. And by his side was Hephaestion, his lover since boyhood and sole keeper of his most intimate affections. Within days, however, Alexander's world began falling apart around him.

Dignitaries, commanders, and foot soldiers alike settled into a life of luxury at Alexander's expense. The athletic games, theatrical performances, and heavy drinking began in earnest. At one of these parties Hephaestion fell ill, possibly with typhus or malaria, or perhaps something more sinister. He languished for a week, tended by his physician Glaucias, and then seemed to improve. On the eighth day, Alexander was attending an athletic display by Greek youths when he was summoned with news that Hephaestion's condition had suddenly worsened.

Hephaestion had already died by the time Alexander pushed his way through the crowds to the palace. The news of his death spread through the city and into the encampment beyond. Hephaestion Amyntoros, the second most powerful man in the empire, had fulfilled the final act of the *Iliad's* tragic hero. Hephaestion had become Patroclus in death as in life, and had left his lover to grieve in spectacular Homeric fashion.

Rumors that Hephaestion had been poisoned were rife in the following days and weeks. But any assassin would have required nerves of steel and questionable motivation. Killing Hephaestion while leaving Alexander alive would be a suicidal act. Our sources are silent, and only the unfortunate physician was ever punished. Glaucias was executed by crucifixion, probably for incompetence rather than suspicion of murder.

Descending into a welter of grief and mourning, Alexander refused food and drink for days. According to Arrian, Alexander "flung himself on the body of his friend and lay there nearly all day long in tears, and refused to be parted from him until he was dragged away by force by his Companions."[4] He had the manes and tails of army horses docked and he cut his own hair, just as Homer said Achilles had done at the death of his beloved Patroclus.[5] By this act, Alexander repeated the heroic identification between himself and Hephaestion that he had displayed at Troy ten years before.

Alexander dispatched envoys to distant Siwa in Egypt to persuade the priests of Ammon to grant Hephaestion rites of worship as a god. In Persia, Alexander demanded that the sacred flames of Ahura Mazda be extinguished, leaving the god's fire temples in darkness. However, for the Persians, such an act was reserved for kings.[6] Since Hephaestion was not a monarch or even a royal, the Persian magi interpreted this action as an evil omen foretelling Alexander's own death.

A mood of dark depression settled over Ecbatana. There was no possibility in Alexander's mind of burying or cremating Hephaestion in the city of his death. Lashing out in fury, Alexander destroyed the local temple to Asclepius, the Greek patron deity of physicians. Today, all that remains to commemorate the tragedy is the so-called Lion of Hamadan, a typically Greek lion sculpture—the traditional form of funerary monument—that Alexander erected on the place of his bereavement.

Alexander also broke the rules of Macedonian tradition by ordering that Hephaestion's body be embalmed. In this he unwittingly set a precedent for his own mummification, which made his corpse a monument and a legend as enduring as the universal fame he achieved in life.

Embalming was unheard of among Macedonians. Their traditional burial rites were either interment of the whole body or ritual cremation, with the ashes stored in a casket beneath a burial mound, or tumulus. For Alexander, it was essential to preserve the body until it could be given a proper funeral in Babylon. Alternatively, Alexander may have intended to display Hephaestion's lifelike remains in a grand mausoleum.

Or did he perhaps envision being laid to rest beside his alter ego in the same way Achilles and Patroclus were buried at Troy?

Several months later, the army somberly assembled outside the city walls to watch Hephaestion's cortege file out through Ecbatana's gates. It was said that Alexander himself drove the chariot carrying his companion's body for a short distance.[7] Perdiccas, who was hastily appointed grand vizier to replace Hephaestion, was charged with conveying the body to Babylon.

As the winter of 324 approached, according to Plutarch, the king attempted to "lighten his sorrow" by launching a brief, bloody raid on the Cossaeans—mountain tribesmen who made a living from brigandage. Notably they had rustled 100,000 of the royal Persian horses grazing in the Nisaean fields. Alexander hunted them down mercilessly, slaughtering the entire male population, it was said, as a bloody offering to the spirit of Hephaestion.[8]

In early spring 323 Alexander finished with the Cossaeans and led the army back down to the Mesopotamian plains. Approaching Babylon from the east, he was met by a deputation of Babylonian priests who delivered a stark warning: death awaited the king if he entered the city.[9] The prediction, they said, was based on astrological calculations of the heavenly bodies.

When Alexander first entered Babylon after defeating Darius at Gaugamela in 331, he found the great ziggurat—the temple of Babylon's patron god Marduk that towered above the city—neglected. Ever respectful to the gods (Greek and Barbarian alike), Alexander had ordered it's restoration. Likely the priests had siphoned off temple revenues and now feared being found out. Alexander ignored the warning, perhaps in order to conduct Hephaestion's funeral.

No expense was spared for Hephaestion's funeral rites. Money, craftsmen, labor, and tribute were directed to Babylon from across the empire for what was probably the most expensive funeral in history. It has been estimated that an astonishing ten or twelve thousand talents—perhaps twenty-five tons of gold—were spent on the proceedings.

Private donations came from Alexander as well as the marshals, the Persian aristocracy, and foreign diplomats and envoys who wished to curry favor with the king. Diodorus records that the marshals and close companions commissioned chryselephantine (gold and silver) likenesses of the dead hero used to decorate a funeral couch or perhaps just as offerings.

To build Hephaestion's tomb, Alexander sought out an architect whose name is variously given as Stasikrates, Deinocrates, or Cheirokrates.[10] Stasikrates had rebuilt the temple of Artemis at Ephesus and would become the main architect of Alexandria in Egypt. Sometime before 331, he had suggested an astonishing project to Alexander. As Mount Athos in Macedonia had the general appearance of a human body, he said, it could be carved and worked into a vast statue of the king. This truly Olympian Alexander would have his feet in the Aegean and his head in the clouds; his left hand would hold a city of ten thousand, and from his right would pour a river from a huge bowl as a libation into the sea.[11]

Alexander famously declined the offer: "Let Athos stay as it is . . . the Caucasus shall show my imprint, as will the Himalayas . . . and the Caspian Sea."[12] Alexander also recalled how the Persian king Xerxes had cut a canal for his ships through the Athos peninsula during his invasion of Greece in 480 B.C.E. Since then the name "Athos" had become a byword for hubris.[13] Nonetheless, Stasikrates's project would have been an unprecedented memorial. Clearly his bravado appealed to Alexander as he contemplated Hephaestion's funeral. Unfortunately it seems the architect was unavailable.

We do not know who eventually designed Hephaestion's huge funeral pyre, but descriptions of it suggest influence by Marduk's ziggurat or more likely the mausoleum of Halicarnassus. It was built of wood on foundations of baked tiles, and it stood some 230 feet high in seven stories. Each level was decorated with a distinctive theme and style. The fascias were molded of unbaked clay and probably gilded.[14] Alexander demolished a section of Babylon's city wall to make room for the pyre and obtain tiles needed to build the support platform. The pyre was hollow inside to facilitate burning and built entirely of highly combustible palm trunks.

Since this was probably the most expensive funeral in history, it merits Diodorus's full account:

Upon the foundation course were golden prows of quinqueremes [warships with five levels of oarsmen] in close order, two hundred and forty in all. Upon the cat heads each carried two kneeling archers four cubits in height, and armed male figures of five cubits high, while the intervening spaces were occupied by red banners fashioned out of felt. Above these, on the second level, stood torches fifteen cubits high with golden wreaths about their handles. At their flaming ends perched eagles with outspread wings . . . while about their bases were serpents looking up at the eagles. On the third level were carved a multitude of wild animals being pursued by hunters. The fourth level carried a centaurmachy [battle between Greeks and centaurs] rendered in gold, while the fifth showed lions and bulls alternating, also in gold. The next higher level was covered with Macedonian and Persian arms. . . . On top of all stood Sirens, hollowed out and able to conceal within them persons who sang a lament in mourning for the dead.[15]

Hephaestion's pyre was as much an overblown victory monument as it was a commemoration of Alexander's dead companion. Even in his grief, Alexander could not resist making a self-serving political statement in a dazzling hybrid of Macedonian and Persian features. There were symbolic weapons, archers, battleships, and lion hunts (representing the idea of Alexander as the victorious hunter of Persian civilization). The battleships likely referred to the fleet of ships Alexander commissioned to conquer Arabia.[16]

The eagle was the symbolic animal of Zeus, and Alexander's coins depict it being grasped by the god. The snake serves the same function for Ammon, and Ptolemy later used it as an emblem of Alexander's cult in Alexandria. The struggle between Greeks and centaurs, steeped in ancient myth, had been used as an allegory of the war between Greece and Persia ever since Xerxes's invasion of 480 B.C.E. The lions and bulls, emblems of the Babylonian deities Ishtar and Adad respectively, were the protectors of both body and pyre.[17] At the top of the pyre, Alexander and his men dedicated their arms, a symbol of mourning as well as militarism. As a final gesture, they threw gold and ivory figurines onto the pyre.

During excavations in Babylon in 1904, archaeologists digging just inside the ancient city walls uncovered a large mud-brick platform still standing to a height of twenty-four feet after two thousand years. The scorch marks told of a fierce conflagration, as did the preserved impressions of burned palm tree trunks.[18]

Although the base of the pyre survived, there is no trace of the tomb, and ancient sources are silent on the matter. Diodorus's description is graphic and detailed but does not mention the funeral or the impressive mausoleum Alexander intended for Hephaestion. Only Arrian mentions the funeral games, briefly: "The festival was far more splendid than ever before both in the number of competitors and in the money spent upon it. In all 3,000 men competed in the various events."[19] An event costing ten thousand talents merits only three lines by a single author.

As for the funeral itself, we are left to imagine the scene, piecing together evidence from other descriptions. After sunset on the appointed day, the pyre was set ablaze, possibly by Alexander himself. Perfume, incense, and the aroma of roasting meat sacrifices mingled and wafted through the wide avenues and along the narrow streets and alleys of Babylon. The night air crackled and sparked with the burning palm trunks as well as laments, prayers, and the sound of horns blowing. Alexander's war elephants trumpeted their deep resonating battle cries, and the massed ranks of Macedonian soldiers clattered their shields and shouted to the gods. Alexander, the companions, army commanders, and ambassadors had a ringside view as the pyre exploded in flames and the costly edifice collapsed in on itself and crashed to the ground.

As memorable as this scene would have been, it is nowhere mentioned. Not a single word survives on the funeral of Alexander's lover and closest friend. Hephaestion's most telling obituary is the silence that surrounds it.

Different theories have sought to explain the silence. Some believe the elaborate pyre was the tomb, and that Hephaestion was buried and not cremated. The burned brick platform seems to argue otherwise, as does the fact that a templelike pyre of flammable materials could be built in months or even weeks, whereas a stone tomb would have taken far longer. Diodorus's description is surely an account of the completed pyre, but did it cost ten thousand talents to build? Or did this fantastic amount include the tomb Alexander envisaged? Alexander's last plans—although abandoned by his marshals and the army after his death as too expensive and ambitious—include the construction of Hephaestion's tomb, so we must assume it was never built.

Macedonian royal tradition decreed cremation but did not mandate it, and full-body burial or inhumation was practiced as well. What the difference meant at the time is unknown. If we believe Diodorus that the Babylonian structure was a funeral pyre, then we can compare it to others uncovered by archaeologists in Macedonia and Cyprus.

Looming above the lush green pastures of the Gardens of Midas in western Macedonia, Tomb II at Vergina is the most famous example. Above the tomb were found burned remains of animal bones, arms, armor, and ivory figurines presumed to be decorations from a funeral couch.[20] At Salamis in Cyprus a similar example was found—a thirty-three-foot-high tumulus yielding the fire-damaged relics of arms, armor, golden wreaths, and human statues covered by a stone pyramid.[21]

The Salamis pyre was a memorial and probably a tomb, and likely Alexander intended to convert Hephaestion's elaborate pyre into an equally grand mausoleum built on the same spot.[22] Hephaestion's pyre, in other words, was a tinderbox replica of what would later be built in stone.[23]

Alexander's expensive plans for Hephaestion's tomb were abandoned when Alexander himself died. And so history's most expensive funeral proved as ephemeral as the poorest—no tomb was built and Hephaestion's body was never mentioned again. Remains would be placed in a ceramic funerary urn or a golden box known as a larnax, normally reserved for royalty. Both the historical and the archaeological record are silent on the fate of these remains. The man Alexander loved above all others disappeared from history amid the thick black smoke of his funeral pyre.

The embers of Hephaestion's pyre were hardly cold when Alexander turned to the only work he knew—military conquest. The ambition that had driven him since childhood overshadowed this grievous personal loss. His immediate concern was to finish converting Babylon into a port for launching a thousand warships against Arabia.

In late May 323, Alexander's envoy to Siwa returned. The oracle of Ammon had pronounced that Hephaestion could be accorded the status and rites of a hero but not worshiped as a god.[24] Alexander jubilantly ordered the establishment of a hero cult in Pella, Hephaestion's hometown, and another in Athens. Alexander sent an official letter ordering his Egyptian satrap Cleomenes to build two hero shrines in Alexandria and ensure that every business contract was sanctified by invoking Hephaestion's name. At Babylon, Hephaestion's cult engaged in sacrifices to the gods and nightly drinking parties. Alexander was in good spirits; the army was massed and ready, and Hephaestion's name had been immortalized.

Nearchus, Alexander's Cretan-born admiral, would spearhead the seaborne invasion of Arabia. Alexander threw a lavish banquet in his honor one evening in early June. Later that night, Alexander and his closest companions were invited to a second party by another friend, Medius of Larissa. Not surprisingly, this proved to be a monumental binge-drinking affair.[25] The drunken session ended with grand toasts, and Alexander is said to have drained a twelve-pint flagon of undiluted wine. Diodorus, our earliest source, describes what happened next.

> Instantly he shrieked aloud as if smitten by a violent blow and was conducted by his Friends who led him by the hand back to his apartments. His chamberlains put him to bed and attended him closely, but the pain increased and the physicians were summoned. No one was able to do anything helpful and Alexander continued in great discomfort and acute suffering. When he, at length, despaired of life, he took off his ring and handed it to Perdiccas. His Friends asked: "To whom do you leave the kingdom?" and he replied: "To the strongest."[26]

This dramatic version of events supports the accusation of poisoning. More sober accounts are given by Arrian and by Plutarch in his *Life of Alexander*. Both writers apparently drew on the so-called Royal Diary or *Ephemerides*—a day-by-day account of Alexander's affairs written probably by his secretary, Eumenes.

According to this common source, Alexander developed a fever at Medius's party. After resting for a day in his quarters in the palace of Nebuchadnezzar, he resumed planning the coming invasion. Another meal and drinking session with Medius followed. Six days later, his condition had become critical and he was confined to bed, guarded by his senior companions. Two days later, his soldiers forced their way into his room fearing he was dead. Arrian records the moment: "Lying speechless as the men filed by, he yet struggled to raise his head, and in his eyes there was a look of recognition for each individual as he passed."[27] Shortly after the final soldier had left, the king lost consciousness.

Alexander died in Babylon on June 10, 323 B.C.E., age thirty-two. Two traditions arose: his death was natural and his death was suspicious. Only Roman descriptions of Alexander's death have survived, and the earliest was written three hundred years after the event. Not one of these sources is free of contamination: retrospective propaganda, self-serving lies, half-truths, and fantastical legend grew by accretion during the three centuries between Alexander's death and Diodorus's first account. Unless Alexander's body is found, the truth of his untimely death will never be known. What is certain is that at the moment of death, Alexander was reborn as a universal myth of how humans can stretch the boundaries of the possible.

Conspiracy theories flourished at the time and have been joined in recent years by an equal number of scientific explanations. Alexander may have been poisoned or he may have died of natural causes, his death hastened by overindulgence, the cumulative effects of battle wounds, the loss of Hephaestion, and possibly some unknown disease.

Alexander's mother, Olympias, believed her son was poisoned, and at the first opportunity she desecrated the tomb of Iolaus, accusing him of murder.[28] Iolaus was Antipater's son, and Alexander's cupbearer and so a natural suspect. What kind of poison might Iolaus have administered? Arsenic was widely known, and its symptoms of abdominal pain, shock, and hypertension fitted Alexander's decline. Strychnine was also known among Aristotle's followers. But these are both quick-acting poisons, however, and Alexander lingered for ten days. White hellebore (*Venatrum album*)—a well-known purgative—is also a possibility.[29] It weakens the heart, brings on fever and stomach pains, and ends in death. A teaspoonful disguised in strong wine would suffice.

But what assassin or group of assassins would want Alexander to die slowly and possibly take revenge on those he suspected of poisoning him? For the next two years Alexander's body lay in state in Babylon.

Read one way, this inertia suggests political and administrative gridlock: strategic indecision and an empire in denial. If Alexander had been the victim of conspiracy, a plan surely would have been enacted.

This lack of direction can also be argued to suggest that the conspirators took their time to let things cool down and kept a collective grip on the empire while they divided it among themselves. In this view, it might not be surprising that it took two years for the marshals to reach a workable deal.

Poison remains a possibility, and it is a suspicious coincidence that Hephaestion died under similar circumstances only months before. But Alexander's symptoms are only vaguely described and the timing remains a problem. And besides, there are other possible explanations.

Malaria also explains some of Alexander's symptoms, such as fever, weakness, and delirium. As many ancient and modern authors have pointed out, Alexander had spent weeks sailing down the Euphrates, exploring the marshes at its mouth in order to improve drainage and canal irrigation, and could easily have been infected. If malaria was the culprit, this was an ironic and unlucky death, as the disease was endemic in Macedonia at that time (and remained so until the twentieth century), where Alexander spent the first twenty years of his life without contracting it.

Typhoid is another suspect, causing fever, stomach pain, peritonitis, and delirium, with severe cases being fatal within two weeks. If Hephaestion died of a fever in Ecbatana, then Alexander could have contracted it from him.[30] One of typhoid's more striking symptoms is creeping paralysis. Victims bear the impression of death for days before it actually occurs. This might explain why Alexander's companions and embalmers, visiting the body six days later, saw that "no decay had set into it and that there was not even the slightest discoloration. The vital look that comes from the breath of life had not yet vanished from his face," according to Curtius's account.[31]

Alexander may have died of West Nile fever, a viral encephalitis that can be transmitted by mosquitoes, with birds serving as ideal hosts and often exhibiting strange behavior as a result.[32] Plutarch describes an incident in which ravens attacked each other and fell dead at the king's feet near the gates of Babylon.[33] Observing bird behavior was a divinatory art at the time; the unusual behavior constituted a serious omen.

In the final analysis, we are left with a royal corpse. What should we do with it? The consequences of the marshals' decision—or indecision—laid out a course we are still following two thousand years later.

A corpse has to be attended to. Yet even in this, Alexander was different. He lay unattended for six days before the marshals and the embalmers examined him again, only to find no signs of decay. In the ovenlike heat of high summer this was an unnerving discovery and clearly unsettled the embalmers, as Curtius recalled. So it was that, after being instructed to see to the body in their traditional fashion, the Egyptians and Chaldeans did not dare touch him at first since he seemed to be alive. Then, praying that it be lawful in the eyes of god and man for humans to touch a god, they cleaned out the body.[34]

Cleaning out the body is a euphemism for a gory procedure.[35] The embalmers were justifiably nervous, as Greeks and Macedonians did not mummify their dead, and so were ignorant of the bloody procedure.[36] They began eviscerating the cadaver, uneasy perhaps that their actions could easily offend the Macedonians and lead to their own execution for desecrating Alexander's body.

Why Alexander was embalmed remains a mystery, though he himself set the precedent with Hephaestion at Ecbatana the previous autumn. But Alexander, unlike Hephaestion, was a king, and mummifying his corpse broke with royal Macedonian tradition in spectacular fashion. Faced with silence in the ancient sources, we must assume that after days of wrangling, the marshals collectively sanctioned it. In keeping with his view of himself as divine and as king of Asia as well as Macedonia, Alexander was now being preserved for all time and all peoples, though this may not have been what the marshals intended.

It seems likely, following the example of Hephaestion, that Alexander's body was embalmed to preserve it for later cremation or burial in its final resting place. Perdiccas, Ptolemy, and Seleucus probably did not intend Alexander to be mummified for eternity.

Alexander's embalmed body was lifted into a golden coffin lined with scented herbs. Perdiccas, according to one account, placed Alexander's body in the casket, covered it with a robe and purple cloak, and tied the royal diadem across his forehead. The body was anointed with perfumes mixed with honey, and the sarcophagus was draped with a purple cover.[37] On hearing of Alexander's death, the Athenian orator Demades is said to have exclaimed, "Alexander dead? Impossible; the whole earth would stink of his corpse."[38] Demades's clever quip was well wide of the mark.

Death reunited Alexander with Hephaestion, and perhaps not just in the afterlife. It is not impossible, though no ancient writer mentions it, that Hephaestion's remains, probably a casket of ashes, were temporarily laid to rest somewhere near Alexander's coffin in a final and brief act of respect by the marshals. After a lifetime together, Alexander and Hephaestion went their separate ways in death—one to obscurity and the other to everlasting fame. Had Alexander lived, Hephaestion would have shared his universal renown. But when Alexander died, he consigned his lover to the darkness: his death unexplained, his tomb unbuilt, his remains forgotten, and his name hardly spoken again.

The marshals likely intended to cremate, not preserve, Alexander's remains. If so, events soon outran the plan. As days turned into months, the lifelike Alexander lay encased in gold, ruling their thoughts and fueling their growing personal ambitions. When they did not immediately dispose of Alexander's body, Perdiccas, Ptolemy, and Seleucus became its prisoners. The gilded corpse took on a life of its own and became a weapon in the deadly game of legitimacy and succession that pitted the successors against one another. Mummified, the king faced an extraordinary future.

STEALING THE BODY
AND THE MEMPHIS TOMB

As THEY GAZED ON THE LIFELIKE FACE OF Alexander's embalmed remains lying in Nebuchadnezzar's palace, Perdiccas, Ptolemy, and Seleucus held the fate of the empire in their hands. Absent were Craterus, now leading ten thousand veterans homeward through Asia Minor, and Antipater, Alexander's regent in Macedonia and Greece.

The immediate succession, according to Curtius, was decided on Alexander's deathbed. He "bade his friends draw near . . . and then took his ring from his finger and handed it to Perdiccas."[1] But this, everyone knew, was a temporary arrangement. The Meleager affair, and Philip Arrhidaios's compromise for sharing power with the infant Alexander IV, naming Perdiccas as regent, had brought an uneasy truce. Each marshal was greedy for power and except the aged Antipater had belonged to Alexander's inner circle since boyhood. None could emulate Alexander, but each had his own design on the empire and its treasury.

In the temples and palaces of Babylon, intrigue and jealousy were palpable, and the tension, like the heat, inescapable. The future was uncertain, and the truce likely to hold only as long as it took to lay Alexander's corpse to rest.

Perdiccas, Ptolemy, and Seleucus argued over every conceivable resting place for the dead king's remains. No record survives of the horse-trading and negotiations that stretched over the next two years, fueled by mutual suspicion over Alexander's postmortem future, but they must have been intense. Never before had a corpse so influenced the conduct of the living and even the future shape of the world.

These men knew Alexander's mind, tactics, and plans, and had acquired great wealth as the Macedonian juggernaut rolled across Asia. Each surrounded himself with a clique of supporters. Relationships were built along the fault lines of ambition and were liable to shift with every new rumor, suspicion, or news item from abroad. Alexander's domineering personality and the breakneck speed of events during his life channeled the marshals' energies and kept their rivalries in check. But now he was gone.

The marshals divided into two uneasy factions. Perdiccas, supported by Seleucus and Eumenes, was opposed by Ptolemy and his commanders. Perdiccas enjoyed the advantage as regent and had been a trusted friend of Alexander, being appointed one of the royal bodyguards, then promoted marshal, and finally named grand vizier after Hephaestion's death. Now he was the official protector of Alexander's wife, Roxanne, and her son, Alexander IV—the touchstone of continuity and legitimacy in the struggle for succession. Seleucus, the son of a Macedonian general, threw in his lot with Perdiccas, as did Eumenes, Alexander's chief secretary and the empire's master administrator. Perdiccas, with some justification, believed he held the advantage and could keep the empire together, ostensibly in the name of the two corulers.

Perdiccas's chief rival was Ptolemy, another of Alexander's boyhood companions and one of his most capable generals. Riding at Alexander's side through Asia, Ptolemy shared the perilous desert journey to Siwa in 331 and personally captured Bessus, a pretender to the Persian throne. Ptolemy had sided with Perdiccas during Meleager's revolt, but he was wary of Perdiccas's growing power and personal ambition.

Craterus—tough, daring, and probably the most gifted of Alexander's generals—and Antipater—Alexander's viceroy in Europe—were sidelined for the moment. The power lay in Babylon with the three marshals, their lieutenants, and the royal army—the ultimate arbiter of Macedonian power. Perdiccas, Ptolemy, and Seleucus engaged in seemingly endless negotiations, each aiming to possess what was fast becoming the ultimate symbol of legitimacy—Alexander's body.

Alexander's corpse was a key to the future of the Hellenistic world he had brought into being. His reputation as the greatest conqueror in history made his body a magnet for soldiers who would flock to the banner

of his successor. Alexander's tomb would become the center of a religious cult. He was a god in Asia, if only a peerless king in Macedonia
and Greece. According to Macedonian rites, the one who buried a king
received honor and legitimacy as a potential ruler himself. The power of
ancestor worship and the wealth and prestige generated by cult rituals
were compelling incentives to control the dead king's remains.

The obvious site for Alexander's mausoleum was Babylon, which
made more political sense than the dunes of Siwa. Yet some, including
the conservative army ranks, favored transporting the body back to
Macedonia for interment in the royal Argead burial ground at Aegae
(Vergina). Here Alexander would rest with his ancestors, perhaps alongside his father, beneath a huge pyramid symbolizing the international
empire he forged.

Alexander may have wished to be buried with his claimed supernatural "father" Zeus Ammon at Siwa, the desert oracle that first confirmed
his divinity.[2] In the months following Hephaestion's death, Alexander
had drawn closer to Ammon. But after the king's death, his wishes
counted for little. In life, he had everyone at his mercy; in death his fate
was in the hands of others.

Perdiccas was the most senior figure, but his position was far from secure. His regency was conditional and depended on protecting Roxanne
and her child, keeping the army placated with pay and largesse, administering the empire, and maintaining its military security. He also had to
keep the other marshals and their lieutenants in check and maintain
good relationships with Antipater back in Macedonia.

Perdiccas also had longer-term issues to consider. He would run the
empire only until Alexander's son reached maturity. Controlling the final
destination of Alexander's body and administering Macedonian funeral
rites was vital if he was to act as a strong and effective regent who could
count on the backing of the army. It was a difficult balancing act.

Perdiccas's dilemma was Ptolemy's advantage, and he was the only marshal who had a clear plan of action. His aim was to possess the rich and
self-contained satrapy of Egypt, not succeed Alexander as lord of Asia.
The fate of Alexander's corpse is the story of Ptolemy's rise to power—a
meteoric rise for a Macedonian general, ignited and propelled by a brilliant combination of caution, subterfuge, bribery, and decisive action.

Perdiccas, Ptolemy, and Seleucus agreed on one point: Alexander's corpse should lie in state in Babylon during the time it took to build the funerary car, a period extended to accommodate their endless and tortuous negotiations. Once they reached a workable compromise, an imperial announcement was made that the hearse was ready.

While the future of the empire and the disposition of Alexander's body were being debated, his hearse gradually took shape in the royal workshops of Babylon. Wheelwrights, goldsmiths, carpenters, and portrait painters labored ceaselessly to create an astonishing catafalque to transport the mummified conqueror to an unknown destination.

Perdiccas gave day-to-day responsibility for overseeing construction of the hearse to Arrhidaios (not to be confused with Alexander's brother, King Philip Arrhidaios). Arrhidaios played a crucial but mysterious role in the fate of Alexander's remains.

The catafalque's magnificence inspired a long description written by the contemporary historian Hieronymus of Cardia, an abbreviated version of which survives in an account by Diodorus.[3] It measured some thirteen feet wide by twenty feet long. In keeping with Greek tradition, it was designed as a scaled-down temple whose Ionic columns were adorned with golden acanthus tendrils. On each of the four corners perched a Nike victory statue, and a golden olive wreath on a stylized palm stood on the top of a barrel roof fashioned from golden scales. Two golden lions guarded the entrance to the temple's interior, where the mummified Alexander lay in his gold sarcophagus flanked by four large paintings. One showed Alexander in a chariot with his companions and Persian Royal Guard, a second depicted Indian war elephants ready for battle, the third was a cavalry scene, and the fourth represented war galleys ready for action. A golden net hid the body from prying eyes and formed a shimmering veil separating the young man-god from the profane world of mortals. Diodorus says it took sixty-four richly caparisoned mules to pull the giant carriage on wheels decorated with lions grasping spears in their jaws.

The hearse was a powerful statement of the multiethnic empire Alexander forged, and it was a political instrument in its own right. While most of the design was Greek or Macedonian, some features, such as the wheels and harness, were of Persian style. The idea of a wheeled funerary cart was Asian, not Greek.

The hearse's martial appearance spoke of imperial military power rather than mourning. The decorative imagery was triumphal and heroic. The visual message was Alexander's astonishing triumphs, as well as the power now wielded by his successor marshals, of whom Perdiccas stood supreme.[4] The whole unwieldy contraption embodied Perdiccas's vision of the empire extending into the future under his command.

With the hearse finished, all that remained was for Alexander's sarcophagus to be heaved into place and transported to an agreed destination. Perdiccas now charged Arrhidaios with leading the funeral cortege on its long journey; the destination, whether to Aegae or Siwa, was still unclear.

Perdiccas now made a critical error of judgment. Early in 321 he left Babylon to march the Royal Army north to the strangely sculpted landscape of Cappadocia. He desired to conquer the region for his staunch ally Eumenes, who had received it when the empire's provinces were divided. Alexander had failed to subdue it in his rush to confront Darius at Issus in November 333, and the region was now in open revolt under the native leader, Ariarathes.

This miscalculation was compounded by what Perdiccas now recognized as his misplaced trust in Arrhidaios and his failure to gauge the lengths to which Ptolemy would go to acquire the royal corpse. While Perdiccas was hunting down Ariarathes, events in Babylon took a startling turn that would shape the Hellenistic world until the Roman era.

As the fierce heat of the Mesopotamian summer gave way to autumn in 321, Babylon's inhabitants watched in amazement as Alexander's funeral cart trundled through the city's gates out onto the dusty plain. Thousands of admiring spectators lined the route as the cortege rolled northwest along the royal highway. Inquiring minds must have wondered why the regent Perdiccas was not present.

It is impossible to accurately reconstruct the machinations that led to this remarkable scene, or the consequences that spilled from it. Events came thick and fast, overlapping and interweaving each other. Our ancient sources are patchy and partisan, omitting detail and insight that could guide us. The fact that Arrian, Diodorus, Curtius, and others wrote their accounts hundreds of years later and from a Roman perspective suggests that the truth was deliberately hidden or had simply disappeared by that time.

Earlier in 321, Perdiccas probably decided on Aegae rather than Siwa as Alexander's final resting place. This was a popular choice in the army and also back in Macedon. In the two years since Alexander's death, Ptolemy—confirmed as satrap of Egypt and based in the capital at Memphis—had become Perdiccas's enemy. Ptolemy murdered Cleomenes under suspicion of loyalty to Perdiccas and seized the treasury, pocketing eight thousand talents of gold and silver. Such a fortune could buy a large and loyal mercenary force.

It was impossible for Perdiccas to send Alexander's body to Siwa, as this would have played into Ptolemy's hands. Possessing the body would confirm Ptolemy's legitimacy and supply a rallying point for the army. What Macedonians would stand against former comrades in arms who possessed and wielded the body of immortal Alexander?

As Ptolemy turned against Perdiccas, Antipater was making friendly overtures to him. While Perdiccas was fighting his way across the Cappadocian mountains, Antipater sent him an offer of his daughter Nicaea's hand in marriage. Macedonia suddenly loomed larger as the destination of choice for the heavily laden funeral cart. Alexander seemed destined to head home to lie alongside his father.

The political winds shifted again a few weeks after Antipater's overture to Perdiccas. When Olympias, Alexander's mother, heard of Antipater's offer to Perdiccas, she made one of her own—the hand of her daughter Cleopatra, Alexander's sister.

A flurry of marriage proposals criss-crossed the Aegean as Perdiccas marched from Cappadocia into neighboring Psidia. Olympias's next letter informed Perdiccas that Cleopatra was in Sardis to his north, and the two began secret negotiations of which we know nothing. Olympias gambled on Perdiccas's ambition; he could hardly refuse the prospect of marrying into Alexander's family, which might legitimize his bid for the throne. Yet there was a price to pay. Perdiccas knew that accepting Olympias's offer would antagonize Antipater.

Perdiccas did not consider his options carefully enough. He fell out with Antigonus One-Eye, the veteran general Alexander left in control of Asia Minor. Antigonus promptly fled to Macedonia, telling Antipater of Olympias's offer and its likely consequences. The die having been cast, Perdiccas had to open a second front at the Hellespont. He appointed Eumenes to defend Asia against Antipater's revenge.

Perdiccas likely decided to keep the body in Babylon until the situation became clearer. Perdiccas's subsequent actions made clear that Alexander would never rest at Siwa.

It was already too late. Ptolemy, as wily as ever, was ahead of the game. While waiting in Babylon to hear from Perdiccas where to convey Alexander's body, Arrhidaios began intriguing with Ptolemy and kept him abreast of Perdiccas's thinking on the fate of Alexander's corpse. Eventually Arrhidaios threw in his lot with Ptolemy, and the two men devised a plan to seize the dead king's body.

Perdiccas learned that Alexander's hearse had left Babylon probably within days. He sent two brothers-in-law, Attalus and Polemon, with a small armed force to intercept the slow-moving cortege. The squadron of horsemen sped across the Taurus mountains and down onto the Syrian plain, catching up with Arrhidaios near Damascus. They failed to talk Arrhidaios out of his treason, and soon Ptolemy and his larger force arrived with suspiciously perfect timing.[5] The funeral procession now turned south toward Egypt. More crowds gathered along the route, watching in awe at the jangling shiny hearse and wondering what was happening.

Many questions hang over Ptolemy's hijacking of Alexander's catafalque, but our sources provide no answers. Did Ptolemy strike on hearing that Perdiccas had decided to transport Alexander to Aegae in Macedonia? Did Arrhidaios ignore a command from Perdiccas to keep the body in Babylon? What explanation did Ptolemy give his soldiers for stealing the god-king's body?

Perdiccas's reaction on hearing that Ptolemy had snatched the hearse can only be imagined, though it was clearly a treasonable act. For Perdiccas, Alexander's royal corpse was a symbol of imperial legitimacy. And now his archenemy Ptolemy had seized it and, as events were soon to reveal, had also joined Antipater in an alliance against Perdiccas.

Ptolemy gambled and won. His daring move was enabled by Perdiccas's disastrous mistake of leaving Alexander's body in Babylon to prosecute a war against a small-time enemy. Ptolemy learned well the lesson of this drama: he held on to Alexander's remains throughout his life. Perdiccas, we can assume from his actions, was desperate to regain Alexander's body, repair his badly dented prestige, and reverse the humiliation of Ptolemy's coup.

Ptolemy escorted the funeral procession south, hugging the coast of Palestine and Gaza, and then turned west into Egypt. Avoiding the construction work at Alexandria, he led the cortege south along the banks of the Nile to his headquarters at Memphis. The catafalque lumbered to a halt before the gates of Memphis in late 321, and Ptolemy milked the occasion for all it was worth. Sounding suspiciously like rationalizing propaganda, *The Alexander Romance* tells a story that Ptolemy had previously asked the oracle of Zeus at Babylon where he should take Alexander's body and was told to convey it to Memphis. It was the flimsiest of myths.

Ptolemy immediately began arranging Alexander's funeral, keen to inter the king before Perdiccas could react. If Alexander could be buried quickly enough, then Perdiccas's dilemma would become a crisis. It was one thing to seize an unburied body, quite another to desecrate a tomb in order to retrieve it.

None of the ancient writers tell where the sarcophagus was deposited to await the funeral, though the huge temple of the Egyptian creator god Ptah—where Alexander had offered sacrifices in 332—is a possibility. Ptolemy hastily organized the funeral celebrations, secure in the knowledge that Macedonian tradition bestowed almost kingly prestige on those who buried a monarch. The kudos and legitimacy that flowed from such an act were foremost in Ptolemy's mind as Alexander's rightful heir in Egypt.

The ancient writers are silent on exactly where Ptolemy finally buried Alexander and are vague about the funeral. Pausanias records that Ptolemy "proceeded to bury it with Macedonian rites in Memphis, but, knowing that Perdiccas would make war, he kept Egypt garrisoned."[6] (Diodorus mislocates the event to Alexandria but describes Ptolemy "entombing him and honoring him with heroic sacrifices and magnificent games."[7] An anonymous inscription on the Greek island of Paros—known as the Parian Marble—records for the year 321–320 that "Alexander was interred in Memphis; Perdiccas marched on Egypt and was killed."[8]

These fragments reveal Ptolemy's skill under pressure: he succeeded in burying Alexander before Perdiccas invaded Egypt. Even more adroit, Ptolemy avoided alienating his Macedonian forces and gave Alexander only traditional hero rites. Deification could wait until there was time to create a divine cult for Alexander and transfer the body to Alexandria. Among his own men at least, Ptolemy now wore the mantle of Alexander's successor in Egypt. Bolstered by the gold and silver bullion he plundered after murdering Cleomenes, Ptolemy and his well-motivated, well-paid army turned to face the regent Perdiccas by the banks of the Nile.

Ptolemy possessed Alexander's body, but Perdiccas and his lieutenant Eumenes had the next best thing—the dead king's armor, diadem, and royal scepter. Perdiccas and Eumenes countered Ptolemy's control of Alexander's corpse with a novel strategy. They wielded the symbols of the living Alexander, evoking the god-king's presence and laying claim to Perdiccas's legitimacy as the rightful heir.

The power of Alexander's aura to inspire and mobilize the only force that mattered in the world—the Macedonian army—was brilliantly displayed when Eumenes conjured Alexander's ghost. Alexander's former secretary claimed to talk with Alexander in dreams, and consequently the army followed Eumenes's orders as if the words of the immortal Alexander. Eumenes gave material form to this deception by setting up a throne adorned with Alexander's royal arms and accoutrements.[9]

Eumenes subsequently galvanized his men and tarnished the luster of Ptolemy's possession of the actual body. But the future was ominous; if Alexander's dreamlike image and empty throne energized Eumenes's army, then what effect would the mummified body have on Ptolemy's behalf? For months, two Alexanders contended with each other for the legacy of empire: Alexander's immutable body legitimizing the actions and aspirations of Ptolemy in Egypt and Alexander's indomitable spirit and royal paraphernalia supporting the cause of Perdiccas in Asia.

Leaving Eumenes to defend the Hellespont against Antipater, Perdiccas marched on Egypt in the spring of 320, probably within weeks of Alexander's burial at Memphis. Leading the Royal Army out of Psidia and with Roxanne, the infant Alexander IV, and King Philip Arrhidaios in tow, Perdiccas's invasion force swept down through Syria, Gaza, and into Egypt, shadowed by his fleet offshore.

Just as Perdiccas arrived, Ptolemy was summoned from Memphis to the eastern frontier of Egypt. He was tried by an assembly of the Royal Army and acquitted of the charge of rebellion. A majority of both armies did not want a civil war between the two marshals and preferred to negotiate. Perdiccas, enraged, marched the Royal Army to the banks of the Nile in late May or June, striking camp within sight of Ptolemy's stronghold known as the Fort of Camels.

Two of Alexander's best generals now faced each other across the great river, but the pressure was on Perdiccas to advance and reclaim Alexander's body. Perdiccas had the Royal Army and wore Alexander's signet ring, but Ptolemy's strategic genius—together with his cunning use of bribery and spies—gave him the advantage.

Perdiccas attacked at dawn, sending his armored war elephants and soldiers across the Nile in an all-out assault on Ptolemy's position. Ptolemy responded in Alexander-like fashion by leading the defense in person, blinding the lead elephant and killing its rider *(mahout)*. Out-fought and outmaneuvered, Perdiccas was forced to retreat.

Perdiccas now gambled everything on a single bold move, leading his men on a night march south to outflank Ptolemy and strike behind his lines at Memphis. In one lightning thrust he would seize the capital, re-trieve Alexander's sarcophagus, and destroy Ptolemy's forces in a ham-mer blow from the rear.

But imaginative strategy was not enough. Perdiccas was not Alexan-der, and his second assault also foundered. Perdiccas's men struggled to cross the river but only made it to one of the islands that divided the Nile in sight of Memphis's harbor walls. The sheer number of soldiers and elephants wading across the shallow part of the river undermined the sandy bottom, and men and beasts lost their footing and were swept away. Weighed down with armor, more than two thousand of Perdic-cas's veterans were either drowned or eaten alive by crocodiles.[10]

The Royal Army had had enough. Frustrated by Perdiccas's refusal to negotiate with Ptolemy, suffering defeat at the Fort of Camels, they were now humiliated again, watching helplessly as thousands of their comrades lost their lives for nothing. The consequences of failure were dire for Perdiccas: his troops mutinied and senior officers stabbed him to death.

Ptolemy played the generous and respectful victor. As he crossed the Nile the following day, he was offered the vacant regency by the officers and men of the Royal Army. He refused the regency, seeking only to tighten his grip on Egypt. He was confirmed in his position at a conference of the marshals, which included Antipater and the two kings, at the royal hunting park at Triparadeisos in Syria a few months later.[11]

Ptolemy's mastery of strategy and timing paid off again, but luck also played a decisive role. Two days after Perdiccas was murdered, news arrived that his lieutenant, Eumenes, had fought and won a great battle against Antipater's generals Craterus and Neoptolemus, who had crossed the Hellespont and invaded Asia on his behalf.

This was dramatic and unexpected news. Perdiccas had just promoted the former administrator Eumenes to general, and Craterus was regarded as Alexander's most brilliant commander. Antipater's army had been defeated, and he lost his two generals. It was even said that Eumenes had slain Neoptolemus in single combat. This was staggering news and could have changed everything had it arrived forty-eight hours earlier.

Perdiccas's aspirations would have been realized in Eumenes's victory: the regency would have been unassailable, Antipater humiliated and sidelined, and Ptolemy's position untenable. Few if any Macedonians would have stood against Perdiccas and Eumenes after such an overwhelming victory. And Alexander's mummified body, disinterred and returned to Perdiccas, would have made a very different journey through history.

As Perdiccas fought Ptolemy for control of Alexander's royal body, the gold-encased mummy waited in a tomb somewhere in Memphis. Alexander's rushed burial had been forced on Ptolemy by strategic necessity. Now victorious, Ptolemy reflected on the need to tighten his grip on Egypt, reshape it as a Greco–Egyptian kingdom, and transform Alexander from a heroic Macedonian king into a universal god. Memphis, Ptolemy soon realized, was the ideal place for such a stunning transformation.

A sprawling city on the banks of the Nile, Memphis (alternating with Thebes) was the capital of Egypt throughout most of the pharaonic period. It was three thousand years old when Alexander arrived at the head of his army in 332—a cosmopolitan city that attracted people from all over the Mediterranean world. Alexander arrived in Memphis to offer sacrifices in the Temple of Ptah, an act that Egyptians regarded as a royal prerogative and made him a divine pharaoh in their eyes. From that time on, Memphis was the center of Alexander's imperial government for the satrapy of Egypt.

Memphis was sacred to the Egyptians, a center of religious, political, and cosmological importance, dedicated to and dominated by the cult of Ptah. The Greek name for the entire country, Aigyptos, derived from the Egyptian Hekaptah, "the palace where the spirit of Ptah dwells." Its connection with Ptah and the political realities confronting Ptolemy during those dangerous times make Memphis an important, if often overlooked, part of the mystery surrounding Alexander's entombment.

For Egyptians, Memphis radiated an ineffable spiritual power. In the scented chambers of its great temples the gods were born and cosmic order was established. Memphis was the ideal burial place for Alexander: he was reborn as a god alongside the pantheon of Egyptian deities whose ancestry stretched back to the beginning of time.

Ptolemy determined to create a hybrid Greco–Egyptian society with himself as king. By possessing and burying Alexander's remains, Ptolemy aimed to legalize and sanctify his rule over Egypt. And by establishing a divine Alexander cult, he hoped to further endow his rulership with an aura of auspicious authority, as if Alexander himself had blessed Ptolemy's rule. Here, at Memphis, Ptolemy devised an imaginative fusion of Alexander, Ptah, and himself that recreated Egypt as a Ptolemaic kingdom.

Ptolemy's ambition was welcome news to the powerful Egyptian priesthood of Ptah. A royal cult of Alexander worship at Memphis would strengthen the priests' influence, tying them ever closer to Ptolemy as he reconfigured the religious politics of Egypt.

Magic, mythmaking, and power politics were entwined in Ptolemy's plans for the future. He forged older Egyptian beliefs and traditional Macedonian cultic rites into an enduring and intimate relationship between Memphis, himself, and the Ptolemaic dynasty he intended to found. And from the reign of Ptolemy V (Epiphanes) in 197 B.C.E.,

Memphis, specifically the temple of Ptah, was the sacred place where Macedonian pharaohs were crowned. Each new Ptolemy was acclaimed the "chosen one" of Ptah.

Ptolemy had the future of Alexander's body and tomb firmly in his sights from the beginning. He buried the king at Memphis with a vision of later moving the body to a grand tomb in Alexandria. His first priority now was to reshape Egypt's religious and political landscape to support the various cults that would establish a regime of Ptolemaic rule sanctified by the living god Alexander. Ptolemy's strategy, especially how he planned to turn Alexander's tomb into the most famous mausoleum of the ancient world, is revealed by the strange hybrid world he created in the years following his defeat of Perdiccas.

Ptolemy's invaluable ally was the high-ranking Egyptian priest Manetho, who schooled him in the bizarre cults and practices of the city, as well as the intricate web of myths and legends supporting them. Manetho's advice is not recorded, but we can reasonably infer that it included insights into Egyptian cosmology, cultic practices, and the confabulations of myth and history that fascinated Egypt's new Macedonian ruler.

The city was the focal point of the Egyptian cult of Apis the sacred bull, regarded as the reincarnation of Ptah. The Apis bull was kept in Ptah's temple in Memphis; after it died it was mummified and interred at Saqqara on the city's western outskirts. Here the dead bull's immortal soul joined those of its mummified predecessors, which were collectively worshiped as Osiris-Apis or Oserapis, a name shortened by the Greeks to Serapis, and whose great necropolis temple they called the Serapeum.[12]

The Apis bull cult appealed to Ptolemy and he, with Manetho's guidance, reconfigured Serapis as a new hybrid deity. Over time, Serapis incorporated aspects of Olympian Zeus, Dionysus, Helios, Asclepius, and Hades. Images of the new Serapis bore no resemblance to Oserapis. Rather, they depicted a Greek man with long curly hair and full beard with a *kalathos* or corn basket perched on his head as a sign of fertility.

Ptolemy and Manetho bound Serapis to Alexander to promote a god sacred to Egypt's native inhabitants and its new Macedonian elite. In one tradition, Alexander was said to be responsible for the cult of Serapis. This story was heard by Plutarch, who included it in his *Life of*

Alexander. Alexander, Plutarch says, founded Alexandria after visiting the shrine of Zeus Ammon at Siwa. Alexander saw the god in a dream and asked for help in his conquests, and in return ordered a Serapeum temple to be built in the god's honor at Alexandria. This has the trademark of a local Alexandrian legend, aimed at binding the cult of Alexander as the city's founder with the worship of the Apis bull at Saqqara.

To consecrate the worship of Serapis, Ptolemy built temples and shrines, approved the official Hellenized appearance of the god, created a liturgy, and paid for a priesthood to oversee the cult rituals. Oserapis had been worshiped by Egyptians and Greeks living in Egypt long before Alexander's time, but Ptolemy's Serapis was strikingly different. Seeking to transform Egypt from a satrapy to a kingdom, Ptolemy and Manetho devised Serapis as a composite deity that coexisted with Oserapis in the Serapeum on the outskirts of Memphis.

Cavernous and otherwordly, the great Serapeum temple rose above the desert scarp of the city's western edge. Since Early Dynastic times, around 3,000 B.C.E., this limestone ridge, known as Saqqara, had been packed with tombs along its nearly four-mile length. They had been used, reused, and plundered on countless occasions. Grand funerary and religious monuments stretched in all directions: the stepped pyramid of the Old Kingdom pharaoh Djoser had stood since 2650 B.C.E., and nearby was the huge temple enclosure of the cat god Bastet, the temple of Anubis (the dog-headed god of the underworld), and a vast subterranean world of catacombs in which tens of thousands of mummified ibises, baboons, and hawks had been entombed. By Alexander's time, Saqqara was a vast city of human dead flanked by a mortuary zoo of embalmed animals.[13]

To reach the Serapeum, priests and worshippers trudged along the Serapeum Way—a winding brick avenue lined with stony-faced sphinxes that snaked its way up from the Nile valley to the ridge. In the final decades before Christ, the Roman traveler Strabo followed in their footsteps, leaving a vivid description of the towering monuments. The Serapeum, he said, is "in a place so very sandy that dunes . . . are heaped up by the winds: and by these some of the sphinxes which I saw were buried even to the head."[14] Today there is nothing to see. Every sphinx has been reclaimed by the desert.

In this sacred area, the Serapeum stood supreme, facing both cosmically important directions: east to the rising sun, the Nile, and the urban sprawl of Memphis, and west to the setting sun, the endless desert, and the kingdom of the dead. As Strabo sweated his way toward the Serapeum's impressive facade, he passed a small temple dedicated to the Egyptian Oserapis and built by Nectanebo II, the last native pharaoh of Egypt.

At the point where the Serapeum Way met the entrance to the Serapeum's subterranean vaults, pilgrims and priests of Strabo's age were confronted by eleven life-size statues of Greek philosophers arranged on a semicircular podium.[15] The surprising presence of Greek sculptures in the midst of Egyptian religious architecture has suggested to some that Alexander was laid to rest in the vicinity, perhaps even in the small adjacent temple of Nectanebo II.[16]

At the end of the Serapeum Way, the path descends underground into the dark. In the subterranean maze of musty rock-hewn galleries lay the tombs of the Apis bulls, embalmed as Osiris-Apis and deposited in huge sarcophagi, some of wood but most of red and black granite weighing up to sixty-five tons. The long continuity of this tradition is evident from the fact that the earliest mummified bulls belonged to the Nineteenth Dynasty of Rameses II (1279–1213 B.C.E.).

The Serapeum stood on the boundary between life and death, a pivotal location for a world and a country being reinvented by Ptolemy in the momentous aftermath of Alexander's conquests and Ptolemy's victory over Perdiccas. During the time Alexander lay in Memphis-Saqqara, Ptolemy built Alexandria and a great tomb for Alexander. Ptolemy also devised and perfected Alexander's cult and condoned (perhaps instigated) the popular rumors and legends that were later written down as the foundations of *The Alexander Romance*.

For Ptolemy, the most useful of these fabulous stories establishes the enduring relationship between Macedonia and Egypt, Alexander and the pharaohs. This legend rewrites history by denying that Alexander was Philip's son and making him the offspring of Nectanebo II, who fled Egypt for Macedonia in 343 B.C.E. There, disguised as Zeus Ammon, he fathered Alexander on Queen Olympias.[17] Thus Alexander was the son of Ammon and Nectanebo II, the legitimate heir to the throne of Egypt, a pharaoh and a living god.

For Ptolemy, this was powerful propaganda passed on by oral tradition and appealing to the illiterate farmers and artisans who made up most of Egypt's population. By promoting himself as Alexander's heir, Ptolemy created a sacred genealogy linking himself to the ancient line of Egyptian pharaohs with Alexander as the linchpin.

Enveloped in this farrago of political myths and urban legends, Alexander's body was too important to be venerated only in the Egyptian tradition. For Ptolemy and his Macedonian rivals, if not the wider Greek world, the mummified royal corpse was a uniquely potent political instrument. And Ptolemy had ambitions far beyond Memphis.

From the beginning, Ptolemy planned to take the body with him to Alexandria. Having gained possession of the corpse, he could never let it go. Losing it would have been worse than never possessing it. By stealing it and then burying it at Memphis, Ptolemy transformed the gilded mummy into a magical touchstone for his royal and dynastic aims in Egypt.

Alexander's body waited in Memphis as the grand tomb took shape in Alexandria. Only when it was finally laid to rest in his eponymous city, amid cult and grandeur, could Ptolemy propel the living god on a journey into the future.

WHO MOVED
ALEXANDER'S CORPSE?

ALEXANDER'S GHOST HOVERED ABOVE Memphis-Saqqara as his empire disintegrated. As Ptolemy looked on, Alexander's former marshals conspired, maneuvered, and murdered their way to ultimate victory and a royal future.

Political fault lines sharpened and then shifted as the Hellenistic era took shape. Ptolemy strained every sinew to tighten his grip on Egypt, revitalizing old institutions, giving birth to exotic new cults, and cloaking Greek gods in Egyptian costume. Above all, he built Alexandria, a lustrous pearl gleaming on the Mediterranean shore, whose spiritual center was the sepulchre fashioned to receive the gilded mummy of the now deified Alexander.

As vast quantities of gold poured into Egypt from Nubian mines, Ptolemy diverted some of it to his royal mint and turned it into coinage to pay for his army and finance the construction of Alexandria. On the coins Ptolemy issued we catch sight of the energetic, gifted man who rode across Asia with Alexander and outlived his more flamboyant and ambitious contemporaries.

In the face staring from his gold and silver drachmas, we see a firm chin and eyes that project steely determination. These miniature portraits show a pragmatist, not a dreamer. Ptolemy, son of the Macedonian nobleman, Lagus, was a master of realpolitik, the art of the possible: shaping Egypt into a unique hybrid kingdom ruled by himself and his dynasty in perpetuity. He had no interest in reviving Alexander's vast unwieldy empire, though he did want to secure his vulnerable eastern border by annexing the area that is today Palestine and Lebanon.

After hijacking Alexander's hearse and defeating Perdiccas, Ptolemy engaged in a deadly game with his rivals. For years they maintained the fiction that they were satraps holding the empire in trust for two power-less kings: the young Alexander IV and the retarded Philip Arrhidaios. In reality, they functioned as monarchs in all but name, and Ptolemy as the absolute ruler of Egypt.

Ptolemy had to work ceaselessly to secure his position because despite his authority, Macedonians and Greeks were a small minority in a sea of Egyptians. Ptolemy decided to resurrect a variation of his earlier ruse in which he had circulated the story that Alexander was the son of Nectanebo II and thus the rightful heir of the Egyptian pharaohs. With Manetho's aid, Ptolemy reprised this legendary sleight of hand by circu-lating rumors that he was actually not the son of Ptolemy Lagus but the illegitimate offspring of King Philip II, and thus the half brother of Alexander and his rightful heir.

As propaganda, this was gold in a world where mythical relationships between important figures enjoyed great currency. Fabulous stories about Alexander's or Ptolemy's "true" parentage spread like wildfire among the illiterate peasants who made up the bulk of the population. Such stories created a favorable aura around Egypt's past, present, and future kings—Nectanebo, Alexander, and Ptolemy.

Ptolemy's fingerprints are all over this rumor, and it is inconceivable that he did not at least approve of such mythmaking. We see an elaborate web of deception, rumor mongering, and propaganda designed to appeal to the lower classes and interlock with the higher-class cults and Alexan-der's tomb that Ptolemy was devising in tandem. He was appealing to all levels of Egyptian society, persuading them to accept the new order that he was creating. Although he concocted legendary connections for the peasantry, Ptolemy aimed mainly at convincing the elite.

Alexander's body was the keystone of Ptolemy's plan, and its cultic display in a grand mausoleum his ultimate aim. But Alexander was in Memphis and the tomb in Alexandria. Conferring with Manetho in Memphis, Ptolemy considered a multilayered strategy. Transferring the body to the coast involved two crucial considerations: when should it be done, and should Ptolemy himself move it or should he leave it to his son Philadelphus? But first, Alexandria and the tomb had to be readied.

Alexandria was founded by Alexander on April 7, 331, but it was Ptolemy's masterpiece. It was a perfect North African port, perched on a spit of land oriented to the sea and separated from its hinterland by Lake Mareotis. A grand canal was planned to link the city to the Nile Delta, and the ambitious Heptastadion causeway was planned to link the small island of Pharos to the mainland, immortalized in history as the name given to the world's first lighthouse.[1]

Alexander's strategic eye recognized the potential of this location, but it was Ptolemy's bold vision that revolutionized the city's role in the post-Alexander world.[2] Envisaging a metropolis dedicated to Alexander and dominated by his tomb, Ptolemy planned temples, palaces, and colonnaded streets, interspersed with spacious parks and groves adorned with Alexander's statues and busts. Alexandria would be Egypt's new capital and Ptolemy's royal residence, moving to the rhythm of hymns, prayers, processions, and sacrifices dedicated to the cult of its divine and eponymous founder.

The cults would underwrite the connection between Alexandria's architectual splendor and Ptolemy's dynastic rule. The Alexander cult and the newly invented Serapis cult would hold Ptolemy and his family in a divine embrace, presenting to the world a single and indivisible dynasty.

Alexandria's exquisite skyline took shape along the grid line of streets that Alexander had laid out. Ptolemy kept a keen eye on the building site, bringing in Egyptian engineers, Greek sculptors, woodworkers, goldsmiths, and planners to build the cosmopolis that became known as the Mistress of the Sea. Ptolemy *was* Alexander now, to all intents and purposes. The tomb, the cult, the wealth, and the future belonged to the boyhood friend turned general, then marshal, now satrap and monarch-in-waiting. Once the gilded mummy was in place and Ptolemy's kingship proclaimed, the doors to divinity would open and the Ptolemaic ship of state would slide effortlessly down Alexandria's slipway into the harbor waters. Alexandria was about to receive the tomb of the ultimate hero and take its place as one of the greatest cities of the ancient world.[3]

Alexander's cult actually comprised two cults. In typical Greek fashion, he was revered as Alexander Ktistes—the city founder—the talismanic individual who patronized Hellenism's ideal of cultured city life. The founder's cult took on grandiose dimensions under Ptolemy's successors. In his book *On the Shrines of Alexander* the Roman author Jason mentions an Alexandrian shrine commonly regarded as dedicated to Alexander as founder, probably located in the city's marketplace.[4]

But Ptolemy required more than a commonplace founder cult to transform Alexander into the symbolic and sacred protector of an entire dynasty. What was in fact demanded was a second cult for the divine Alexander, in which Ptolemy, his family, and successors could be intimately linked and be seen to rule with Alexander's blessing.

Ptolemy conceived Alexander's tomb and personalized cult as revolving around himself and his dynasty, with rituals focused on the mausoleum.[5] To glorify and administer the cult, he created a priesthood with a high priest who was the top-ranking religious official in Egypt.

The full-blown Alexander cult came into being between 311, when Alexandria had become Egypt's capital, and 285, when Ptolemy coruled the kingdom with his son and successor, Ptolemy II Philadelphus.[6] However, no ancient writer even alludes to the event. Thus we are left to imagine how Alexander arrived. Was he dragged across the desert from Memphis? Or, more likely, floated on a garlanded mortuary barge down the Nile and into the delta, coming ashore in Alexandria's southern harbor on Lake Mareotis?

Alexander's move from Memphis-Saqqara to Alexandria was a pivotal moment in Egypt's three-hundred-year transition from native pharaonic grandeur to the advent of Roman rule. Yet we cannot be sure when it occurred or who was responsible.

Our sources belong to Roman times, several centuries later. Rome was the new superpower, and while its emperors saw Alexander as a heroic conqueror, they held the Ptolemies in contempt as effete, corrupt nonentities. Not surprisingly, Strabo and Diodorus—our two earliest Roman sources—are not overly concerned with such dynastic niceties as which Ptolemy moved Alexander's body, or when.[7]

Strabo and Diodorus, writing during the last fifty years before Christ, assert that Ptolemy buried Alexander in Alexandria but do not mention his brief stay in Memphis. A century later, the Roman rhetorician and proconsul Quintus Curtius Rufus mentions the Memphis burial, saying that Ptolemy transferred Alexander's body to Alexandria a few years later.[8] Despite the confusion, Diodorus paints a vivid scene.

> Ptolemy decided . . . to keep it [Alexander's body] in the city that [Alexander] had founded. . . . There he built a precinct that was worthy of the glory of Alexander both in its size and in its construction. Laying him to rest and honoring him with heroic sacrifices and magnificent games, Ptolemy was rewarded richly, not only by men but also by the gods. . . . [M]en gathered in Alexandria from all sides and eagerly enrolled in his army.[9]

Diodorus spins a colorful but careless tale. He fails to mention Memphis and mistakenly assumes that Ptolemy buried Alexander in Alexandria in 321, long before the city was built.

These were dangerous times. Perdiccas was at the gates of Egypt, and Ptolemy would never have left Alexander's remains in Alexandria while he was in Memphis. And Perdiccas would never have gambled his army on Memphis if the golden body lay elsewhere. Diodorus conjures a magnificent funeral, but it could describe either Alexander's interment at Memphis or his reburial at Alexandria; perhaps it is a composite of both.

Five hundred years after the event, around 150 C.E., the Roman writer Pausanias put the finishing touches to his *Description of Greece*. He says that Ptolemy's son, Philadelphus, took Alexander's remains to Alexandria.[10] How can these contradictory accounts be untangled?

The answer may lie inscribed on a missing fragment of the Parian Marble, an anonymous monument carved on the Greek island of Paros. It is the earliest example of a Greek chronological table. Its sequence of inscriptions is a year-by-year record of major events between 323 and 299–298 B.C.E. It tells of Alexander's burial in Memphis in 321 but is silent on reburial in Alexandria. In fact, the inscriptions end in 264, but the last thirty-four years are absent on a segment that has never been found.[11] Sixteen years of these missing dates—between 298 and 283— fall within Ptolemy's lifetime—any one of which could have seen him bring Alexander's corpse to Alexandria.

Ptolemy, as wily as ever, was looking for the right time to move Alexander. He was content to remain satrap in name as long as his rivals did the same, and as long as Alexander's royal Argead line survived. His decision to finally proclaim himself king culminated a decade of dramatic events outside Egypt's borders.

The bloodletting had begun in September 317 B.C.E. Alexander's mother, Olympias, murdered Philip Arrhidaios, Alexander's half brother who had been proclaimed King Philip III by the Royal Army in Babylon just six years before. This act of regicide showcased Olympias's ruthless streak, which she then flaunted with a spate of political murders that included Cassander's son and supporters. Olympias's bloody reign ended in the spring of 316, when Cassander had her stoned to death in public.[12]

In the space of a year, Alexander's mother and brother were murdered, and in 309, his Persian mistress Barsine and their illegitimate son Heracles suffered the same fate. Mother and son were seized in Pergamum in Asia Minor and then dragged along on an invasion of Macedonia by General Polyperchon, who intended to depose Cassander and install the eighteen-year-old Heracles as a puppet king. Cassander reckoned that if he took the field, his soldiers would desert him for Alexander's illegitimate son, and a speedy execution would follow.[13] Just as Polyperchon was succeeding, however, he threw away his winning hand. When Cassander offered to return his estates and appoint him general in his army, Polyperchon had no further use for Barsine and Heracles and killed them.

A few months later, Cassander eliminated his last legitimate rivals by poisoning Roxanne and her son Alexander IV at Amphipolis and then burying them in unmarked graves. It was a timely murder, since Alexander IV would soon turn fourteen, when he would become a royal page and would be invited by the army to claim his father's inheritance. Cassander would not have survived the succession.[14]

The royal bloodline was thinning, leaving only Cleopatra, Alexander's sister, as a source of royal legitimacy for a would-be successor. Having lost two husbands already in 322, Cleopatra had ignored overtures from several of Alexander's former marshals. Now she changed her mind, judgingly rightly that her future, and probably her life, lay with Ptolemy in Egypt. With the tragic events of 309 surely playing on her mind, she began corresponding with Ptolemy and arranged to meet him in Greece. As she was leaving her home in Sardis, Cleopatra was set upon and murdered by a group of women under the direction of Antigonus One-Eye and ultimately Cassander. It was an act of terrible and symmetrical irony: what Olympias began with the killing of Philip Arrhidaois was completed when her archenemy Cassander assassinated her daughter Cleopatra: Alexander's entire family, legitimate and illegitimate, had been extinguished. The Argead dynasty that had conquered Greece under Philip II and the known world under his son Alexander disappeared from history in a welter of jealous feuding, conspiracy, and murder.

Cassander concealed his killing of Alexander IV for three years. The news leaked out in 306, and the effects were immediate. With no Argead left alive, the successors crowned themselves kings. But who would reign where, and what would be the consequences for Ptolemy and for Alexander's remains?

Antigonus One-Eye, now almost eighty years old, assumed a royal diadem and referred to himself as *basileus* (king) in 306. Antigonus aspired to rule the whole empire and believed himself to be Alexander's true imperial successor, issuing gold and silver coins stamped with his name and new royal title. In Pella, Cassander styled himself king of the Macedonians, and Seleucus in Babylon and Lysimachus in Thrace also took up the title of king.

The Hellenistic era was born in treason and blood. Ptolemy alone had legitimacy, by virtue of possessing Alexander's body, a talisman now more potent than ever. Once again, Ptolemy's foresight and planning came into its own. Apart from those buried in unknown graves, all the murdered contenders for the throne had been cremated according to Macedonian custom. Apart from miniature portraits on coins and the occasional sculpture, they had no share in the world of the living. Alexander alone had been mummified, preserved as in life to be gazed on, venerated, and touched by those privileged to have access to his tomb.

Ptolemy had watched these bloody events from the safety of Egypt, spending the dangerous years between 317 and 306 creating his Greco–Egyptian kingdom and developing the Alexander and Serapis cults. Ptolemy had played it safe and legal; he would not rebel against the two kings as long as they lived, nor be the first to proclaim himself king when they perished. But with each royal murder the day fast approached when Ptolemy could legitimately crown himself king of Egypt. Antigonus's announcement in 306 sealed Ptolemy's royal future.

In 305, in a cleverly orchestrated move, Ptolemy meshed the traditions of Macedonian kingship and the divine office of Egyptian pharaoh. In a brilliant *coup de théâtre*, Ptolemy had himself crowned king and pharaoh simultaneously, and from this moment reigned as king.[15]

Surely Ptolemy considered the pivotal role of Alexander's cult and tomb in his coronation. There was no better time to bring Alexander to Alexandria to consecrate Ptolemy's enthronement as pharaoh-king. Yet the Parian Marble says nothing of this in its entry for 305, and neither does any other ancient writer. Why was such a perfect opportunity ignored?

Ptolemy's astute political sense gave him a keen eye to the future. It would not be out of character for him to forgo the immediate glory of moving Alexander himself for the greater prize of securing his dynasty by allowing his son to do so. Perhaps king and heir hatched a plan, a delayed move and reburial to give Philadelphus an opportunity to create his own personal attachment to Alexander.

The most likely date for such subterfuge is 283–282, the year Ptolemy died and Philadelphus acceded to his throne. If Alexander was not already entombed in Alexandria by this time, Philadelphus would hardly squander the opportunity for such a propaganda coup. He would seal his legitimacy in the Macedonian fashion by burying his father *and* the great Alexander. No record survives of Ptolemy's funeral or Philadelphus's coronation, and the year 283–282 falls on the missing section of the Parian Marble. Consequently we are left to speculate on the role of Alexander's tomb in this event.

One other date would fulfill Philadelphus's self-aggrandizing purposes, 275–274 B.C.E. Philadelphus loved ritual and show, filling his reign with new and ever grander religious cults and festivals. One overblown event early in his reign seems a likely opportunity for bringing Alexander to Alexandria.

Ptolemy died in the winter of 283–282, after an extraordinary life that saw the son of an obscure Macedonian noble transformed into the king-pharaoh of Egypt. Philadelphus wasted no time in deifying his father as Soter—savior god—and establishing a new religious festival, the Ptolemaia, in his honor.

The Ptolemaia set a precedent as an ostentatious display of unbounded wealth enveloped in religious and mythological imagery derived from Alexander's conquests in Asia. It glorified the Ptolemies, emphasizing their legendary connections with Alexander and perhaps bringing together Greco–Macedonian and Egyptian culture.

The Ptolemaia was celebrated every four years at the same time as the Olympic games, attempting to surpass them with its own athletic, musical, and drama competitions, with prizes equaling those awarded at Olympia. As an exercise in realpolitik networking it was triumphant, with political and religious representatives arriving from all over the Greek world to be dazzled by amounts of gold exceeding what any could have imagined. For Philadelphus, the first Ptolemaia was probably tinged with the sadness over his father's death. The second, staged in the winter of 275–274, astonished the ancient world.[16]

A Hellenistic writer known as Callixeinus of Rhodes described what he saw (or heard) in a now lost book called *About Alexandria,* excerpts of which have survived in a much later source.[17] He tells of a flagrantly expensive celebration of Alexander and the Ptolemies organized in a sequence of separate parades. The most famous of these has become known as the Grand Procession of Ptolemy Philadelphus.[18] Callixeinus is a dry, uninspiring correspondent, but the details he supplies make it easy to imagine the awe-inspiring scene.

Philadelphus reclines alongside his new sister-wife Arsinoe II amid a circle of guests seated on 130 golden couches, shaded by the royal pavilion near Alexandria's stadium. Ostentatious wealth glitters beneath a canopy of scarlet and white suspended eighty-two feet above them. Golden goblets and platters overflow with wine, meat, and fruit, supported by solid gold tables. The scent of perfume rises from the flower-strewn floor, which vibrates to the distant bellowing of richly caparisoned elephants, the percussive pounding of drums, and the cadences of human voices accompanied by reedy flutes and the strumming of harps and lyres.

Philadelphus glances toward the harbor, where he sees his pride and joy—ten huge supergalleys, moored and garlanded for the occasion—as well as the largest ship in the world, the *Lady of Alexandria*, boasting twenty banks of oars against the usual seven.

Arsinoe and her courtiers relax elegantly. Full-length diaphanous silk chitons twine seductively around their bodies, teasing the eye with what they do not quite reveal. Glistening and fragrant, their hair is turned and twisted, artfully braided in the latest fashion and surmounted by intricately wrought golden tiaras. Sunlight flashes on pendant earrings, playing across cheekbones smudged with colored powders, highlighting kohl-encircled eyes and producing an unnerving precision to the glance. A few wear intricate wigs in the Egyptian style, and one balances a dazzling conical hat on her raised bun of hair. Queen Arsinoe II and her companions wear the empire well.[19]

Arsinoe rearranges the pale blue silks that cling to her body and fingers the gold serpent that coils up her arm. Suddenly Dionysus appears, standing twenty feet tall and pulled on a four-wheeled cart. He is surrounded by musicians and dancers. Philadelphus nods his approval as the spectacle he helped design unfolds before him. It is overpowering, and the symbolism is clear. Dionysus's mythical exploits in India are known throughout the Greek world, but so are those of Philadelphus's legendary ancestor Alexander, who in many ways surpassed the god.

Philadelphus and his advisers have drawn parallels between Alexander and Dionysus, emphasizing blood links to this deified duo via Ptolemy's mother, a previous Arsinoe, whose family claimed descent from Dionysus. Strengthening this bond, another branch of Philadelphus's family traced ancestral origins to Alexander himself. Dionysus imagery in the grand procession, especially the segment called the Return of Dionysus from India, artfully ties the Ptolemies to Alexander and presents them as his rightful heirs.

Alexander spent vast sums on entertaining his troops at Ecbatana and planning for Hephaestion's funeral and burial in Babylon. But he never amassed such exotic splendor in one place for purposes of self-aggrandizement. Times had changed, and Ptolemy's son was no Alexander, though he benefited from the vast wealth Alexander had acquired, which now belonged to Alexandria's treasury. In Philadelphus's world, opulence and propaganda were replacing military conquest as the basis of dynastic rule.

Philadelphus brought the world to Alexandria in the Ptolemaia of 275–274. But did he bring Alexander? From every corner of his kingdom and beyond, people, animals, gold, silver, and gems paraded before the royal box and then out of the stadium and along the city's marbled streets. The scene was a paean to gigantism that impressed itself deeply into memory, inspiring perhaps the grand triumphs that would become such a feature of imperial Rome in the centuries to come.

Philadelphus and Arsinoe sipped their Mareotic wine, white and sweet, its bouquet appealing to their cultivated palates. They sank back onto the pillows in their gold couches, cooled by a fragrant mix of sea breeze and myrrh. Then this epitome of high culture was confronted with a procession of animals from the barbarous margins of the world. Camels appeared for the first time in Egypt, swaying under loads of saffron and frankincense strapped to their bodies, followed by tightly bound lions and panthers in a cacophony of noise.[20] The exotic plumage of caged parrots, guinea fowl, and peacocks excited spectators. For those in the know, the big cats were Dionysian symbols and the strutting peacocks emblematic of Alexander.

The Roman writer Aelian recorded that the brightly colored bird enjoyed a special relationship with Alexander beginning in India. He tells how Alexander was entranced by their beauty and placed them under royal protection. Anyone who killed a peacock was subject to severe punishments. In the years following Alexander's death, the peacock was adopted as a religious symbol by the Ptolemies, and in a curious turn of events became an image of Christian resurrection.[21] Philadelphus was pleased; even his choice of wildlife proclaimed the links between himself and Alexander.

The animals were followed by groups of boy charioteers, followed by men dressed as lusty satyrs and Ethiopians carrying bundles of pure white elephant tusks and logs of blue-black ebony. Others appeared heaving containers filled with gold dust, silver, and pearls. Alexandria's engineers contributed a giant automata in the shape of a snail, sliding along and leaving a trail of mucous in its wake. Another was a statue with a hidden mechanism that made it continuously stand and sit on its own. And somewhere in the melee, Philadelphus knew, was a gigantic cart with a cave gushing forth two springs, one of wine, the other milk.

Alexander appeared twice, according to Callixeinus, his giant images lumbering along on oversize floats. First came his statue accompanied by Ptolemy, both sitting on thrones, sporting golden diadems fashioned to resemble Dionysus's crown of ivy leaves. Elegantly clad women strode dutifully behind in elaborate coiffures topped by golden crowns, each representing a Greek city of Asia liberated by Alexander's army more than half a century earlier. In their wake came a 135-foot golden thyrsos of Dionysus, a 90-foot silver spear, and a 180-foot erect golden phallus tied with ribbons.[22]

No sooner had Alexander left than he returned as a golden statue of the universal conqueror, alongside Athena and Nike, drawn by four war elephants—noisy, exotic, and unpredictable symbols from the furthest reaches of Philadelphus's realm. In the eastern Mediterranean, elephant imagery was already well known and well fingered, at least in the pockets of the rich, as Alexander's portrait wearing an elephant-skull headdress adorned Ptolemaic coins. From 304, Ptolemy authorized the minting of golden staters showing Alexander in an elephant-drawn chariot. Behind these lumbering beasts came altars and thrones piled high with gold, silver, and more golden crowns—the spoils of Alexander's wars in the east and the plunder from Persian treasuries.

For members of the royal court and their guests, enjoying the parade from their cushioned gold couches, Alexander had become Philadelphus's fantasy, a wish fulfillment owing little to Alexander himself, his behavior, or his historic significance. Alexander had been tamed and reconfigured as a public relations bonanza. The modern fascination with Alexander owes much to Philadelphus's fantastic creations in the winter of 275–274.

As the procession passed out of royal view, it exited the arena and made its way through the city, almost certainly past Alexander's garlanded tomb. Alexandria was swollen with visitors from Egypt and beyond, with perhaps several hundred thousand people pressing forward to catch a glimpse of the wondrous display. Shouting and jostling, singing and drinking, the odor of sweat mingling with the aroma of roasting meat, the pungent alchemy of incense, and elephant dung conjured by the heat. Rich and poor, jeweler and thief, soldier and civilian—all pushed and shoved in the porticoes of magnificent buildings and the shade of marble colonnades.

The pomp and pageantry had an edge, for behind the sumptuous display a war loomed. Everyone knew it was coming, and Philadelphus incorporated a military parade into his procession, made up of 23,000 cavalry and 57,000 infantry. This Ptolemaia was part of a mobilization for the forthcoming campaign, the First Syrian War against the Seleucid King Antiochus I. The war began soon after the procession and ended in victory for Philadelphus in 272.[23]

Philadelphus intended his revels to evoke the majesty and opulence of his divine kingdom and its intimate associations with immortal Alexander. Although no source mentions it, this astonishing display of wealth created the perfect opportunity for Philadelphus to bring Alexander from Memphis and rebury him in the tomb Ptolemy had prepared.

Such an act would have been a focal point of the celebration, and its absence from our sources is not definitive proof against it. Callixeinus's book survives only in fragments, and the year 275–274 is on the missing part of the Parian Marble. Many believe that Alexander's body was already in Alexandria when the Grand Procession took place. Whether already entombed or being prepared for reburial, Alexander's mummified remains likely have played a key role in the celebrations of which we have not a single word.

Alternatively, if Alexander was already in his tomb and thus unavailable for a grand entrance, Philadelphus had another candidate at hand. In his determination to draw links between himself, his father, and Alexander, Philadelphus proclaimed his intimate relationship with Nectanebo II, the Egyptian pharaoh announced by Ptolemy to have been Alexander's father.

Learning from his father, Philadelphus saw the logic of allying his dynasty with Nectanebo's, drawing lines of continuity and legitimacy between Macedonians and Egyptians.[24] Philadelphus took a great interest in Nectanebo's home city of Sebennytos in the Nile Delta and even completed a temple that the pharaoh began but abandoned during the Persian invasion of 343 B.C.E. Might Philadelphus have brought Nectanebo II's green stone sarcophagus to Alexandria during the Ptolemaia, perhaps portrayed as a symbolic reburial of Alexander's legendary father?

Philadelphus, although not the great general his father had been, inherited his deft touch in matters of religion and cult. In 272–271, celebrating perhaps his victory over Antiochus I in Syria, Philadelphus deified himself and his wife Arsinoe II as the Theoi Adelphoi (brother–sister gods), alluding to the sibling marriage of Zeus and Hera. Perhaps viewing his military victory in the east in light of Alexander's glorious campaigns, Philadelphus attached his new cult to the Alexander cult, changing the high priest's title to Priest of Alexander and of the Theoi Adelphoi.[25] Just a few years after his Grand Procession, Philadelphus joined himself and his wife to Alexander directly, without his father's intercession.[26] The center of this grand if unwieldy cult was Alexander's mausoleum.

After two thousand years, we cannot say whether Ptolemy or Philadelphus reburied Alexander in Alexandria. Each had powerful incentives and ideal opportunities. Ptolemy, perhaps, attempted to legitimize his kingship and sanctify Alexandria by bringing Alexander to his new capital sometime between 298 and his death in 283. Alternatively, his mastery of dynastic strategy may have persuaded him to let his son and successor Philadelphus transfer the body as part of Ptolemy's burial rites and Philadelphus's accession, or perhaps during the Ptolemaia of 275–274.

As Eumenes had discovered fifty years before, possessing Alexander's ghost and royal paraphernalia had potent consequences. Ptolemy's canny sense of the politics of the dead and Philadelphus's access to astonishing wealth combined to make Alexandria a city worthy of the world's most famous corpse. When Philadelphus staged his grand procession, Alexander had been dead for half a century, spending about twenty years somewhere in Memphis or the Saqqara plateau. By 274, Alexander was in his Alexandrian tomb, his spirit abroad in the colonnaded streets he had planned as a young man almost six decades before.

Alexander was now enthroned in death, deified and immortal in lifelike perfection and joined by Ptolemy, the architect of his postmortem fame. Alexander was now a universal deity who had hijacked good fortune from the gods themselves, and bestowed it in turn on Ptolemy and Philadelphus. But where was the mausoleum, and what did it look like? What kind of tomb could hold such a restless spirit, so eager to grasp the future in the grip of the past?

THE ALEXANDRIAN
MAUSOLEUM

IN DEATH, AS IN LIFE, PTOLEMY REMAINED in Alexander's shadow. Similarly, wherever Alexandrians walked there were sculptures, statues, paintings, terra-cottas, ivories, and cult rituals invoking the immortal conqueror. Stifled by the heat bouncing off marble streets and columns, they turned a corner and were struck by the cool Etesian winds breezing up from the sea as Alexander had planned. No one could escape the shadow of this extraordinary man now dead for over half a century.

Ptolemy and Philadelphus, father and son, created something unique when they built Alexandria. The city was a living tomb, a sprawling urban memorial park whose foundation, street plan, and dazzling architecture conjured up a heady mix of Alexander's power, wealth, and destiny. Ptolemy's genius brought these elements together, giving them material form and infusing them with tangible political presence. Ptolemy knew that the city and its ethos could shape the religious attitudes and everyday behavior of Alexandria's inhabitants. *The Alexander Romance* captured a part of this truth in a divine prophecy supposedly given to Alexander, that "the city which you are building will be your grave."[1]

Philadelphus extended and beautified what Ptolemy built—magnificent colonnaded avenues, marbled streets, and imposing temples, a royal court adorned with gold and ivory, scented by perfume, and softened by opulence of every kind. But it was Alexander's tomb that bestowed on the city its universal fame and mystique and created the political power wielded by its dynastic Ptolemaic kings. Although the mausoleum was the best-known sight in Alexandria, little survives to suggest where it was or what it looked like. How did one of the most remarkable and renowned buildings of antiquity disappear virtually without a trace?

Ptolemy or Philadelphus brought Alexander's golden sarcophagus to Alexandria sometime between 298 and 274 B.C.E. But as the funeral cortege passed through Alexandria's city gates, Alexander disappeared from view. It is difficult to know where to look for him because we have little idea of what the original city looked like. Ancient sources belonging to the Roman age describe an enlarged and reconfigured city. Like a shroud, Roman Alexandria covers Ptolemy's city. The outlines can be traced, but what lies beneath—between thirty and forty feet down—remains largely unknown.

Strabo saw Alexandria less than a decade after Rome conquered it in 30 B.C.E. He is our best guide to Ptolemy's city, reminding us that he lived there for a long time, probably between 24 B.C.E. and 20 B.C.E.[2] Romanization had already begun: the population was increasing, and demolition and rebuilding were changing the face of the city, gradually burying Ptolemaic streets and buildings under many feet of imperial Roman construction.[3] Nevertheless, during Strabo's time, Alexandria was still recognizably the city of the Ptolemies.

Strabo paced Alexandria's streets, stylus at the ready, watching a city in transition. Scratching his observations onto papyrus, he noted that Alexandrian life revolved around the royal quarter—the so-called Palaces District—and Alexander's impressive tomb nearby. He tantalizes us with a brief but graphic description.

> The city has extremely beautiful public precincts and also the royal palaces, which cover a fourth or even a third of the whole city. . . . Also part of the royal palaces is the so-called Soma, which was an enclosure containing the tombs of the kings and that of Alexander.[4]

Strabo furnishes two vital clues about Alexander's tomb. He explicitly says that he saw the mausoleum in the northern Palaces District, making no mention of the central part of the city named after Alexander. In fact, Strabo says virtually nothing about the city center, its grand Ptolemaic municipal buildings, or the agora,[5] which may have featured the Founder's Shrine dedicated by Alexander himself.[6] If the grand mausoleum had been located anywhere other than the Palaces District, Strabo would surely have mentioned it.

In a passing comment, Strabo reveals that Alexander must have had two tombs in the city. Ptolemy originally buried Alexander in a solitary tomb. When Strabo tells of "the tombs of the kings and of Alexander," we realize that someone must have moved the body to a second larger and collective mausoleum. It was this second tomb that Strabo saw, surrounded by the sepulchres of the Ptolemies and flanked by their royal palaces clustering tightly around the base of the Lochias peninsula.

Ptolemy spent at least fifteen years planning and building Alexander's first Alexandrian tomb, which disappeared without a trace and hardly a mention. What might Ptolemy have built, and what could have inspired him?

Ptolemy was as impressed as everyone else in Alexander's army when he and his men finally broke through the walls of Halicarnassus in September 334 and gazed on King Mausolus's towering burial monument. Earlier that year, Ptolemy had watched as Alexander and Hephaestion stripped off their armor and ran naked in a circuit around the great tomb mounds of Achilles and Patroclus at Troy. Ptolemy was at Alexander's side when the two men rode into the shadows cast by the pyramids at Giza, and he had stooped to follow his king into the solitary burial chamber of Cyrus the Great at Pasargadae. Ptolemy had seen and touched the tombs of great men, and had witnessed the grandeur of Hephaestion's funeral pyre in Babylon. Reflecting on the hubris of men and the jealousy of the gods, Ptolemy had not forgotten the fate of Hephaestion's tomb, which Alexander planned to raise above the pyre but never began.

Never slow to learn, Ptolemy drew on all these experiences when it came to burying and commemorating Alexander in Alexandria. He knew that a monumental tomb enveloped in a web of cult rituals would capture people's imagination and loyalty, and that wealth and power would accrue to those who administered the afterlife of the world's greatest conqueror.

Of all the tombs that Ptolemy had seen he may have been inspired most by the mausoleum at Halicarnassus, a tomb so gigantic that it became a universal symbol of the city, as well as one of the seven wonders of the world.[7] Ptolemy foresaw Alexander's tomb as the emblem of Alexandria, which the dead king had founded but Ptolemy was building. The city and the tomb were one in his mind, and both would be a constant reminder of the magical presence of Alexander's incorruptible body, and of the legitimacy and kudos that settled on Ptolemy's shoulders as his chosen successor.

For decades Alexandria was the largest building site in the Mediterranean world. As surveyors laid out their papyrus plans in thick layers of fine white marble dust, huge blocks were lifted and heaved into place, and the clanging of stonemasons' mauls filled the air. Planning the public buildings, royal palaces, and shrines of Alexandria, Ptolemy intended that he and his successors would eventually be buried near the founding hero and also receive honors as gods.

This aim shaped the size and design of Alexander's first tomb, but none of our sources mention these deliberations. For Ptolemy, Alexander's mausoleum would at least equal Mausolus's in size and magnificence, and Alexandria would easily outstrip Halicarnassus in the political economy of the eastern Mediterranean. Yet Alexander's first tomb, unlike Ptolemy's other innovation—the Pharos lighthouse—was never considered one of the seven wonders of the ancient world.

This first tomb, almost invisible in the ancient sources, may have been built in the center of early Alexandria, possibly in the neighborhood known as Alpha for Alexander. At this time, Alexander served as a religious and ideological point of reference amid the construction activity, focused by a founder cult that Ptolemy and his successors had an interest in fostering and elaborating; it was to be cleverly interwoven with a new cult of the ruler—Ptolemy himself.

Alexander was fascinated by the tombs of the great men of Asia but gave little thought to the shape of his own final resting place. While Siwa may have loomed large as a destination in his final days, the idea of being buried in Alexandria probably never occurred to him. The Alexandrian tomb reflected Ptolemy's dynastic aspirations rather than any discernible wish of the dead king.

Alexander's journey from Memphis-Saqqara and his burial in Alexandria must have been a spectacular event, accompanied by all the pomp and pageantry Ptolemy could muster. If the golden mummy traveled overland, it may have come on the same funeral hearse that brought it from Babylon several decades earlier. More likely it sailed down the Nile, into the western branches of the delta and straight into one of Alexandria's harbors. However grand the event, whatever the appearance of the tomb, and wherever it was located, Alexander's stay proved as temporary as his initial interment in Memphis-Saqqara. Alexander's mummy rested for less than a century in the tomb Ptolemy built before being moved to an even grander mausoleum.

Writing over one hundred years after Strabo's viewing, Zenobius, a second-century C.E. teacher of rhetoric, offers a glimpse into the possible fate of Alexander's first Alexandrian tomb after the body had been reburied elsewhere. Zenobius says that Alexandrians soon lost interest in the now empty sepulchre,[8] though it continued attracting devotees of the Alexander cult for a while.[9] Zenobius was writing three hundred years after the event, by which time Alexander's first tomb may have fallen into disuse even as an empty shrine; or perhaps it was built over and forgotten.[10]

Strabo's clue demonstrated that every historical encounter with Alexander's tomb surviving from antiquity refers to the second and not the first mausoleum. Alexander now had two sepulchres in Alexandria, though the second would eclipse the first in myth and memory. The inevitable questions arose: Who built Alexander's new tomb, when, and why?

Strabo also creates an enigma that remains a puzzle after two thousand years. He uses the Greek word *soma* (body) to describe the funerary enclosure for Alexander's second tomb. In many literary traces of what other ancient writers saw and heard, the Greek term *sema* or tomb is used instead.[11] Over several hundred years, from around 20 B.C.E. to 400 C.E., Roman sources used these two terms interchangeably, applying them variously to Alexander's mummy, his tomb, the whole mausoleum enclosure, and even the district in which the mausoleum was located.

This curious confusion of names may have a local inspiration. City residents passed by the Soma every day as they went about their business. Allusions and colloquialisms concerning Alexander's tomb likely were common currency. In this way, *soma*—the body—could have been a local place-name for Alexandria's grandest tomb *(sema)*, reflecting the degree to which Alexander's presence had embedded itself in the city's collective psyche.[12]

Strabo walked through the royal funerary park, past sepulchres housing the long-dead Ptolemaic kings, interspersed with fountains and groves, and surrounded by perimeter walls. He probably knew this was not Alexander's first resting place in Alexandria and assumed his readers knew it too. What was obvious to Strabo only becomes clear to us from later writers—Zenobius and a third-century C.E. novelist called Achilles Tatius.

Zenobius was writing during the reign of the Roman emperor Hadrian (117–138 C.E.), who loved all things Greek and fervently admired Alexander.[13] According to Zenobius, Alexander's second tomb was built by Philadelphus's grandson, Ptolemy IV Philopater, who built the imposing new royal mausoleum sometime during his reign, between 221 and 204 B.C.E. Philopater, Zenobius says, gathered together and buried the bodies of Alexander and his own royal predecessors in a different location somewhere in the middle of the city.

Zenobius adds flesh to the bones of Strabo's earlier hint about the Soma. Achilles Tatius is more oblique in the surviving fragments of his erotic novel *Clitophon and Leucippe,* which takes place in Alexandria.[14] In Tatius's story, Clitophon enters the city through the great Sun Gate in the eastern walls. Strolling down a long colonnaded street toward the central crossroads, he is amazed by what he sees in the neighborhood named for Alexander. It is like a town within a town, arranged in squares and full of columns.[15] Tatius's brief description of this great enclosure has been interpreted as an eyewitness account of Alexander's walled mausoleum, added to spice up the novel's imaginative plot.[16]

Tatius was writing some 400 years after Philopater built the mausoleum, and about 150 years after Zenobius; Alexandria had seen huge changes during this time. In his glowing account of Alexandria's opulence and grandeur, Tatius never once refers to the Soma by name.[17] Clitophon, however, is described standing next to the ancient world's most famous monument. Seeing through Tatius's eyes, Clitophon is far more impressed by right-angled streets and columns, an astonishing missed opportunity for a fiction writer. The truth is inescapable: Tatius never saw the Soma because he never traveled to Alexandria, and Clitophon's city stroll is an anachronistic fantasy.[18]

Philopater had good reasons for building a new funerary park. He understood that monumental tombs are political symbols for the living as much as they are memorials to the dead. A century or so had passed since Ptolemy first buried Alexander in Alexandria, and since that time the number of dead Ptolemies had been accumulating. Following his family's obsession with grand public displays, Philopater judged the time was right for rejuvenating his dynastic links with Alexander by regrouping his family and the city's founder. His plan was to cluster this charmed circle of royal cadavers and cinerary urns in a walled enclosure near his royal palace.

When exactly did Philopater build the new mausoleum and why at that particular time? What impulses led him to construct such an expensive communal sepulchre and then disinter, move, and rebury these remains? Philopater's personality was one factor, and his political situation another. Philopater had a penchant for inventing new cults and displaying the dead. When the deposed Spartan king Cleomenes III took refuge in Alexandria and subsequently died, Philopater had him flayed and put on public display.[19]

In all probability, politics rather than personality was the deciding factor. Two events in the summer of 217 may have tipped the balance. On June 17, having survived an assassination attempt the night before, Philopater took the field against an invading army of the Seleucid King Antiochus III at Raphia near Gaza, winning a famous victory.[20] Philopater built the new Soma as a way of expressing his piety and gratitude to the god Alexander and the deified Ptolemies, first for cheating death and second as a commemorative monument to the only military triumph of his reign. If the tombs and enclosure took two or three years to complete, then the bodies would have been moved and the mausoleum opened in 215 or 214.

Philopater found this deadline appealing and perfectly timed. He saw how dynastic continuity and spectacle could be combined, as 215–214 was an Olympian year that also included Alexandria's Ptolemaia festival, celebrating the cult of Alexander and the Ptolemies. Philopater capitalized on this conjunction by adding a personal ruler cult that included

Ptolemy and his wife Berenice, as well as himself, to the existing priest-hood of Alexander and the Ptolemies.[21] In a *coup de théâtre* typical of the Ptolemies, Philopater proclaimed to the Hellenistic world that the new mausoleum and its reconfigured and extended cults were open for dynastic business.

Behind the scenes, prosaic and pressing reasons played on Philopater's mind. After the victory at Raphia, Egypt's economy slumped, forc-ing Philopater to abandon the silver standard for coinage and adopt a debased copper one instead. What better way of dropping money in the pockets of Alexandria's fractious inhabitants than by state-funded job creation resulting in a new sepulchre to their favorite and patron deity Alexander? The foresight of Ptolemy and Philadelphus in joining Alexander's cult with their own was paying handsome dividends for king, stonemason, and laborer alike.

Gazing into Philopater's world and trying to determine why and when he built Alexander's second tomb leaves us struggling to locate the Soma within the Palaces District that Strabo knew. Zenobius's observa-tion that the new mausoleum was "in a different place" to Alexander's first tomb may imply that Alexander's body was brought the greatest distance, perhaps from a more central part of the city. Philopater, as Zenobius records, was consolidating the royal remains in one place, and it is difficult to reconcile this with building the new tomb farther away from (rather than closer to) the center of power that was the hub of royal palaces at the base of the Lochias peninsula.

Philopater brought Alexander's mummy to join the Ptolemies, and soon the prospect of a peerless cluster of royal sepulchres in one place was a reality. Alexander was now resting alongside, at the very least, Ptolemy, Ptolemy II Philadelphus, and Ptolemy III Euergetes. What do we know of this highly desirable piece of Ptolemaic real estate, and can we locate it more precisely?

Strabo calculates that the Palaces District, with "its beautiful public precincts," covers between one-quarter and one-third of the city. This general area occupied the northern and northeastern parts of the city, stretching out south and west from the base of the Lochias peninsula. As the new mausoleum lay within this high-class neighborhood, where was the "different place" that Zenobius refers to for Alexander's first tomb? In all probability it lay further south from the Palaces District in the city's civic center.

Strabo walks us through the Palaces District, observing the shrines, statues, and works of art dedicated by the Ptolemies and other members of the ruling family and royal court. It was heavily patronized, consisting almost exclusively of royal buildings, shrines, and pleasure gardens, with the museum and library situated probably toward (but not on) the harbor shore to the west.[22] Strabo's familiarity with the city, born of tramping its streets, is our loss, for he sees no reason to explain precisely where these buildings were located.

He does, however, lead us farther along the polished marble avenues of Alexandria's past. Strabo briefly refers to a smaller, even more refined neighborhood within the Palaces District that he calls the inner palaces. His comment is seductive but fleeting, noting that the area was composed of royal palaces and pleasure parks, as well as expensive high-class residences built on the lower Lochias peninsula connecting this exclusive sector with the city beyond.

Between the lines of Strabo's eyewitness account we can discern clues to the crucial role of the Lochias peninsula in identifying where Alexander's new mausoleum was located. Today the peninsula is known as the Silsileh promontory. It is far smaller than in Strabo's time, due mainly to the combined effects of subsiding land and rising sea levels.[23] Compounding this loss, large stretches of the ancient city's shoreline disappeared during the nineteenth century, when Alexandria was remodeled and the famous corniche was laid down. The present-day topography in this area distorts our view of Strabo's city, confounding our efforts to gauge the size and location of the inner palaces.

Striding through this high-class neighborhood—in his day the headquarters of Roman administration—Strabo tramped over land that today is sea. His eyewitness calculation that the Palaces District covered a third of Alexandria included this substantial but now submerged area. When this lost land is restored to Strabo's assessment, the southern boundary of the Palaces District moves northward, away from the city center and toward the coast. This probably reduces the search area for the Soma, but we are hard-pressed to be sure, and only archaeology can bring us closer to the truth.

Zenobius's comment that the mausoleum lay in the "middle of the city" requires explanation. Zenobius was writing three centuries after Philopater opened the mausoleum around 215 B.C.E. During that time, Roman Alexandria spilled out over the city's eastern walls[24] and underwent dramatic development by the imperial Roman authorities.[25] As Alexandria expanded, the city center moved. If Alexander's tomb lay in the northeastern Palaces District in 215 B.C.E., city growth left it stranded in Zenobius's hazily defined middle by around 100 C.E.

Strabo and Zenobius are ambiguous in regard to the location of the Soma. They lead us in fits and starts through Alexandria's streets, taking us close to Alexander's tomb but never arriving there. They make it clear, however, that Alexander's second tomb was integrated into a grandiose funerary park that promoted Philopater's dynastic links to Alexander and his predeccesors. It almost certainly lay just to the south or south-southwest of the Lochias peninsula.

Everyone in ancient Alexandria knew where to find Alexander's tomb, and nobody needed to have it written down. The landscape of the city was a topography of wonder, inspired by its eponymous founder and magnified by the Ptolemies as the guardians of his memory in the cult located at the Soma. Alexandria's ritual life and architectural splendors were a code that inscribed Alexander's legacy on the minds and bodies of its inhabitants.

Although innumerable eyes saw the grand sepulchre and its image was etched in countless minds, it is hardly mentioned in our ancient sources, nor are there any artistic representations of it. While Alexander's tomb was arguably the most famous monument of the Hellenistic and Roman world for six hundred years, not one confirmed image of it survives.

In the Hermitage Museum in St. Petersburg and the British Museum in London we find some small clues. Roman terra-cotta lamps are humble items, decorated with illustrations of recognizable ancient vistas. A few of them depict miniature panoramas of an ancient port, which some interpret as representing Alexandria during the first century of the Christian era. In the space of a few inches, the artisan traced harbor scenes against an urban backdrop that includes a building with a pyramidal roof identified as Alexander's Soma.[26] Some of these lamps are forgeries, while others depict not Alexandria but third-century C.E. Carthage in North Africa or the ancient Roman port of Ostia.[27] Alexandria may have inspired some of them, but ultimately the lamps fail to penetrate the gloom surrounding the Soma. More promising, perhaps, is a scene that comes straight from the afterlife.

Julius Philosyrius, except for his name, is anonymous. Living in Ostia sometime during the fourth century C.E., he may have been a merchant trading with the Levant (his name means lover of Syria). Philosyrius was buried in Ostia, inside a magnificent sarcophagus sculpted with an image of himself set in a harbor scene of people fishing in boats accompanied by mythical winged figures playing musical instruments.

The port is reminiscent of Alexandria, specifically the perspective that greets the visitor arriving by sea. The Pharos lighthouse lies to the west, Diocletian's column (popularly known as Pompey's pillar) straight ahead, and to the east a palace adjacent to a round tower with a conical roof identified as the Soma.

Philosyrius's sarcophagus seems to bring the Soma and Diocletian's column together in the same field of vision. The emperor Diocletian erected his column in 298 C.E. after a six-month siege of Alexandria, which may imply that the Soma was still standing on the verge of the fourth century. Alternatively, Philosyrius's sculptor may have created a composite picture of the city's most famous monuments, past and present.

The imagery on the sarcophagus seems allegorical of Philosyrius's life (and perhaps business interests) in the eastern Roman empire—and centered on Alexandria. Alternatively, it may be an idealized picture of Ostia, which had its own, albeit smaller, Pharos. Whether Philosyrius had a realistic or idealized view of Alexandria sculpted on his sarcophagus we cannot know for sure. Ironically, our best view of Alexander's tomb may be a decoration on the sarcophagus of an unknown merchant buried in Italy.

The terra-cotta lamps and Philosyrius's tomb attribute a common feature to the building interpreted as Alexander's tomb. The circular tower capped with a conical roof reappears on a sixth-century C.E. mosaic from St. John the Baptist Church at Jerash in Jordan. The craftsman captioned his work "Alexandria," and dominating the view is a domed-roof building crowned by an unidentified sculpture, possibly a winged Nike—the Greek goddess of victory.[28]

If this is Alexander's Soma, it is a strange anachronism. Why would Christians commission an image of an infamous pagan tomb in a Jordanian church a century or more after the original had disappeared in Egypt? There were other Alexandrias in the region, and no obvious reason why this should be Alexander's Egyptian city.

Alexander's Soma and the Pharos lighthouse were the two architectual masterpieces of Alexandria, and they were emblematic of its unique status in the ancient world. Yet, although the Pharos is well described and shown on several images, Alexander's tomb is only briefly alluded to in the written sources and is not represented in art.

The Roman poet Lucan (36–65 C.E.) was the nephew of Seneca the Younger and came to an early end when Nero forced him to commit suicide after being implicated in a failed assassination attempt against the emperor. At the time of his death, Lucan was working on an epic poem called *Pharsalia*, an account of the civil war between Julius Caesar and Pompey the Great. The poem takes its name from the Battle of Pharsalus in Greece in 48 B.C.E. in which Caesar finally defeated his rival: it includes two passages that describe the Soma in unique and priceless detail.

Lucan tells of Caesar's visit to Alexander's tomb and his dismissive attitude to Alexandria's other appealing sights. "No thing of beauty attracted him, neither the gold and ornaments of the gods, nor the city walls; but in eager haste he went down into the grotto hewn out for a tomb. There lies the mad son of Philip of Pella."[29] Elsewhere Lucan refers to the sacred grotto where Alexander's mummified remains lay, as well as the sepulchres that surrounded it, where "the dead Ptolemies and their unworthy dynasty are covered by indignant pyramids and mausoleums."[30]

Lucan's insightful detail is the work of an eyewitness, either Lucan or his Uncle Seneca. Caesar's descent into a subterranean cavern carved out of the rock furnishes a clue as to the form of Alexander's burial chamber, though not the architecture of the mausoleum that enclosed it. Lucan denigrates the Ptolemies and seems to resent that the ancient and venerable form of the pyramid now had to entomb their unworthy remains.

This comment likely refers to a pyramid-shaped roof on top of a mausoleum rather than replicas of the huge pyramids of the pharaohs.

Lucan paints a picture of the Soma as it was around 60 C.E. when he began the *Pharsalia,* and thus it was mainly the same monument that Strabo had seen eighty years before. Lucan was writing as the Christian age was dawning, and his account shows that the sprawling funeral park of the Soma was as popular as ever, and was packed with Ptolemaic sepulchres in various styles.[31]

Lucan uses the word "mausoleum," and Halicarnassus was a Ptolemaic possession during Philopater's reign. This may suggest that the tomb Strabo saw and Lucan described was similar to Mausolus's great sepulchre.[32] If true, then the Halicarnassus mausoleum may have influenced both Alexander's first and second Alexandrian sepulchres. But this is a tenuous argument, and we need to search for more substantial clues to the Soma's appearance.

The Roman general Octavian became the Emperor Augustus after defeating Anthony and Cleopatra at the Battle of Actium in 31 B.C.E., and again at Alexandria in 30 B.C.E. The death and entombment of Augustus offers a different perspective on what Alexander's tomb looked like.

Augustus's mausoleum on Rome's Campus Martius was inspired by several funerary traditions, especially the circular earthen burial mounds of the Etruscan civilization, whose cemeteries dotted the countryside north of Rome. Yet Augustus was a man of the world, and he planned his mausoleum to reflect his life, not just Rome's Etruscan heritage. Augustus's conquests in the east made his name and shaped his destiny, and the royal tombs and cults he saw there influenced his own imperial afterlife. Augustus imitated Mausolus's great sepulchre at Halicarnassus on his own tomb by including many freestanding sculptures and capping the summit with a great bronze statue of himself.

Augustus was deeply influenced by a visit to Alexander's mausoleum in Alexandria in 30 B.C.E.[33] Lucan describes Caesar descending into a subterranean grotto; in Macedonian tradition, this may have been covered with a circular earthen grave mound adorned with Greek columns and statues. Alexander's tomb may have been a hybrid of styles, ancestral and contemporary, that would have appealed to

Philopater's obsession with grand architectural gestures, as the whole Soma complex shows.

The possibility that Philopater created a circular or cylindrical mausoleum for Alexander finds intriguing support from two later tombs in Algeria—Medracen and the so-called Tomb of the Christian—both dating to a hundred years after Philopater's grand opening of Alexander's new tomb.[34] The Algerian tombs incorporate some sixty columns into their structure, and each has a flattened conical summit that could have supported freestanding sculptures or a small pyramidal roof.

Given the widespread fame of Alexander's mausoleum, the Medracen and the Tomb of the Christian could have been inspired as miniatures of the Soma in Alexandria.[35] The striking similarity between the Algerian tombs and Augustus's cylindrical mausoleum may suggest that Alexander's tomb was a prototype for both.[36]

Augustus walked through the Soma enclosure and saw Alexander's tomb for himself, and so did the emperor Hadrian—an avid Hellenophile and admirer of Alexander. Hadrian drew inspiration for his own funerary monument in Rome from Augustus's mausoleum, copying both its cyclindrical shape and cluster of decorative statues. The tomb was completed in 140 C.E. by Antoninus Pius, and is known today as the Castel Sant' Angelo.

In a delicious irony, Hadrian's pagan mausoleum later housed the private apartments of Rome's medieval popes. Alessandro Farnese, who sat as Pope Paul III between 1534 and 1549, decorated these rooms—the Sala Paolina—with painted scenes from Alexander's life.[37] Farnese probably knew of Hadrian's admiration for Alexander, but he didn't know about the Soma's influence on the building he was occupying. Alexander—the ultimate pagan—was a hated figure to the early Christian fathers. But within a millennium he was looking down benevolently on the head of the Catholic Church from the walls of a tomb that was an imitation of his own Alexandrian mausoleum built by a Roman emperor for whom he was the ultimate hero.

There is no record of Hadrian's visit to the Soma, though it can be inferred from the fact that he visited Alexandria and held Alexander in high regard. If the shape and style adopted by the two Roman emperors is in part an architectural legacy of Alexander's tomb, then all three tombs were made possible by the same Egyptian engineering skills that built the Pharos lighthouse. Looking today at the mausoleums of Augustus and Hadrian in Rome and Medracen and the Tomb of the Christian in Algeria, we may be seeing more than a glimpse of the Soma.[38] Attempts to miniaturize these huge structures may account for the cylindrical towers with conical roofs that peer out of Roman lamps and Philosyrius's sarcophagus.

Alexander's tomb is mysteriously absent from contemporary images of Alexandria that adorn the coins and medallions that were part of everyday life during Hellenistic and Roman times. Many of Alexandria's architectural wonders peek out from finger-worn scenes on bronze coins minted in the city during Roman times. The Alexandrian mint, unlike others in Roman Asia, produced coins showing the city's older monuments and secular buildings, not just the temples of the Roman age.[39] Over a thousand of these image-bearing coins have been studied, and not one shows Alexander's tomb.

There are depictions of the Pharos lighthouse, the great Serapeum temple, and lesser-known cultic places such as the Isis-Harpocrates shrine and the Isis pylon.[40] In this era of imperial Roman visits to the tomb by Caesar, Octavian, Hadrian, and others, the invisibility of the Soma remains an enigma.

Might the Soma's absence from art be more apparent than real? Every society has its own artistic conventions, configured by the culture that produced it. Where outsiders see ambiguous miniature coin images, Alexandrians would recognize a world of everyday meaning, common metaphors, and symbols representing the ideas and buildings they knew so well. Does the Soma exist on coins and medallions without being recognized?[41]

The Alexander Romance tells a story about a great serpent that slithered out of the ground when Alexander founded Alexandria, causing consternation among his followers. Alexander ordered it killed and had a monument erected on the spot. This snake, called the *agathos daimon*, was venerated by Alexandrians on the anniversary of the city's founding, and the festival included sacrifices to Alexander as the serpent-born hero. Alexander's identification with the serpent probably refers to Zeus (whose symbolic animal it was) and possibly also to the fascination his mother Olympias felt toward snakes. Alexander and the *agathos daimon* may have been worshiped as one entity in the endlessly overlapping Greek cults.[42]

The temple images on Alexandria's coins are approximations— miniature symbols of large-scale realities—and their identity is often more tentative than certain. The earliest Alexandrian building shown on Roman period coins is the so-called Agathos Daimon altar, a structure with a portico, six Ionic columns, a frieze of shields, and a female figure. One image shows the *agathos daimon* serpent on one side of the altar and a serpent wearing a two-horned sun disk on the other.[43] No one is sure what is being shown; could it be that this is a "lost" image of Alexander's tomb?

Between 300 B.C.E. and 400 C.E., everyone who lived in or visited Alexandria saw one or the other of Alexander's two tombs. Yet the location of the sepulchres remains a mystery, and not a single undisputed image of either is known. We may never discover the shape and form of Alexander's first tomb, though the huge drumlike mausoleums of Augustus and Hadrian may suggest the appearance of the Soma built by Philopater.

What Caesar, Strabo, Octavian, Lucan, and others saw as they stood before the great conqueror's second mausoleum is lost to us now. But the tomb itself has a vivid afterlife stretching across the centuries from Philopater's foundation in 215 B.C.E. to its eventual disappearance in the turbulence engulfing Alexandria in 391 C.E.

Between these years, the Soma reached its peak of fame. Resurrected from the lethargy of an effete and despotic Ptolemaic regime, Alexander's tomb was reinvented by visitors whose councils with the dead king became encounters with the numinous. The ineffable spirit of Alexander confirmed each man's genius and destiny, shaping Alexander for the next two thousand years.

ANCIENT VISITORS

6

ALEXANDER, GOLD-ENCRUSTED AND DIVINE, held court after death in the magnificent mausoleum Ptolemy built. A unique and potent relic, Alexander's lifelike presence drew thousands of visitors to Alexandria, embedding itself in the psyche of the city's inhabitants and lining the pockets of the Ptolemaic kings who administered the eponymous cult.

Touring "the body" was de rigeur for visiting royalty, diplomats, generals, scholars, and the curious. Disembarking from ships, dismounting from horses, or walking through the city's marbled streets, eager pilgrims were drawn to Alexander's tomb.

Outside the Soma's perimeter walls, visitors pushed their way through a noisy throng of traders and stalls offering goods and services: rooms for rent, food and drink, trinkets and souvenirs touched by Alexander's good fortune; sellers of ivory, glass, incense and spice, perfumed oils, and purveyors of more fleshly desires.

Passing through the gates of the walled enclosure, visitors entered Alexander's realm. Walking through the grand funerary park Philopater had created, they dipped their hands into a cooling fountain and rested on marble seats in shady groves. They gazed on huge monuments dragged from ancient Egyptian temples and admired Greek statues and the grand royal sepulchres of the Ptolemies. Incense curled in the air, mingling with the aroma of roasting meat and spiced wine.

All gazed on Alexander's tomb, though not on the mummy enclosed in its grotto, where the cool temperature helped preserve it. No ancient writer tells how many visitors were allowed to see Alexander's body, but practically speaking it must have been a fraction of those who came.

Viewing the mummy may have been easier in the early days of Alexander's first Alexandrian tomb, with more restrictions being put in place after it was moved to Philopater's grand new mausoleum.

Playing politics with the dead, the Ptolemies had a winning hand. Alexander was the talisman of every Ptolemaic king and the pivot of Alexandria's cult activities. Alexander tourism was the most profitable example of postmortem commerce until the discovery of Christ's tomb turned Jerusalem into the hub of Christendom's pilgrimage industry. In the pagan world, Alexander's tomb was a heady mix of propaganda, legitimacy, universal fame, and material wealth—part hero worship and part heritage attraction, overloaded with legend and myth.

Even in death, Alexander drew the powerful men of history to his side. The attraction depended on the politics of the time, and the motivation of those who wielded power. Those who did not share an imperial and military outlook considered Alexander—in Lucan's famous words—as "the mad son of Philip." With the joint suicides of Anthony and Cleopatra in 30 B.C.E., the Hellenistic era ended.[1] When the Romans arrived, Alexander was reborn, a peerless emblem for a new breed of men who saw themselves as his natural heirs and sought to emulate his achievements.

Julius Caesar routed Pompey the Great at the Battle of Pharsalus in Greece in 48 B.C.E. Pompey was Rome's most successful general, styling himself after Alexander, adopting the trademark windswept coiffure, tilting his head, and adding the suffix "Great" to his name. At Pharsalus, Pompey's military skills failed to match this conceit, and Caesar chased him across the sea to Egypt.

Before Pharsalus, the Ptolemaic court had shamelessly flattered Pompey, but they stabbed him in the back as he strode ashore near Pelusium. Caesar disembarked two days later in Alexandria expecting to take custody of his enemy, but was greeted instead with Pompey's signet ring and severed head.

Untrustworthy and sycophantic, the royal court at Alexandria revolved around the child pharaoh Ptolemy XIII and his willful sister Cleopatra VII. Both were offspring of a weak and ineffective father, Ptolemy XII, ridiculed by the sobriquet Auletes, the flute player. Carpeted by Cleopatra and putting the young Ptolemy under his guardianship, Caesar found time to visit Alexander's tomb, one genocidal despot paying homage to another, as Lucan commented.[2]

Caesar set a new precedent for visiting the Soma. Every Roman saw in Alexander what he wanted to see in himself. Caesar, the dictator, considered Alexander the ultimate exemplar, proving that strong personal authority worked. Years before, in 69 B.C.E., Caesar had wept, it was said, at how little he had achieved by comparison to Alexander, who had conquered the known world by the age of thirty-two.[3] Standing before Alexander's tomb as master of the empire, Caesar had finally matched his illustrious predecessor.

Caesar's murder in Rome on the Ides of March 44 B.C.E. was avenged by his nephew and ultimate successor Octavian, who ruled the empire as Augustus between 31 B.C.E. and 14 C.E. In the wake of his crushing naval victory over the forces of Cleopatra and Anthony at Actium in September of 31 B.C.E., Octavian took possession of Alexandria the following year. Alexandrians saw Octavian as Alexander's literal successor, not only due to his victories but also because Octavian entered Alexandria at the same age as Alexander when he died.[4]

Octavian was forthright in his desire to see Alexander. When asked if he wished also to see the tombs of the Ptolemies, he replied, "I wished to see a king, not corpses," according to the Roman historian Dio Cassius,[5] a view echoed almost word for word by the imperial biographer Suetonius.[6] Octavian chose his words and his tone with conviction, for he loathed the degenerate Ptolemies whose dynasty he had just destroyed.

Octavian's dismissive comment seems to imply that the Ptolemies were buried intact and mummified like Alexander. Yet royal Macedonian burial rites incinerated the bodies and interred their ashes in a burial urn or a golden larnax. Philadelphus and his sister-wife Arsinoe II are known to have been cremated because their burial urns were exhibited to the public. But it is unclear how the bodies of previous and later Ptolemies were treated. Traditional cremation sits awkwardly with Octavian's comments.

Octavian ordered "the sarcophagus and body of Alexander the Great brought forth from its inner sanctum, and, after gazing on it, showed his respect by placing upon it a golden crown and strewing it with flowers."[7]

A possibly apocryphal anecdote says that when Octavian bent over to kiss Alexander, he accidentally damaged the king's nose, perhaps breaking it off.[8]

Alexander would have had little use for a gold crown in his original fitted, golden mummy case. Strabo, living in Alexandria less than a decade later, tells a story that the shimmering sarcophagus was stolen by Ptolemy X (107–88 B.C.E.) and replaced with one made of glass (possibly alabaster or rock crystal).[9]

Alexandria was the center of a revolution in glassmaking, which drew on the vast deposits of silica and natron south of the city in the mineral-rich area known as the Wadi Natrun. This raises the intriguing possibility that Alexander's replacement casket could have been the largest and most sophisticated glass object up to that time. The dazzling beauty of Ptolemaic glass preserved in modern-day Alexandria's Greco–Roman museum gives a hint of what would have been an extraordinary object.[10]

Only Strabo mentions the glass-for-gold episode, adding that Ptolemy X melted down the original sarcophagus to mint gold coins to pay the mercenaries who retook Alexandria for him after he had been ejected by the city's rioting population.[11] Ptolemy X's return in 89 B.C.E. was short-lived. Outraged by the desecration of Alexander's tomb, the city's inhabitants rioted again. Ptolemy fled and later drowned off the coast of Cyprus.

Ptolemy X and his successors mismanaged Egypt's economy so disastrously that Alexander never again rested in a golden sarcophagus. As Octavian stood beside the hallowed remains, the tomb had been stripped of all golden ornaments. Cleopatra herself was the most recent looter. Following the defeat at Actium, she ransacked the Soma and the sepulchres and temples of her ancestors to raise money to continue her fight against Octavian, which finally ended with her suicide.[12] The Jewish historian Flavius Josephus says that Cleopatra took gold from Alexander's tomb.[13] When Octavian placed the golden crown on Alexander's body, it was a mark of respect and perhaps a gesture of reparation, restoring a little of the precious metal to the great conqueror who had once been completely encased in it.

Caesar and Octavian blazed a path to Alexander's tomb followed by many later Roman emperors. A personal encounter with Alexander evolved into a powerful symbolic statement for the autocratic rule of the Roman emperors. The flair for battle that Caesar and Octavian possessed cast them in the same mold as Alexander. Soma tourism was raised to a new level as Alexander's legacy was hijacked by new men of power.

The affinity that the emperor Gaius, better known as Caligula, had with the great conqueror was based on psychology. He imagined himself as Alexander reincarnated, journeying to Alexandria to consecrate his delusions. Details of Caligula's visit are few, but it seems he was unable to resist taking away Alexander's breastplate (cuirass), which he wore as he pompously paraded around Rome.[14] Caligula's passion for imitating Alexander and indulging in ostentatious displays of wealth once led him to don Alexander's breastplate and drive his chariot at top speed along a bridge of boats tethered across the Bay of Naples.[15]

Following Caligula, who met a bloody end at the hands of his own Praetorian Guard, imperial visits to the Soma declined. The emperors Claudius and Nero were either unable or unwilling to travel to Alexandria. In 69 C.E., Vespasian, the governor of Syria, was acclaimed emperor by the Roman legions in Egypt and ruled for the next ten years. Vespasian's legions were commanded by the emperor's trusted prefect, Tiberius Alexander, and soon the emperor moved his headquarters to Alexandria. We know that Vespasian visited the Serapeum temple overlooking the city, and it is inconceivable that he didn't also walk through the Soma precinct and stop at the tomb of Alexander, his chief supporter's namesake. No record survives of Vespasian's visit, nor any made by his son and heir, Titus (79–81 C.E.), who was with him at the time and returned in 71. It is a virtual certainty that father and son gazed on Alexander's mummified remains.

Nothing more is heard of Alexander's tomb for some forty years until Hadrian ascended the imperial throne in 117 C.E. Hadrian loved all things Greek and spent most of his reign traveling in the East. In 130 C.E., he began a grand tour of Egypt and entered Alexandria in a four-horse chariot known as a *quadriga*. In response to the enthusiastic welcome he received, Hadrian paid for statues and building renovations. Although no record survives of dedications to the Soma, we can assume that he made them.

Hadrian stressed his imperial association with Alexander and com-memorated his visit by minting distinctive coins. A bronze drachm, dat-ing to the year of the imperial visit, shows Hadrian in his *quadriga* chariot being greeted by Alexander as a personification of the city and possibly wearing his tusked elephant-scalp headdress.[16] A brass medal-lion depicts Alexander clasping Hadrian's hand as if to kiss it.[17] Since Hadrian authorized Alexandria's mint to issue these items, it is unlikely that he did not visit and perhaps improve Alexander's mausoleum.

Hadrian's admiration for Alexander went beyond Caligula's delu-sional aspirations. In his imperial entourage, Hadrian included not only his wife Sabina but also his handsome favorite, a youth called Anti-nous.[18] On October 22, 130, while sailing lazily on the Nile, Antinous somehow drowned, and Hadrian—like Alexander after Hephaestion's death—was inconsolable. As if prompted by his knowledge of Alexan-der's life, Hadrian ordered the worship of Antinous throughout the em-pire, identifying him with the Egyptian god Osiris and naming him Osirantinous. Antinous was one of the last pagan gods created before the advent of Christianity.

In his grief for his dead lover, Hadrian exceeded Alexander in one crucial respect. Perhaps inspired by Alexandria's function as a city tomb for Alexander, Hadrian built a new city, Antinoopolis, on the eastern bank of the Nile where Antinous had died. He ordered it built in Greek style and filled it with colonists from the city of Ptolemais and from Greek towns in the Fayum region on the western side of the river. As they began arriving in Antinoopolis, they brought with them a startling new form of burial custom—a hybrid Greco-Roman-Egyptian tradition begun a hundred years earlier.

Mummy cases were now being decorated with a painted face panel that depicted the deceased in an eerily lifelike fashion. Glowing with a flame of immortal life, they gaze out across two millennia through almond-shaped eyes, adorned with elaborate coiffures, glittering jew-elry, and expensive clothing. These mummies, with their unsettlingly modern photographic stare, are known as the Fayum portraits.[19]

Hadrian's Antinoopolis survived until the early nineteenth century, when it was scavenged for building stone. During the 1880s, the painted-face mummies began to appear in Europe and the United

States.[20] One of them takes us straight back in time to Hadrian and Alexander. Known as the Portrait of Two Brothers, it was discovered in 1898–1899 and is now housed in the National Museum in Cairo.[21] Two thousand years vanish as we gaze at the two young men. A miniature golden figure of Alexander hovers above the right shoulder of the younger man. Considered in light of the inexorable spread of Christianity into the Roman empire, it is fitting that Alexander appears as a funerary talisman on a painted mummy discovered in the last pagan city founded in Egypt, by an emperor who admired all things Greek, and Alexander especially.

No known imperial visits were made to Alexander's tomb for fifty years. There is no record of Antoninus Pius, Marcus Aurelius, or Commodus visiting the tomb. Half a century after Hadrian, Septimus Severus (193–211 C.E.) became emperor and paid his respects at the Soma. The curious events surrounding his encounter with Alexander throw light on how times had changed for Alexandria and the Roman empire.

> [Severus] inquired into everything, including things that were very carefully hidden; for he was that kind of person to leave nothing, either human or divine, uninvestigated. Accordingly, he took away from practically all the sanctuaries all the books that he could find containing any secret lore, and he locked up the tomb of Alexander; this was in order that no one in future should either view Alexander's body or read what was written in the above-mentioned books.[22]

There is an undercurrent of menace here. Long gone are the gold and silver riches that once adorned Alexander's tomb, lost to greedy men and women. Implicit but unspoken acts seem to connect Alexander's body, his tomb, and unknown secret books. The concern with magical scripts over worldly goods suggests a very different environment than that of Hadrian's time just a few decades before. What happened in Alexandria during this time, and how did it affect the Soma?

Septimus Severus was a good pagan emperor, a devotee of the Greco-Egyptian god Serapis, into whose mystery cult he had been initiated. Ever since Ptolemy created Serapis five hundred years before and linked the god's worship to Alexander's cult, the two deities had been closely related. But much had changed since then, not least Octavian's banning of all cult activity that invoked the hated Ptolemies. This left Alexander, Serapis, a host of local mystery cults, and a rising tide of early Christian beliefs overlapping in unusual ways.

Severus arrived in Alexandria in 199 after his war against the Parthians, and was enraged by what he saw. The city was alive with bizarre occult practices, its population obsessed with divining the future through interpreting strange signs. Severus regarded these activities as undermining official Roman religion and threatening the public good. He was particularly troubled by the easy and widespread availability of books and manuals on magic and alchemy, which he removed from circulation by sealing them up in Alexander's tomb.[23] Making the Soma a hiding place for esoteric texts suggests there was more going on than meets the eye.

Dio Cassius says that Severus worried about the safety of Alexander's body and was determined to stop people from reading—in other words consulting—the obviously not so secret books. This is contrary to assumptions that these two acts were simply a coincidence of opportunities, with Severus sealing the tomb to protect the corpse and removing the books from circulation.

Alexander had been displayed in Alexandria for half a millennium, surviving natural and man-made upheavals. What now endangered his precious remains? No ancient writer tells us that Alexander's tomb was sealed after Ptolemy X pillaged its golden sarcophagus or Cleopatra took the other items. And it is difficult to believe that the Soma was the most secure hiding place in the city for books. Did Severus perhaps see a dangerous link between the official Alexander cult and the rampant belief in magic?

In the absence of ancient clues to guide us, we can only surmise that Alexander's cult had frayed at the edges in the two centuries since Octavian outlawed the veneration of the Ptolemies. Most Alexandrians were native Egyptians, with a predilection for magic, secret formulas, and amulets. Their beliefs bore little resemblance to the official Roman state religion. The Ptolemaic dynasty was gone, and Alexander's cult had been hijacked by Rome, its heroic mythology adopted by the emperors, and its rituals incorporated into state religion. What Severus saw, perhaps, were attempts by Alexandrians to reclaim Alexander by infiltrating his cult and identifying his body and tomb with the Egyptian fascination for sorcery and divination.

Severus's concern for Alexander's remains could have been prompted by a new role for Alexander's corpse as the focal point for common magic with nationalistic overtones. After all, Alexander was the eponymous hero-god of Alexandrians, not Romans. Instead of just paying their respects, perhaps the tomb's visitors were invoking Alexander in a new way that was more meaningful to people living in 200 C.E.

To Severus, such a revitalized and reconfigured Alexander was a potentially explosive development. If Severus's angry reaction on arriving in Alexandria is any guide, the combustible compound of Alexander and alchemy was already subverting and disrupting the orderly life of Roman Alexandria, based on Roman law and backed by the Roman state religion. Almost as bad, in Severus's mind, altering Alexander's cult dangerously reconfigured Alexander's symbolism as an exemplar of Roman imperialism, making the dead conqueror's tomb a focus for nationalistic Egyptian impulses.

Severus's concern for the safety of Alexander's body may have focused on the way the body was being viewed and manipulated in religious terms. Alternatively, the obsession with divination, alchemy, and magical objects gripping Alexandria's inhabitants may have led them to acquire parts of Alexander's body or tomb for the talismanic power they were believed to possess. When Severus sealed Alexander's tomb with the secret books inside, he removed potent magical objects from public access. Severus may have calculated that the sanctity of the Soma would deter Alexandria's famously volatile inhabitants from any violent reaction.

This brief glimpse into the turbulent religious life of Alexandria around 200 C.E. may conceal a different reading of events. Dio describes Severus as taking "away from practically all the sanctuaries all the books that he could find containing any secret lore" and then "locked up the tomb of Alexander." Dio does not explicitly link these two actions. Perhaps they were separate and were only brought together by Dio in his history. This in turn might explain why there is no further mention of these magical texts in relation to the Soma. What prompted Severus to these two curious acts remains as murky as ever.

Severus's son, Marcus Aurelius Antoninus Caracallus (Caracalla), was with his father in Alexandria and probably visited the Soma at the same time. Caracalla developed a lifelong fascination with Alexander, whom he emulated as a personal hero. Severus's problem with Alexandria's troublesome inhabitants was not lost on the young Caracalla, and he still harbored a grudge when he visited Alexander's tomb in the early years of the third century.[24]

Caracalla sailed into Alexandria's harbor in the summer of 215 to a rapturous welcome. Crowds lined the heavily perfumed streets, showering the royal party with flowers, the scented air reverberating to the music of drum and flute. Like his father and so many others before him, Caracalla wished to see Alexander. The historian Herodian picks up the story:

[Caracalla] . . . went to the tomb of Alexander where he took off and laid upon the grave the purple cloak he was wearing and the rings of precious stones and his belts and anything else of value he was carrying.[25]

But Caracalla was no ordinary emperor, and his visit to the Soma went far beyond paying his respects to the great Macedonian conqueror. Caracalla was a dangerous megalomaniac, whose adulation of Alexander was an obsessive and bloody fixation with the worst of his hero's excesses. Disturbing insights into Caracalla's character appear in an anonymous fourth-century source describing how his visit to Alexander's remains affected the emperor.

After he had inspected the body of Alexander of Macedon, he ordered that he himself should be called "Great" and "Alexander," for he was led on by the lies of his flatterers to the point where, adopting the ferocious brow and neck tilted towards the left shoulder that he had noted in Alexander's countenance, he persuaded himself that his features were truly very similar.[26]

Imitation did not satisfy Caracalla, who decided he was in fact Alexander reborn. Driven to commemorate his astonishing transformation, Caracalla ordered statues and images that showed his true identity.

When they were displayed publicly, Alexandrians heaped scorn and ridicule on the emperor. One particularly ludicrous painting showed a single heroic body whose head was split into two faces, one of Alexander and the other of Caracalla.

Caracalla even drank his wine from goblets supposedly belonging to Alexander that he had taken from the mausoleum. He had statues of Alexander erected in military bases and throughout Rome. He went further, Dio says, by creating an anachronistic army unit called the phalanx of Alexander, in which sixteen thousand native Macedonians were equipped with ersatz Alexander-period weapons. Caracalla amazed everyone by parading around Rome followed by elephants as Alexander had done, announcing to an astonished Roman senate that Alexander had entered his body so that he could live longer, since he had died so young.[27]

Caracalla loathed the arrogant Alexandrians who poked fun at him. They gleefully detailed awful allegations about the emperor: how he murdered his brother Geta, practiced incest with his mother, and made ridiculous claims to be Alexander reincarnated when he was a ludicrous underachiever. Caracalla's exploits gave Alexandrians plenty of scabrous ammunition, but they should have kept their peace, for Severus's son was not the forgiving type.

Caracalla indulged his bloodlust in the days following his encounter with the numinous in Alexander's tomb. He enticed the city's young men to gather in the stadium to be enrolled in a special Alexander phalanx of infantry.[28] Once assembled, Caracalla ordered his soldiers to kill everyone and then rampage through the streets raping and slaughtering anyone they found. Caracalla's vengeance left Alexandria awash with blood but, we must suppose, left Alexander's tomb intact.

In the wake of this mass murder, Caracalla decided to fortify the old Palaces District that housed the imperial administration. This protected area became known as the Brucheum, and it was surrounded by a huge wall that cut through the heart of the city.

Whether the Soma enclosure survived unaltered is unknown; the walls may have been demolished or incorporated into the ramparts, perhaps supplying raw material for the giant towers that reinforced the new wall at regular intervals. Caracalla's adoration of Alexander suggests that he likely included the mausoleum within the Brucheum.[29]

Possessed by some inner demon, Caracalla was driven to imitate everything about Alexander. It was to be his undoing. Massacring unarmed Alexandrian youths was not in the same league as the visceral experience of battle. With his blood up, and mistaking easy murder for hard-fought combat, Caracalla rode with the army out of Egypt believing he could emulate Alexander's Asian conquests by fighting in Syria.

At the Temple of the Moon at Carrhae, Caracalla was assassinated by one of his own centurions. As this most terrifying of would-be Alexanders lay dying in the Syrian desert, back in Alexandria the Soma was sliding away from history. Caracalla's devastating visit was the tomb's last historically secure appearance in the written sources.

Caracalla's wall in Alexandria defined the city's new Brucheum district, which included civic and temple buildings, and probably the Soma as well. If the emperor believed that his massive ramparts would protect this area, events proved otherwise. The wall put the Soma at greater risk than ever before in Alexandria's five-hundred-year history.

Alexandrians loathed Rome but consistently misjudged the politics of power from Caesar to Caracalla. Within a few years of Caracalla's death, Alexandrians recklessly adopted the Roman prefect Marcus Julius Aemilianus as emperor against Gallienus, who had been proclaimed in Rome. Gallienus's general Theodotus appeared outside the walls of Alexandria with his imperial legions in 262. Aemilianus took refuge in the Brucheum, where Theodotus launched one bitter attack after another to dislodge him. Open war raged through Alexandria's streets in the neighborhood of the Brucheum and Soma for two years before Aemilianus was captured and executed in 264. No mention is made of Alexander's mausoleum, and we can only guess whether it was damaged or destroyed.

Only five years later, the Brucheum was again at the heart of destruction. In 269, the beautiful and wily Queen Zenobia of Palmyra renounced her kingdom's alliance with Rome and invaded Egypt. Under her general, Zabda, the Palmyrene armies besieged the Roman garrison in the Brucheum. Zenobia's son Wahballath ruled the city, minting coins bearing his own likeness, at first with the new emperor Aurelian's head on one side and later with only his own likeness accompanied by the imperial title. The new dawn faded fast, and Wahballath and his army were expelled by Aurelian's general, Probus (himself a future emperor), between late 270 and the summer of 271.

Both armies may have honored Alexander's tomb during these two years of constant fighting, treating it as sacred and neutral ground. If the Soma was inside the Brucheum, it was probably safeguarded by Roman legionaries. If outside the perimeter, it would have been protected (and visited) by Wahballath, as his mother claimed royal descent from Cleopatra VII and thus had Ptolemaic blood running through her veins. The ancient writers, sadly, are silent on this intriguing possibility.

Zenobia ordered the retreat from Alexandria, but this did not save the Brucheum. As her armies marched back to Palmyra, Zenobia's ally—a wealthy businessman named Firmus—seized control of the city, taking up residence behind the Brucheum's walls. It is said that Firmus adorned his house with glass windows, a rare and expensive luxury at the time.[30] If Alexander's tomb still stood, Firmus must surely have visited it, though no ancient writer records it.

In Syria, the Emperor Aurelian had just routed Zenobia's army when news of Firmus's insurrection arrived. He swept through Egypt with his army, camping outside Alexandria's walls and besieging the city. Aurelian devastated the Brucheum area in 272, razing parts of the famous museum library before capturing Firmus and putting him to death.[31] We hear nothing of the Soma and can only speculate that either it survived or its destruction was so embarrassing that none of the ancient writers recorded it. Perhaps both sides agreed to spare Alexander's tomb, though any such arrangement may not have included the sepulchres of the Ptolemies.

After years of bloodletting and destruction, Alexandria enjoyed a few peaceful decades. The city's willful inhabitants rediscovered their confidence, only to once again misread the political landscape. Provoked by Roman tax reforms and rampant inflation, and spurred on by an individual known only as Achilleus, Alexandrians supported Lucius Domitius Domitianus in a bid for imperial power in 297.

During his inevitably brief reign, Domitianus issued anachronistic coins in the Ptolemaic style that played to Alexandria's past glories and pleased the Alexandrian crowds. Domitianus, an otherwise anonymous pretender, made great play of Alexander as the embodiment of the city; presumably he visited the Soma if it was still standing.

Domitianus and Alexandria rebelled during the reign of the tough soldier-emperor Diocletian, who was in Syria fighting the Persians. Newly appointed to the throne by his own legions, Diocletian turned his anger on the rebellious Alexandrians. He swathed through one Egyptian town after another and arrived at the gates of Alexandria in late 297, besieging the city for eight long months.

Alexandria was eventually betrayed from within, and a vengeful Diocletian sacked the city in the spring of 298. The memory of Caracalla was invoked when Diocletian ordered a mass slaughter of Alexandrians, especially Christians. This murderous reprisal ended when the emperor's mount suddenly collapsed beneath him, unexpectedly fulfilling a command he had made—that killing would cease when blood flowed around his horse's knees.[32]

Diocletian commemorated his victory by raising a red granite column bearing his name that still today towers eighty feet above the remains of the Serapeum temple. Surveying the wanton destruction his legions had wrought, it is a moot point whether Diocletian could see the Soma on the other side of the city.

The third century of the Christian era brought bitter conflict, ruin, and abandonment to large swathes of Alexandria. In the eye of the storm was the Brucheum, an area at whose heart lay Philopater's grand funeral park. No ancient writer mentions it despite the ravages of Theodotus, Zenobia, Aurelian, Firmus, and Diocletian.

A stray comment by the fourth-century historian Ammianus Marcellinus writing one hundred years after these events suggests the mausoleum's survival. Ammianus records the destruction, adding that "the greater part of the district called Brucheum was destroyed."[33] The slenderest of hopes is that the tomb was spared in the part of the Brucheum that Ammianus infers survived.

The destruction of the Soma would have been a propaganda gift to the Romans who idolized Alexander, Zenobia who claimed Ptolemaic descent, and the Alexandrians for whom he was the deified founder and resident "genius." The silence of the ancient sources may indicate that the tomb somehow survived. War damage may not have been worthy of comment in such perilous times, but total destruction would surely have left some written trace.

By 298, Alexander's tomb had entered the realm of rumor and legend, half-truths, possible sightings, romance, and deception. The succession of imperial Roman visitors, rebellious upstarts and vengeful emperors, added a sharper edge to the image of Alexander himself. The extraordinary achievements and appalling crimes perpetrated by imperial visitors to the Soma blended imperceptibly with Alexander's own, creating a composite but vibrant memory that has burnished our fascination with the great Macedonian.

Although the era of imperial visits was over, Alexander's encounters with the great figures of history were not. The next visitor differed from all who had come before, and he did not come in person. Of all who had fought Alexander in life or visited him in death, none were such as this. The meeting between Alexander and Jesus was to have unforeseen and far-reaching consequences, as might be expected when a confrontation between the dead takes place in the world of the living.

Both men were spirits of their age—Alexander of Hellenistic paganism, Jesus of a new Christian faith that elevated the primacy of the soul over the body. The consequences were a spiritual and temporal struggle of epic proportions. Ironically, without Christianity's conquest of paganism, the obsessional search for Alexander's tomb might never have begun, since it would never have been lost.

THE TOMB DISAPPEARS

IN 312 C.E., THE FUTURE EMPEROR CONSTANTINE the Great was poised to traverse the Alps and invade Italy, his soldiers' shields emblazoned with the sign of the cross. On the eve of battle, Christ had appeared to Constantine in a dream and advised him to adopt the Christian emblem if he wished to defeat his enemies. This was the beginning of the end for the Soma in distant Alexandria.

Constantine was a lifelong pagan who was still being hailed by the pagan gods and their priests in 311. Intent on overthrowing Emperor Maxentius in Rome, Constantine was unsettled by the news that his enemy was mobilizing the city's ancient gods, resorting to divination, and invoking Sibylline prophecies. Constantine needed a supernatural ally to counter Maxentius's advantage, and he found one in a vision of the Christian faith.

Constantine and his God defeated Maxentius at the battle of the Milvian bridge north of Rome. Twelve years later Licinius, Constantine's last rival for the imperial purple, was defeated at Chrysopolis and later murdered, leaving Constantine as sole emperor. In 324, he dealt the first of many blows against paganism by declaring Christianity the only religion of the empire, though the old beliefs were still tolerated. Over the next ten years, Constantine closed down, robbed, and destroyed many Greek temples, sacking famous oracles such as Didyma, stealing their treasuries, and stripping their cult statues to adorn his new capital of Constantinople.

Persecution, execution, and torture of pagans began under Constantine and continued under his successors. Glories of the ancient world were destroyed in an orgy of religious zealotry. Libraries were set aflame and magnificent marble temples disappeared in smoke as they were burned into lime. The Soma became ensnared in a web of propaganda and fell victim to a sleight of hand that reveals a hitherto unidentified connection between Alexander and Christ.

The mystery begins with Constantine. Eager to celebrate his Christ-given victory over Licinius, the emperor announced he would tour his new imperial possessions in the east. Egypt was the jewel in his itinerary, and not just for strategic and political reasons. Constantine was hoping to catch sight of the mythical Phoenix—a bird adopted by the Christian Church as a symbol of resurrection and the beginning of a new age.[1] To glimpse the beautiful asexual creature that made itself from its own ashes would be auspicious indeed. Ancient papyri record that Egypt readied itself for the emperor's imminent arrival.[2]

Bishop Ossius of Cordova in Spain was Constantine's most intimate confidant in spiritual matters. Ossius journeyed east to prepare the way for his emperor, arriving at Antioch in early 325 and then traveling on to Alexandria. As soon as he arrived inside the city walls, Ossius convened a synod of local Egyptian bishops. The fight against schism and paganism was uppermost in Ossius's mind, and he found himself being briefed on the state of religious affairs in Alexandria. Like all visiting dignitaries, Ossius probably toured the city, being shown Alexandria's churches and the resting place of St. Mark, as well as the two centers of the old and hated pagan beliefs—the Serapeum and the Soma.

Constantine, meanwhile, was approaching Egypt when he heard about activity among proponents of the Arian heresy, a controversy concerning the nature of Christ's divinity. Constantine stopped in his tracks and made his way back to Antioch, where he gave a rousing speech to the assembled Christians on Good Friday 325. During this extraordinary address, known as the "Oration to the Saints," Constantine bitterly attacked pagans, singling out the idolatry and polytheism that characterized paganism's flexible, accommodating approach to religious belief.

On his travels throughout the empire, Constantine and his advisers saw the continuing presence of paganism and its sacred places. Constantine realized that if Christ's victory was to be complete and consolidated, alternative places would have to be set up that coopted the symbolic language of the old religion and replaced it with a different message.

Constantine, as a former pagan, understood his enemy well. Paganism's roots lay in age-old beliefs of the sacredness of special places, where spiritual forces gathered and lingered—thresholds between worlds where humans encountered the numinous and felt the pull from another world. Mountains, caves, freshwater springs, wells, and unusual geological formations were places where the membrane between different dimensions might rupture. Some of the greatest pagan oracles—Delphi, Claros, and Didyma—were built over or incorporated unusual natural features.

And most of all, Constantine knew, pagans were devoted to their tombs, especially those of heroes who transcended humanity, and the kings and warriors who imitated them. The grander and more richly appointed the tomb, the more potent it became. Such ideas were anathema to Christians and their focus on the immaterial world beyond the present world, and their driving obsession with the soul and the body's eventual resurrection. Paganism's grand temples, statues, ancestral tombs, and treasuries full of golden idols embodied and provoked the zealous Christian's fear and loathing of a world saturated in idolatry and superstition—the work of the devil himself. Playing pagans at their own game, Constantine knew that Christianity lacked what paganism had in abundance—a supremely sacred place, a tomb.

Not long after addressing the meeting at Antioch, Constantine welcomed the Church Fathers to a second meeting—the famous Council of Nicaea in June-July 325. Also present were Bishop Makarios of Jersualem and Ossius, the president of the proceedings, who had recently returned from Alexandria.[3] Their endless discussions must have included Ossius's experiences in Alexandria. Ossius likely brought up the Soma and its continuing fascination for pagans and Christians alike. Whatever transpired on this topic between these three ambitious and powerful men, the consequences were dramatic. Constantine ordered Makarios to start searching for Christ's tomb, or perhaps Makarios requested permission to do so.[4]

The three men must have agreed that Christianity needed a counterweight, a grand tomb for Christ that would eclipse Alexander's mausoleum and all the non-Christian funerary monuments so beloved of pagans. If Christ's tomb could be found, it would drive another nail into paganism's coffin and offer Christians and potential converts a focus for their devotion and a place to visit on pilgrimage. The only analog for the power and influence of Christ's tomb, should it be found, was Alexander's, and images of the latter's magnetic attraction must have been fresh in Ossius's mind.

Makarios returned to Jerusalem and within weeks was informing Constantine of his stunning and almost immediate success. Constantine, overjoyed, announced the discovery of Christ's tomb at a site near Golgotha where Jesus had been crucified some three centuries before.[5] Makarios's find was a masterstroke and an unparalleled propaganda coup for Constantine. The uniqueness of Alexander's mausoleum was destroyed in one stroke, and a Christian rival appeared that spoke in the language of sacred space to Christians and pagans alike.

This was a remarkable sequence of events. Did Ossius's sighting of Alexander's tomb and its milling crowds inspire the idea of finding Christ's tomb? The circumstantial evidence is intriguing and suggestive. It answers questions hitherto judged unanswerable. Why, after three hundred years, was there a desperate need to provide Christ with a tomb? Why did Constantine order the search for it within weeks of Ossius's return from Alexandria? And how was it discovered almost immediately and against all odds?[6]

The rock-cut tomb identified as Jesus's resting place was one of several and had no distinguishing features. No method of identification is recorded, and it appears to have been a random choice that somehow felt appropriate. Professor Martin Biddle of Oxford University spent years investigating Christ's tomb and was forced to admit that "for reasons never stated, one of these tombs was immediately hailed as the Tomb of Christ."[7]

Constantine followed his momentous announcement by declaring his intention to build a basilica over the tomb, transforming it into a suitably grand focus for Christian pilgrimage and devotion. Ten years later, in 335, it was consecrated as the Martyrion and has survived to the present, despite waves of destruction and rebuilding, as the Church of the Holy Sepulchre.

Whatever led to this probably arbitrary identification of Christ's tomb, the result was clear: Constantine had created a paganlike cave tomb for Christianity. It was a physical place that could be visited and couched in terms that recently pagan Christians and potential converts could identify with. It spoke their own language of landscape and place. Whether faith or fraud, the sudden discovery of the tomb was a victory for the emperor and all Christians.

Christianity now had its own sepulchre—a place that focused Christian thoughts and emotions on the true meaning of life, which lay, paradoxically, in the other world. Christ's tomb, unlike Alexander's, was not an architecturally impressive location with a body on which the pilgrim could gaze, but a symbolic and empty tomb, a portal to the spiritual world of resurrection for all who embraced the new Christian faith—a material place for the contemplation of the immaterial world.

Constantine out-tombed Alexander and made Christianity more user-friendly in the process. Christ's tomb would trump the Soma and all the lesser pagan tombs of the empire. Alexander's mausoleum would soon disappear and Christ's tomb would evolve into the central and iconic pivot of Christendom. Soon after it was discovered, Christ's tomb was linked to other holy Christian sites at Bethlehem and the Mount of Olives that were identified by the Byzantine empress Helena during her high-profile visit to the Levant just a year later in 326.

Helena lavished imperial funds on the newly found locations, authenticating them as true sites from the Gospels by her extravagant patronage.[8] In less than a year, the atlas of Christianity was transfigured, the Holy Land peppered with sacred places that materialized the Gospels in the physical world. If Alexander's tomb inspired Ossius, Constantine, and then Makarios, it also played a spectacular role in the future success of the religion that would eventually bring its six-hundred-year existence to an end.

In 361 Julian the Apostate became emperor, and the old religion enjoyed a brief resurgence. But Christianity returned with a vengeance in 364, when the emperor Jovianus, who succeeded Julian, issued an imperial edict ordering the death penalty for anyone found practicing paganism. Jovianus's successor, Valens, persecuted non-Christians with zeal, and in 380 the new emperor Theodosius made Christianity the exclusive religion of the empire, overseeing the destruction of pagan temples and altars across the empire.

Throughout these turbulent years Roman emperors, despite their zealous Christianity, continued adorning their cities with pagan imagery. The Lateran Obelisk was erected in Rome's Circus Maximus in 357, and in 390 Theodosius set up another in the Hippodrome in Constantinople. Did the popularity of pagan decorations for Christian Rome and Constantinople extend to parts of the Soma, or even Alexander's sarcophagus?

In this cauldron of social and religious ferment, which saw pagans and Christians indulging in violence, murder, retaliation, and wanton destruction, two tantalizing glimpses of Alexander's tomb emerge. Ammianus Marcellinus (c. 325–c. 391) was a noble-born pagan from Antioch who served in the army of Julian the Apostate. He was traveling through Egypt in the 370s when he stumbled across a remarkable story.[9] In his history of the period 353–378, known as the *Res Gestae*, Ammianus tells the fate of Bishop Georgias—the city's patriarch around 360–363—and hints at a role for Alexander's mausoleum in Georgias's murder.

Georgias was so unpopular with Alexandria's pagan inhabitants that he needed the protection of the imperial garrison. He persecuted the city's pagan community for years, and Ammianus informs us that he spied on their activities for the emperor Constantius II. But when this rabid Christian cleric threatened the greatest pagan figure of all—Alexander—he sealed his own fate.

As Ammianus tells it, Georgias was making his way through Alexandria's colonnaded streets when he passed the splendid temple to the city's Genius, which was as usual surrounded by a large crowd. Gazing at the magnificent building, Georgias exclaimed, "How long will this tomb stand?" The assembled throng, knowing his reputation, were struck "as if by a thunderbolt," fearing that he would have the great building destroyed. From this moment, Ammianus adds, the crowd "devised secret plots to destroy him."[10]

Ammianus's story turns on the identification of the entity called the Genius. It may refer to the serpent spirit known as the Agathos Daimon or perhaps the god Serapis, or even Tyche—the city's own fortune deity. Yet none of these are tombs. Perhaps Georgias's outburst was aimed at Alexander's still magnificent mausoleum. This view is strengthened by the fact that this passage appears almost immediately after Ammianus mentions Alexander as the city's founder. If Georgias was in fact gazing on the pagan Soma, then the great sepulchre was still standing around 360–361 C.E., and evidently as popular as ever.

Georgias soon paid for his outburst. In 361, Constantius died and Julian the Apostate came to the throne. Julian was a Hellenophile who had been brought up as a Christian but renounced the faith when he became emperor. He reinstated pagan practices and allowed the persecution of Christians.

Julian believed he was a reincarnation of Alexander and planned to recreate Alexander's empire, especially in Persia, with the help of the pagan gods.[11] Ammianus says that Julian sacrificed a hundred bulls at a time, drenching the old altars with their revitalizing blood.[12] Julian was fascinated by acting out the cosmic roles of pagan gods and enjoyed playing the part of Serapis. He authorized the enthroning of the Apis bull at Memphis in 362—the last mention ever of the once dominant cult. Julian must have been concerned to safeguard the Alexandrian tomb of his hero, though there is no record of his visiting Alexandria.

Taking heart from Julian's enthronement, Alexandria's pagans dragged Georgias out of his church, murdered him, and burned his remains in the pagan tradition. They purged the Christian community, crucifying many in imitation of Christ.[13] Paganism flourished in fourth-century Alexandria, even if the tide was moving out on it. If Georgias's threat to the Genius refers to Alexander's tomb, then the Soma was a focus for pagan cult activity and was still open for business around 361.[14]

Alexander's mausoleum may have survived the vicissitudes of the late pagan, early Christian era, but a more serious threat was looming. In the summer of 365, a disastrous earthquake and tidal wave struck the city. Alexandria's population—evenly split between pagan and Christian—saw this as the wrath of the old gods or the punishment of Christ.

Ammianus describes the awe-inspiring event. On July 21, 365, the sea retreated from the harbor waters of many eastern Mediterranean ports, including Alexandria, leaving fish and fishing boats stranded. When the sea returned, now as a giant tsunami, it came crashing onto the land, sweeping before it many magnificent buildings. In Alexandria, Ammianus adds, ships were left high and dry on the tops of buildings.[15]

Sozomenus (400–450), a Christian lawyer from Gaza, gives a more detailed account of the catastrophe, which he attributes to the wrath of his own God. He also tells how ships were left stranded atop city buildings, adding that Alexandria's inhabitants commemorated the event for years afterward with an annual festival.[16] The tidal wave wreaked havoc among the coastal cities of the eastern Mediterranean, though to what extent well-built masonry structures were affected is guesswork.

It seems unlikely that the huge Soma would have been totally destroyed by this wave, though it may have been severely damaged. Even if it was abandoned completely, its 550-year-old location would hardly have been forgotten by the city's inhabitants.

Libanius (314–394) gives us a glimpse of Alexander's tomb at this time, as well as an intriguing insight into the turbulent half-pagan, half-Christian world of the fourth century, in the fifteen hundred letters and the autobiography he left. Libanius straddles paganism and Christianity to a remarkable degree. He was a contemporary of Ammianus and taught him rhetoric in Antioch.[17] Exiled from Constantinople after accusations of sorcery, he became a friend and teacher of the future emperor Julian the Apostate. Libanius's connections to the Christian world were equally impressive. He was rewarded with an honorary prefecture by the Christian emperor Theodosius (r. 378–395 C.E.) and taught rhetoric to the scourge of paganism—the Christian patriarch John Chrysostom. When Chrysostom became bishop of Constantinople in 398, he launched a virulent attack on Alexander the Great.

Libanius was a good pagan who protested the ravages that militant Christian zealots were inflicting on pagan temples throughout the eastern empire. Despite an official policy of religious toleration, Christian mobs went around smashing statues, leveling walls, and appropriating land. In 386 Libanius wrote a letter to Theodosius, hoping to persuade the emperor to save the remaining old temples. Libanius railed against the antipagan activities of the Christian prefect Cynegius in the eastern

Mediterranean, warning against this zealous official committing similar outrages in Egypt.

In 386, it appears, Alexandria had not yet suffered the mass destruction of its pagan buildings that Cynegius had wrought in Antioch and elsewhere. Libanius's concern for Egypt's pagan temples may have focused on the threat to Alexander's mausoleum, as well as the city's great Serapeum temple.[18]

Libanius was tireless in his efforts, writing again a few years later, probably in 390–391, complaining bitterly about the behavior of the region's city councillors. In a visceral attack on what he saw as the unscrupulous moneymaking activities of greedy local officials, he asked the rhetorical question of whether such men could even "keep their hands off temple offerings or tombs?" He went further, saying that the avariciousness of civic authorities is universal "whether you mention Paltus or Alexandria where the body of Alexander is to be seen, whether Balaneae or our own city. They may differ in size, but the same ailment afflicts them all."[19]

The tenor of the letter suggests that Libanius is referring to Alexander's mausoleum in Egyptian Alexandria. The problem of bureaucratic corruption is widespread, and Libanius is comparing the metropolis of Alexandria with the small Syrian town of Paltus, and his own great city of Antioch with another small settlement called Balaneae.

Libanius's comment is intriguing. Was he implying that Alexander's corpse had been dug up from the collapsed ruins of the Soma in the wake of the earthquake and put on display for profit by Alexandria's councillors?[20] Or perhaps he was simply referring to the money-grubbing corruption of local officials in Alexandria, where Alexander's mausoleum had always been a popular (and lucrative) tourist attraction. In the aftermath of the natural and social disasters that had overtaken Alexandria, tourists visiting Alexander's tomb may have been one of the city's few remaining crowd pleasers and an important source of revenue.

Christian officials, Libanius observes, had no compunction about enriching themselves or the Church by stealing, recycling, or destroying pagan buildings and monuments. In the closing years of the fourth century, financial management of the Soma may have passed from pagans to Christians. Perhaps this is what enraged the aging Libanius.

Libanius is being deliberately provocative. He knows that to be convincing, his letter to the emperor must deploy well-known examples of civic corruption, not fantasy and fiction. Can we assume that Alexander's mummy was on display in Alexandria and that this was common knowledge? If so, the Soma was not completely destroyed during the earthquake and tidal wave of 365, and was still open for business as late as the 380s, perhaps even 390–391.

Alexander's tomb has entered the realm of legend and supposition, of circumstantial evidence that teases and frustrates: there are no clear-cut accounts of the tomb's survival or destruction. Libanius is among the last to refer even ambiguously to Alexander's mausoleum. What happened next closed the door on the tomb's history for half a millennium.

In 391 the emperor Theodosius banned paganism throughout the empire, ending the uneasy tolerance that had existed on and off since Constantine's edicts of 324. An ominous future beckoned for Alexandria's pagans and their most sacred cult centers—the Serapeum and, if it still stood, the Soma.

The Serapeum was the focus of pagan worship in late Roman Alexandria. Bloody clashes and riots between pagans and Christians occurred against its massive walls until it was pillaged, abandoned, and ultimately closed in 391.[21] Theodosius personally ordered his imperial prefect Evragius to destroy the Serapeum. Evragius had the help of a raging mob led by Theophilus, the patriarch of Alexandria.

The fate of Alexander's mausoleum hung in the balance. Theophilus and his angry monks focusing attention on the Serapeum may have taken the heat off the mausoleum. Evragius and Theophilus may have found it easier to whip up righteous indignation against the Serapeum than against the popular mausoleum, which was a possible source of revenue for the Christian authorities Libanius had recently complained about.

The Soma, however, was on the firing line, for Theodosius's edict ordered the destruction of all remaining pagan temples in Alexandria. Such was the violence and rage of the crowds unleashed by Theophilus that they may well have destroyed the mausoleum in the days and weeks after they destroyed the Serapeum. It may be around this time that Theophilus is said to have discovered a great treasure from Alexander's era, which the emperor allowed him to use to build and dedicate churches throughout the city.[22]

Yet the rich detail of surviving accounts of the Serapeum's end is counterpointed by a strange silence concerning Alexander's tomb. We read how the statue of Serapis was repeatedly smashed by a soldier and its limbs dragged through the city's streets, and how other parts of the body were set on fire in the city center. Yet not a word concerning the Soma. If the mob destroyed the tomb, we would expect to hear of it—not least in Christian writings that eagerly trumpet their victories over paganism. Perhaps the mausoleum no longer existed or was left alone for some reason.

The last mention of the Soma belongs to a powerful figure of the time. John Chrysostom (340–407 C.E.) was the most influential thinker of the early Church. Sometime around 400, Chrysostom launched a bitter attack on Alexander's tomb in a homily on St. Paul's epistle to the Corinthians.[23] In keeping with his reputation for surpassing eloquence (from which his name Chrysostom, "golden mouthed," derived), he asks a rhetorical question: "Tell me, where is the tomb of Alexander? Show me, tell me the day on which he died."[24]

Perhaps the Soma was now so lost that its location had slipped from documented history and common memory as well. Chrysostom was overjoyed at the demise of the Serapeum, but it was a temple, never a tomb. While Serapis was a pagan god (and a hybrid of Greek and Egyptian deities as well), Alexander was a historical person who had accomplished astonishing things and then become a god—an unsettling (and blasphemous) parallel for Jesus's life and transfiguration. If the tomb of Alexander—the epitome of what a human being might accomplish in life—could be forgotten, then all other physical lives were as nothing compared to the eternal life of the soul that Christ promised.

Chrysostom was making a rhetorical flourish, an allusion to a divided audience still wavering between Christianity and paganism. He was ramming home a religious and philosophical point to the disparate peoples of the empire who had never visited Alexandria but knew of the Soma.

Chrysostom's outburst conceals his economy with the truth. Alexander's second tomb was built by Philopater in 215 B.C.E. and dominated

Alexandria for six hundred years. It is inconceivable that nobody knew where it was or where it had been until recently. It is even more unlikely that no one who was alive around 360 could remember it. Even if the Soma had been destroyed by the earthquake and tsunami of 365, it could not have disappeared from the memory of those who were alive just ten or twenty years before.

Far more likely is that no one who remembered the Soma and its location (likely tens of thousands of people) would have the temerity to say so publicly. Chrysostom's statement referred to religion and philosophy, not Alexandria's urban geography. In Alexandria, the Soma was almost certainly in ruins, its location—perhaps as a source of building materials—well-known. It was less a case that no one knew than no one cared or dared to respond.

Chrysostom's homily includes an ambiguous passage that may recall the magnificence of Alexander's royal corpse and its magnetic attraction to the great men of history. Chrysostom stresses that the simple tombs of poor Christians are more popular than elaborate pagan sepulchres. He has one doubter express the sentiment that "it is a sweet sight to look on a king covered with gold and crowned, and standing by his side, generals, commanders, captains of horse and foot," only to answer that this is as nothing compared to the king who lives in heaven and has an army of angels.[25] Is the doubter referring to Alexander's mummified body and thereby allowing Chrysostom to compare it unfavorably with the simplest Christian burial?

Chrysostom's homily, from which the passage about Alexander's tomb is often lifted, repays a closer look. Time and again the patriarch rails against Alexander, asserting that his military victories and astounding conquests, as well as the buildings and trophies he erected, count for nothing against the achievements of the crucified Christ and his message of resurrection. Both men had died. But Christ's spiritual empire was flourishing and Alexander's worldly domain had been torn to pieces. Chrysostom was using Alexander as a paragon of paganism against which Christianity compared favorably.

Chrysostom further took issue with the Roman senate's decree that Alexander be made the thirteenth god and asked, "How is Alexander a god?" To a modern eye, and probably to many at the time, there is the inescapable feeling that the whole episode is overdone. Was Chrysostom's demonizing of Alexander just a little too fervent? If everything that Alexander stood for—in official paganism as well as in common magic—was so transparently false, then why make so much of it?

Time and again in Christianity's earliest struggles with the pagan world, the Church Fathers invoked the devil's advocate. Alexander serves Chrysostom's purpose because he was so entrenched in the ancient world's collective psyche. The mausoleum (with or without its royal corpse) was probably destroyed by this time, but it was Alexander's universal empire that was the ultimate (if short-lived) achievement that agitated early Church leaders. For Christians, a similarly universal empire of the spirit was the only way to equal and then surpass what Alexander had achieved in the physical world.

Chrysostom and other Church leaders were right to be nervous about Alexander. Despite their zealous fundamentalism and rent-a-mob tactics, they knew that Christianity's ultimate triumph in the Greco–Roman world was bought at the price of compromises with paganism. While Christian emperors destroyed pagan temples and pillaged their artworks, other temples, festivals, and even gods were assimilated, smoothing over the transition from a pagan to a Christian world. It was, as Chrysostom knew, a thin line to tread, as an episode fifty years before in Alexandria had shown.

In 350, the city's patriarch, Alexander, decided to abolish a pagan feast day that was celebrated annually in the great temple known as the Caesareum. Cleopatra had built it to honor Caesar, and later Octavian appropriated it for his own cult as Augustus and for the worship of Saturn. Inside the temple was a huge bronze statue of Saturn to which sacrifices were made. The patriarch intended to abolish the feast and smash the statue as well.

When the plans leaked out, Alexandrians were outraged and forced the patriarch into a compromise. The Alexandrians, he announced, could keep their festivities but dedicate them to St. Michael; the bronze statue would be recast as a cross.[26] This astonishing episode saw Alexandrians forcing a partial climbdown on their Christian authorities, and it is tempting to think that they would have gone even further in trying to protect the grand mausoleum of their city's founder.

Christianity made such accommodations as and when the situation demanded. Some practices, however, were judged too pagan to be acceptable to leaders such as Chrysostom, though their views and edicts were widely disregarded. Wearing amulets, a common practice, dated back to Ptolemaic and earlier Egyptian times. Its origins stretched back into prehistory, and it would become an important feature of medieval Christianity's fascination with relics. Wearing coin amulets, often engraved with such phrases as "Lord, protect the wearer," would become a fashion of its own during the Byzantine age.[27]

Chrysostom and other Church Fathers saw amulets as pagan objects that conjured the devil, and they virulently attacked the wearing of such miniature idols. Nevertheless, Christians were fond of necklaces and anklets made from Ptolemaic coins bearing the head of Alexander adorned with the ram horns of Ammon. Other coins showed Alexander on one side with Nike, the Greek personification of victory, on the other, a doubly potent image of good fortune for the wearer.[28]

In his native Antioch, the devout and austere Chrysostom saw Alexander's image everywhere: "And what is one to say about them who use charms and amulets and encircle their heads and feet with gold coins of Alexander of Macedon."[29] Such practices were neither new nor confined to the middle or lower classes. During the third century, the Roman Macriani family had ascended briefly to the imperial throne, keeping talismanic images of Alexander about their bodies on rings and bracelets, and even having them stitched into their clothing in the belief that fortune would smile on them as it had on Alexander. They even ate from bowls depicting Alexander's face and scenes from his life.[30]

In late Roman society, Alexander's amuletic image spread across the empire. In Rome, distinctive bronze medallions known as *contorniates* were cast that depicted Alexander, Homer, and Roman emperors on one side, and imagery from the Roman games on the other.

Alexander medallions show his bust on one side, dressed as Heracles and wearing the skin of the Nemean lion, with a view of the Circus Maximus and an Egyptian obelisk on the other.[31] They project success and victory, especially perhaps in chariot races. These were typically pagan objects, whose likenesses of Alexander and others invoked the logic of magic in order to bring their owners good fortune. Alexander's image appears especially potent in this respect, as many of the medallions depicting him are also pierced—probably to be worn as talismans.[32] *Contorniates* were especially popular during the reigns of the Christian emperors Valentinian I and Valens (364–378 C.E.), each of whom zealously persecuted pagans.

But there was one type of medallion that must have made Chrysostom's blood boil. It jeopardized the basis of his homilies and messages, and may partly account for his violent attack on Alexander. During the fourth and fifth centuries, many Christians favored a special kind of Alexander amulet that brought together images of Alexander and Christianity on the same medallion.

In the Cabinet of Medals in Paris there are several examples, portraying Alexander as Heracles on one side, with a she-ass and her foal, a scorpion, and the name of Jesus Christ all together on the other. In the Vatican Library, another medallion bears Alexander's head on one side with the monogram of Christ on the other side.

Average Christians, living in a world still shaped by paganism, perhaps saw amulets as a hedging of bets. They desired luck, success, and prosperity in Alexander's material world but were also attracted by the potent message of an immortal soul, salvation, and a spiritual afterlife as promised by Christ. For many Christians—recently pagan—Alexander amulets with Christian symbols were the perfect compromise.

Chrysostom saw these fashionable talismans as ignoring Christ's warning against idolatry and superstition. Satan as well as God worked in mysterious ways, and for Chrysostom the Alexander–Christ amulets were the devil's work. The prospect of Alexander fusing with Jesus to form a new and widely popular deity was anathema to Chrysostom, but typical of paganism's subtle ability to accommodate and incorporate new religions in a flexible and creative way.

Most astonishing of all these objects is a remarkable bronze *contorniate* dating to the reigns of Valentinian I and Valens. Alexander is shown wearing Heracles's lion-skin headdress, but with facial features imitating those of Constantine the Great, who had sponsored Christ's tomb and first outlawed paganism in 324. This was a stunning and dangerous metamorphosis that linked paganism, Alexander, and the founder of the Christian faith as the imperial religion.[33]

Alexander and Christ, Alexander as Constantine! For the proselytizing patriarchs of the early Church, such transformations amounted to blasphemy. Yet the mass of ordinary Christians accepted them, to varying degrees, and probably for centuries. After all, they turned to Alexander not for immortality of the soul, but for good luck and fortune in this life.

Many pagans converting to Christianity found it difficult to embrace a purely spiritual view of life while living in a harsh physical world. Since time immemorial, religions, cults, and beliefs had been built around the physicality of life—and for over half a millennium Alexander had epitomized how far a human could stretch that life. Alexander's amulets were a legacy of his achievements; wearing them might allow the ordinary person to partake of his extraordinary good fortune.

Alexander was the single most famous and influential rival to Christ. Until 325, Alexander was alone in having a tomb to act as a focus for those who wished to worship or emulate him. After 391, and the likelihood of the Soma's destruction, Christ's tomb in Jerusalem stood alone and supreme. Chrysostom singled out Alexander's tomb as an exercise in futility, and by 400, it is easy to see why.

Chrysostom's challenge of "show me where Alexander's tomb now is" and its probable destruction by Theophilus's monks brought Alexander closer to Christ. Now both bodies were lost, and both would live on, albeit in quite different ways, in imagination and memory. The absence of a body lent mystery to Alexander; for Jesus, it became part of a Christian faith that stressed the enduring soul over the transience of earthly life and the corruption of physical remains.

Although Alexander's tomb disappears completely from history at this time, an alternative fate can be suggested. Not for the Soma but for its more portable contents—Alexander's royal mummy.

Christianity's conquest of the Roman empire was far from complete by 400. Paganism was no longer the official imperial religion, but elements of it survived, sometimes mixed with Christianity and sometimes practiced in secret.

Pagan temples still functioned during the fifth century in Egypt, and the Temple of Isis at Philae was kept open until the reign of Justinian (535–537).[34] Christianity's incomplete dominance is shown by Theodosius II's edicts of 450, encouraging good Christians to burn heretical books and cast down pagan temples. In 486, pagan priests discovered at work in Alexandria were swiftly executed, and in 491, worshippers of Zeus were uncovered and murdered on Cyprus. Almost a century later, in 580, more of Zeus's faithful were found at worship and killed in Antioch. Paganism was a spent force in terms of its imperial past, but it lingered into the sixth century after Christ.[35]

In light of this, was it possible that Alexander's body, or parts of it, survived as the most sacred relic from the pagan age and perhaps went on to play a part in the continuing practice of forbidden rites?

Historians can find no record of the destruction of Alexander's mausoleum or his mummified corpse. Yet there had to be an ending—an event that saw Alexander's remains dealt with in one way or another by the people of Alexandria. It is difficult to believe that even with the mausoleum in ruins, Alexander's talismanic corpse would have been left to rot away. While the Soma stood, his remains were probably inviolate. But once the Soma was cast down, the body may have been spirited away by those who clung to pagan beliefs or by others who could turn a handsome profit by selling such unique and powerful relics.

Even the ultimate irony is not impossible. Perhaps Alexandrian Christians were not averse to owning a piece of the great conqueror—maybe the Christian cult of gathering human relics began at the Soma. Chrysostom's dire threats to Christians who wore Alexander amulets illustrate the continuing power of his image. How much better (and efficacious) it would be to own a sliver of Alexander's shroud, mummified flesh, bones, or sarcophagus, rather than a simple coin. Unlike coins, such fragments were anonymous to all but their owner. What peerless talismans such relics might have been to Christians and pagans alike.

Alexander was as restless in death as he was in life. A few years in Memphis, maybe a century in his first Alexandrian tomb, and perhaps six hundred years in the Soma. At this last resting place, before disappearing from view, he received some of the great and notorious men of Rome—ancient visitors drawn to his side out of respect, fascination, emulation, and megalomania.

And what was the fate of his mausoleum and corpse? Were they destroyed by earthquake and tsunami, the devastation wrought by Aurelian and Diocletian, or the rioting monks of Chrysostom's age? The silence of the texts is deafening. Perhaps the mummy was stealthily removed to a safe haven, or maybe it slipped away in countless pockets as good luck charms bought by Alexandria's own feckless population. This at least has the romantic attraction of keeping his body in his own city, albeit in a thousand pieces rather than one. If either was his fate, then the prophecy of *The Alexander Romance* had come to pass—Alexandria was Alexander's city, and his tomb.

THE TWO-HORNED LORD
AND MEDIEVAL WHISPERS

THE PROPHET MOHAMMED DIED IN 632 AT MEDINA, an Arabian trading town that became the second holiest place in Islam. Ten years later, the Muslim warriors of Allah swept across the Egyptian desert and into Alexandria. Speaking a strange language, writing an unfamiliar script, and calling on an unknown god, the Arab invaders brought a new world, where time began again and the calendar was reset to year zero. Alexandria began a new history in 642, and the search for Alexander's tomb continued in a city reshaped by Islam.

In 641 in the fortress known as Babylon-in-Egypt (modern Cairo), the Arab general Amr ibn al-As sat with Cyrus, the Byzantine prefect of Egypt, and discussed terms of surrender. Amr was in a generous mood, and Cyrus was satisfied with the result. Amr gave his Christian guest an eleven-month armistice during which, he assured Cyrus, the Byzantine army and wealthy citizens could leave freely. Those who remained were granted freedom of worship and allowed to keep their property, as long as they paid their taxes.

Amr was a wily desert warrior who left nothing to chance. A month after the agreement was signed, his army appeared outside the city walls, panicking Alexandria's inhabitants. The Arabs had come to collect the first of three large installments of gold bullion—the price Cyrus had agreed to pay for the delayed handover of Alexandria. Then Amr set up camp—a line of billowing Arab tents encircling the Byzantine city. For ten months Amr and his commanders jealously eyed their future prize.

Alexandrians who were able to leave stripped the city of its movable treasures. Laden with their riches, they sailed to Constantinople or Cyprus. Countless Christian masterpieces and probably also Hellenistic and Roman artworks left with the refugees. It is possible, although unconfirmed, that this booty included fragments of Alexander's Soma, such as statues or sculptures, or even pieces of his talismanic corpse. Ordinary Alexandrians who had no hope of escape sank into a mood of resignation.

On September 17, 642, the last Byzantine galleys tacked out of Alexandria's harbor on a rising wind, and almost a thousand years of Greco–Roman civilization ended. Alexandria eventually sank into obscurity, though it remained a large and impressive city for decades after the conquest. As Amr led his army toward the city gates, he was watched by at least 150,000 jittery Alexandrians.

Amr and his desert warriors were astonished at the sights that greeted them as they filed into the city. Many of the great Hellenistic and Roman buildings had disappeared, but much pagan splendor remained, reconfigured for the Christian God. Amr wrote a letter describing his impressions of this momentous event, in which he says there were four thousand palaces, four thousand baths, four hundred theaters, and twelve thousand vegetable sellers, as well as forty thousand Jews.[1]

The Arabs were struck by the intense light that bounced off the marble streets, palatial buildings, and endless rows of polished columns. The tough men of the desert were deeply impressed by this brilliance, as were those who visited the city for the first time during its Ptolemaic heyday. Alexandria in 642 was still unique, a colonnaded Christian city that never shook its Hellenistic past as the city tomb of Alexander the Great.

Arab writers tell how Alexandria shimmered in the light, as bright by night as it was by day. They understood the black clothing of the city's Christian monks as a way of escaping the glare of polished marble. The Arab historian As-Suyuti captured this almost transcendental quality of Alexandria on the eve of conquest.

> it was painful to go out by night: for the moonlight reflected from the white marble made the city so bright that a tailor could see to thread his

needle without a lamp. No one entered the city without a covering over his eyes to veil him from the glare of the plaster and marble.[2]

Ibn Dukmak, a devout Muslim warrior, says that a month spent praying on the shores of Alexandria would be dearer to him than sixty pilgrimages to Mecca. Dukmak captured the magical aspect of a city that had survived a thousand years, witnessing the rise of paganism and Christianity and then Islam, when he remarked that "according to the law of Moses, if a man make a pilgrimage round Alexandria in the morning, God will make for him a golden crown set with pearls, perfumed with musk and camphor, and shining from the east to the west."[3]

The impression that Alexandria made on the minds and imaginations of its new Arab masters raises intriguing questions about Alexander's tomb. How much (and what) remained of Ptolemy's original city and the area of the Soma during Byzantine times and the early years of Arab dominion? There seems an irreconcilable gap between the endless cycles of destruction reported by third- and fourth-century Roman authors, and the magnificence and beauty observed by Arab chroniclers just a few centuries later.

The Coptic bishop John of Nikiou, writing during the seventh century, throws doubt on the total abandonment of the Brucheum area, where Alexander's tomb lay. He says that the eastern walls were still standing. Antoninus Martyr, who walked around the city in 565—just a century before Amr arrived—comments that "Alexandria is a magnificent city."[4] Did traces of the Soma still exist? What did Amr ibn al-As see on that morning in September 642?

Before the Arab invasion, Alexandria was enjoying an economic boom generated by its grain exports to Constantinople. The population was growing, and city officials were building churches and converting pagan buildings for Christian purposes. Between 400 and 600, parts of the city devastated by the earthquakes of 365 and 535 were pillaged for columns and marble slabs. The Soma, ruined by 400, was probably a prime quarry site, a pile of upmarket rubble and debris. The Byzantine transformation of Alexandria probably reused architectural elements of Alexander's mausoleum. In Alexandria, as throughout the Mediterranean, a newly Christian city was beautified with relics from the pagan age. Now change was coming again, and Alexandria's grand avenues echoed to the sounds of the muezzin calling the faithful to prayer.

Arab writers described Alexandria in terms that could apply equally to Philopater's city of 215 B.C.E. There were beautiful gardens flanking the palaces in the city center, streets were colonnaded, and two grand avenues bisected the city—one running from the Sun Gate in the eastern wall to the Moon Gate in the west, the other dividing the city north to south. Where they met, there was a great open space enclosing gardens flanked by architectural wonders. In the distance, perched on the end of Heptastadion causeway, the Pharos lighthouse continued flashing its huge fire-reflecting mirror out into the Mediterranean night. It was a scene straight from Strabo's pen or Achilles Tatius's novel.

As men of the desert, the Arabs were fascinated by water and were astonished by Alexandria's underworld labyrinth of conduits and cisterns. Some were five stories deep, supported on a forest of carved stone columns. They channeled water from the Nile into vast subterranean reservoirs that could supply the city for a year. One Arab writer was moved to say that "Alexandria is a city upon a city: there is nothing like it on earth."[5]

The Arabs in Alexandria, as elsewhere in Egypt, likely spent time digging up ancient sites in search of buried gold.[6] The fabulous wealth associated with Alexander in *The Alexander Romance* and similar accounts in Arabic almost certainly led to diggings in Alexandria, perhaps in search of Alexander's tomb itself.

Amr and his men took possession of a stridently Christian city with undisguisably pagan origins. Monuments such as the Hellenistic Tetrapylus temple and Diocletian's column were still standing, but surrounded by churches, such as St. Mary Dorothea, St. Athanasius, St. Catherine, St. Mark, and St. Theodore. The most impressive of all the pagan-turned-Christian monuments was the old Caesareum, begun by Cleopatra VII for Julius Caesar and completed by Octavian.

Under Augustus the Caesareum was the center of emperor worship. It was located in the greater harbor area, in the sector damaged by the great fire that broke out during Caesar's time and, according to the Roman historian Livy, destroyed 400,000 papyrus scrolls in the famous museum library. In the first century after Christ, Flavius Josephus wrote that the Alexandrian Jew Philo was awestruck by the Caesareum's pagan splendor. Philo remarks on its paintings and sculptures, its plentiful gold and silver decorations, galleries, libraries, porches, courts, and halls, as well as its sacred groves.[7] The luxury and magnificence of this architecture attracted the attention of Constantine the Great, who converted the Caesareum into Alexandria's cathedral, which was dedicated to St. Michael in 350.

Any lingering doubt about the building's new religious direction was dispelled in March 415, when the renowned pagan philosopher Hypatia was murdered. Despite having high-born Christians among her devotees, Hypatia was accused of practicing satanic magic and was dragged into the Caesareum by a frenzied Christian mob and killed.[8] Despite its high-profile Christianization, the grand building was still called the Caesareum when Amr arrived three hundred years later.

Alexandria, the palimpsest of pagan and Christian architecture, retained its Byzantine dimensions for decades after the Arab conquest; in 670 it had changed little since Cyrus. But two centuries later, around 870, it was a pale shadow of itself. The population had declined, probably after a devastating earthquake in 797 that resulted in large areas of the eastern sector of the city being abandoned to the desert and treasure hunters. Alexandria shrank in on itself, contracting behind the walls built by Sultan Ahmed ibn Tulun (c. 868–884 C.E.).

The new Muslim city was smaller than Ptolemy's original foundation. Over the next few centuries much of the old central part of the city, with its maze of alleys and decaying mud brick, emptied out. In 912 an earthquake leveled the Caesareum, and by the eleventh century, Alexandria was a ruin, albeit with five hundred columns still standing.

As Alexandria shrank, fabulous stories grew up about its ruined splendor. Weaving stories that were further embroidered with each retelling, Alexandria's Muslims explained what they saw in the language of their own traditions. The tumbled ruins of the Caesareum and Serapeum were now the works of magical spirits or djinn that haunted them. It is tempting to speculate that somewhere beneath the sand and rubble in Alexandria's abandoned eastern suburbs lay clues to the location of the Soma.

The world that Alexander and the Ptolemies created was reshaped by Rome and later swept away by Christianity. Islam changed it again, and all traces of the pagan Alexander and his Soma might have been buried forever. But it didn't happen. Islam, Christianity, and Judaism are religions of the book—sharing ancestral beliefs and personalities, albeit configured in radically different ways. The Ommayad Muslims who now controlled Egypt were tolerant toward Christians and Jews, extending this tolerance to Alexander, whom they called Iskender.[9] Alexandria is still known as Iskandariya in Arabic.

Alexander—the pagan who enraged the Christian patriarchs—was embraced by Islam. He was Zulqarnein, the "two-horned lord" mentioned in the Qur'an, chapter 18. His horns symbolized physical strength as well as spiritual power, and for this reason Alexander was honored with the title Nabi, or Prophet. As Muslim Alexandria rose from the remains of Ptolemy's city, Arabs began identifying certain places with Zulqarnein. With a change of name, Alexander's spirit was abroad again in the streets of his own city. The connection between Alexander and Islam was to define the search for the Soma.

For all its initial unfamiliarity to Christians, Islam had deep roots in the rich cultural and religious traditions of Hellenistic, Greco–Roman, Jewish, and Christian societies of the eastern Mediterranean and beyond.

Qur'an, which means recital, represents the living words of Allah as revealed to Mohammed his prophet by the angel Gabriel. Mohammed was born in 570 and died in 632. He grew up in the pagan cities of Mecca and Medina, where he learned the legends, folklore, and histories of the age, as well as the great religions—from Judaism to Christianity and Zoroastrianism. Mohammed began receiving Allah's teachings in 610 when he was forty, and they continued for decades. The prophet's mission was to publicly recite the words God sent him so that they could be written down, collated, and standardized; eventually they became the Qur'an.

Mohammed's recitals were stories, some featuring individuals well-known to Christians and Jews, such as Adam, Moses, Abraham, and Jesus, whom Islam regarded as prophets. Alexander was one of them. Alexander's identification as the twin-horned Zulqarnein may have originated in images on coins depicting him wearing the ram horns of Ammon or his elephant tusk headdress.

Despite Church opposition, Alexander coin amulets were popular throughout the Christian east during the fourth and fifth centuries.

During Byzantine times, the coins were incorporated into fashionable jewelry[10] that Byzantine women wore for its potent symbolic imagery.[11] Alexander's two-horned image on coins and other medallions was popular among Christians, pagans, and those who lived beyond the imperial frontier.

These striking objects recalled the historical Alexander, but also conjured the power of legend and myth. *The Alexander Romance*—while Ptolemaic in origin—became an elaborate saga in the centuries after Christ, influenced by the genre of wonder tales and heavily colored by Christian theology. Some manuscripts refer to the "life and acts" of Alexander.[12] Although Alexander's Soma was lost, his image continued to circulate, heavy with amuletic power and recalling his legendary exploits. Zulqarnein was Mohammed's way of turning Alexander's enduring fame and preternatural qualities to the cause of Islam.

Alexander underwent a renaissance at the hands of Muslim scholars. Just a few centuries after John Chrysostom died, Mohammed's recitals put Alexander on a par with Moses and Jesus, in a new religion that superseded Christianity in Alexandria, Antioch, and throughout the former Byzantine empire. Chrysostom preached vociferously against Alexander coin amulets, yet now these items perpetuated the image of Zulqarnein in all his two-horned glory. Alexander's victory over Chrysostom extended even to the Coptic inheritors of the Egyptian Christian tradition, who put Alexander's image—and sometimes even his name—on their religious tapestries.[13]

Alexander, as Zulqarnein, returned in triumph to Alexandria in the years following the Muslim conquest. In 871 the Arab historian Ibn Abdul Hakim compiled a list of Alexandria's mosques and included the "Mosque of Dulkarnein" located near the "Gate of the City and its exit."[14] Some seventy years later, in 943, al-Massoudi commented on perhaps the same building, calling it the tomb of the prophet and king Iskender. These early attempts to integrate Alexander into the religious topography of Muslim Alexandria fueled a tenacious misidentification of Alexandria's mosques with the remains of Alexander's tomb.

After 943 the trail of Alexander's tomb runs cold for half a millennium. These centuries of silence are misleading. Alexander lived on in religion and folklore as Zulqarnein and as a fantastic figure in the embroidered legends and fables so beloved of Arab culture. Alexandria's political status was changing too. Cairo was the new capital, and for the first time in a thousand years political power shifted away from Egypt's Mediterranean coast. Alexandria slipped into obscurity, taking the Soma with it.

Five hundred years after al-Massoudi talked briefly of Iskender's tomb, Alexandria changed hands again. In 1517 the Ottoman sultan Selim I invaded Mamluk Egypt and claimed it for the Turks, who reversed old isolationist habits. The Mamluks traded pepper with the Venetians (Alexandria's southern gate became known as the Pepper Gate), and the new Ottoman regime revitalized and extended trade of all kinds; silver, brass, silk, velvet, saffron, sandalwood, rubies, pearls, spices, perfumes, raisins, oranges, lemons, and capers passed through the city.[15]

Ottoman traders focused their attention on Alexandria's harbors. They ignored Ahmed ibn Tulun's small and sparsely populated walled city, settling instead on Ptolemy's Heptastadion causeway between the Pharos and the mainland. Centuries of silt swept down by the Nile had washed up against this narrow neck of land, producing a broad isthmus that became the center of a new outward-looking city.

Opening Alexandria to the non-Muslim west heralded a new era for Alexander and his tomb. French and Catalan merchants and diplomats journeyed to the city, followed by pilgrims and travelers who visited holy sites and sought out places of antiquarian interest. Diocletian's column became Pompey's pillar in the tourist imagination of the time.

The Renaissance stimulated renewed interest in the histories and philosophies of classical antiquity, and soon collectors were tramping Alexandria's musty alleys and abandoned ruins in search of past glories. Struggling to make sense of the Greek dedication on Pompey's pillar, visitors wondered also at the meanings of mysterious designs inscribed on Cleopatra's needles down by the harbor.[16] Others were driven by a curiously profitable quest for the dead. Egyptian mummies had been used in European medicines for hundreds of years. Now that access to the source was no longer restricted, a brisk trade developed, and by the sixteenth century, "mummy" was a common drug in all the best European apothecaries.

As Alexandria awakened from centuries of sleep, its most famous personality reappeared. If Alexander escaped the ignominious fate—as

Sir Thomas Browne observed in 1658—of pharaoh's being sold for balsams, then his tomb if not his body must lie somewhere in the city.

Leo Africanus (1495–1552) was a Muslim traveler from Fez in Morocco who visited Alexandria between 1515 and 1517, making copious notes of everything he saw. He was captured a year later by Spanish corsairs off the coast of Crete and taken to Italy, where he converted to Christianity.[17] Africanus was a prolific writer who included his impressions of Alexandria in his 1526 *Description of Africa*, which has survived in an Italian translation. After five hundred years, Africanus brings Alexander's tomb back to life, reclaiming it as a venerable Islamic monument.

> . . . in the middle of the city amongst the ruins may be seen a little house in the form of a chapel, in which is a tomb much honored by the Mahometans; since it is asserted that within it is kept the corpse of Alexander the Great, grand prophet and king, as may be read in the Koran. And many strangers come from distant lands to see and venerate this tomb, leaving at this spot great and frequent alms.[18]

Africanus's startling observation does not give the location of the chapel, although his description of the middle of the city contradicts Ibn Hakim's observation that the mosque of Zulqarnein lay adjacent to a grand city gate. Likely these are two separate buildings in different locations.

Marmol, a Spanish traveler, followed Africanus to Alexandria in 1546. He echoes Africanus, describing a temple with a tomb containing Alexander the Great whom the Muslims call Iskander, and is similarly vague as to the tomb's location.[19] A third European visitor, Michael Sierotka, also visited later that century, but he too seems content to repeat Africanus's account.

Alexandria's fortunes dipped again in the late sixteenth century. Her population was declining, and large parts of the city were abandoned. In 1577 the Venetian engineer and probable spy, Filippo Pigafetta, says that most of the city was in ruins and a pitiful sight.[20] It was another thirty years before Alexander's tomb was mentioned again.

George Sandys was an English poet and traveler whose interest and expertise in the classical world led him to translate Ovid's *Metamorphoses*.

During his visit in 1610, Sandys picked up on a story placing Alexander's tomb in a small building in the courtyard of the Attarine Mosque built on the ruins of the earlier Church of St. Athanasius. Sandys published an account of his travels in 1617 as the *Relation of a Journey Begun A.D. 1610.* His brief description, however, seems disappointingly close to that originally told by Africanus and then retold by Marmol.

> There is yet to be seene a little Chappell; within, a tombe, much honored and visited by Mahometans, where they bestow their alms; supposing his [i.e., Alexander's] body to lie in that place: Himselfe reputed a great Prophet, and informed thereof by their *Alcoran.*[21]

Marmol, Sierotka, and Sandys recycled Leo's earlier account to enliven their books with local color and legend. The same cannot be said for the next visitor—known only by his pseudonym, Evilya Çelebi— who came to Alexandria sometime between 1670 and 1682.

Çelebi was born in Istanbul in 1611, the son of a jeweler at the Ottoman court. He spent eleven years of his life studying in a Qur'anic school before launching into a life of travel lasting forty years, a decade longer than his more famous predecessor, Ibn Battuta. In 1640 Çelebi set out on the first of many long journeys across the Ottoman empire, publishing his experiences in ten parts as *Seyahatname,* or "Book of Journeys." In part 10, he describes his time in Egypt, and especially in Alexandria, where he records 348 shops, 7 caravanseries, and a covered market.

Çelebi eventually makes his way to the Attarine Mosque, where he encounters Alexander's tomb. Unlike his predecessors, Çelebi studies and describes the hieroglyphic figures covering all four sides of the sarcophagus: men, genies, cherubim, and all the animals of God's earth. And then he casually makes an astonishing claim—the ancient sarcophagus is serving as a water container for ritual ablutions—inferring, though not explicitly saying, that he observed it being used in this way.[22] Çelebi's eyewitness account is the first to describe Alexander's tomb as a decorated sarcophagus, and the first to hint at its recycled use in Islamic ritual cleansing.

Çelebi was one among many visitors to the Attarine Mosque, which was probably little more than a convenient stopover for sixteenth-century Muslim tourists. The "great and frequent alms" that Africanus saw being left at the shrine suggest a steady income in an otherwise slow economy in a sparsely populated part of the old Tulunnid city. It is impossible to tell whether the mosque was a prominent Alexander shrine because of its location or solely because of the tomb in its courtyard. The ancient Egyptian sarcophagus, covered with indecipherable hieroglyphic inscriptions, was a spectacular stage prop that gave the mosque an edge over its rivals.

When the mosque was built, it is unlikely that the sarcophagus was found conveniently in situ or even in the depths beneath, which had belonged to the previous church. Chancing upon and reusing ancient monuments had always been a habit in Alexandria. Muslim authorities dragged high-quality stonework from abandoned parts of the city for construction during the Mamluk period, likely including the Attarine sarcophagus.

The sting in the tail of this story is an unlikely coincidence. The Attarine Mosque's main attraction was a mysterious Egyptian sarcophagus. In 1617 no one could read hieroglyphs, but when the code was cracked two centuries later, the inscription produced astonishment.

European travelers to Alexandria during the fifteenth and sixteenth centuries described and illustrated Alexander's latest tomb. In 1472 a stylized but wildly inaccurate painted map of the city by Ugo Comminelli appeared. Unfortunately it adds little insight into the town's layout at the time. In 1573 Georg Braun and Frans Hogenberg of Cologne published a book of maps of famous cities known as *Civitates orbis terrarum,* or "Cities of the World." Their compendium included a vivid plan of Islamic Alexandria.[23]

Braun and Hogenberg never set foot in Alexandria. They conjured up their map from the firsthand accounts of a Cologne-based merchant, Constantin van Lyskirchen. Consequently the map's accuracy wavers, caught between the grand myths of the ancient city, van Lyskirchen's memory, and the need to compress the city's layout into an impressionistic vista. It captures, perhaps overemphasizes, the ruination of Alexandria, with clusters of buildings surrounded by empty spaces. The occasional camel, a palm tree, a native in colorful dress, and scattered columns and tumbled ruins complete the picture of decay. Braun and

Hogenberg intended not to provide an accurate plan for the adventurous traveler, but an imaginative escape for the armchair enthusiast.

Filtered through the European imagination as a romantic oriental
ruin, Alexandria's mosques appear more like church steeples than
muezzin's turrets (supposedly modeled on the Pharos). Braun highlights
historical places that recall the city's former greatness—St. Mark's
church and tomb, Pompey's pillar, and the Pharos lighthouse (now Fort
Qait Bey) are all captioned. During his time in Alexandria, van
Lyskirchen heard stories of Alexander's tomb and may have visited it.
He passed on the information to Braun, who included in his map the
first visual clue to the tomb since Philosyrius's sarcophagus more than a
thousand years before.

Dominating the cityscape of Braun's and Hogenberg's map is a natural rise on which are clustered the great buildings of Alexandria. Only
two are named—one is simply captioned "Mosque" and the other intriguingly labeled "Domus Alexandri Magni," or House of Alexander
the Great.[24] Given the inevitable distortion in a painting created from
verbal reports and in a European style, it is unclear which of three buildings is being referred to—a medium-size, domed-roof building, a tall
minaret, or a smaller domed-roof structure—or perhaps all three.

Van Lyskirchen might have seen (and Braun may be showing) the
chapel house referred to by Africanus and others as housing Alexander's
tomb. The adjacent minaret may belong to the Attarine Mosque, where
the chapel lay in the courtyard. There is a plausible but not conclusive
fit between Africanus's text and Braun's image. And Alexander's tomb is
almost certainly the reused Egyptian sarcophagus and definitely not the
grand Soma mausoleum.

The possibility that the Braun and Hogenberg map depicts the Attarine Mosque took on a life of its own. The mosque became a con-
tender for Alexander's sepulchre for the next two hundred years,
exercising a magnetic fascination on European visitors. During the eighteenth century, a favored few Europeans mentioned seeing the Attarine
Mosque's houselike shrine; the Muslim authorities often denied access
to infidels.

A few adventurous spirits managed to steal a glimpse. Eyles Irwin
crept into the mosque for a secret viewing in 1777, and a year later

Charles Sonnini bribed his way in, commenting that the sarcophagus was covered with hieroglyphic figures and was one of the most beautiful objects surviving from ancient Egypt. Like Celebi before him, Sonnini noted that Muslims used the sarcophagus as a water source for ritual bathing.[25] In 1792 the Englishman William Browne caught sight of the tomb, describing it as made of serpentine and used as a water cistern. He found it difficult to gain access from the authorities, who had previously uncovered a plot to smuggle the sarcophagus out of the city and present it as a gift to the king of Germany.[26]

None of these men firmly believed they were gazing on the tomb of Alexander the Great. This identification came later. Perhaps it was simple curiosity and rumor that provoked their interest. Nevertheless, curiosity soon turned to obsession, and by the end of the eighteenth century, the mystery of Alexander's final resting place was rejuvenated by two imperial superpowers fighting in Egypt.

Alexander—as Zulqarnein, the twin-horned prophet—became embedded in the religious and folklore traditions of Muslim Alexandria. The Attarine Mosque possessed the inscribed sarcophagus, but the Nabi Daniel Mosque had the name—the mosque of the Prophet Daniel— which linked it through a tortuous Arab tradition to Alexander.

The Nabi Daniel Mosque lies on the western slope of a hill known as Kom el Demas—the Hill of the Bodies or Hill of the Burials—in the center of Alexandria. Its tentative association with Alexander begins in the ninth century, when two Arab astronomers, Abou Ma'shar and Mohammed ibn Kathir el-Farghani, relate a story that blends Islamic ideas with an earlier tradition of Alexander's magnificent Soma.

Ma'shar and el-Farghani tell how Daniel conquered Asia, how he was acclaimed by the people of Egypt, founded Alexandria, and eventually was buried there in a golden sarcophagus. The Jews then stole the sarcophagus and melted it down to mint coins, putting Daniel's body into a replacement casket made of stone. This story is an enigma. The two astronomers, living two centuries after Amr conquered the city, possessed knowledge that had disappeared during early Roman times.

The heart of the mystery is that only Strabo says Ptolemy X replaced Alexander's golden sarcophagus with one made of glass or alabaster and melted it down to mint coins to pay off his mercenaries.[27] Strabo heard this story in Alexandria around 20 B.C.E., and it is not repeated by Pausanius, Suetonius, Ammianus, Libanius, or any other Roman source. Where did Ma'shar and el-Farghani hear this garbled version of an event that apparently was not mentioned for at least eight hundred years?

It is possible that Alexandrians preserved a folk tradition that mixed the story of Ptolemy X stealing Alexander's golden mummy case with anti-Jewish feeling. Christian–Jewish rivalries exploded frequently in antiquity, as in 38 C.E. under Trajan, in 55 during Nero's reign, and in 115–117, when the Jews rose in revolt and were expelled.

A more likely and fascinating possibility is that Arab scholars possessed copies of Strabo or other now lost written sources and took an active interest in classical texts long before Europeans. Around 943, al-Massoudi had alluded to Alexander's original golden sarcophagus and its replacement by one of marble; perhaps he had access to Strabo's works.[28] In contrast, the Italian humanist Cyriaco of Ancona obtained a copy of Strabo in January 1447 and immediately started translating it.[29]

Greek continued in use as the main language for administrative purposes in Egypt for about a century after the Arab conquest. Fifty years after Amr's men entered Alexandria, the Ommayyad governor Qurrah b. Sharik was corresponding with a man named Basilius, mostly in Greek, and these letters have survived as papyri.[30]

From the 680s, Greek and Coptic texts were translated into Arabic. The Omayyad caliph Abd al-Malik (685–705 C.E.) created a special translation department in Baghdad, and one of his sons had Aristotle's "Letters to Alexander" translated into Arabic. Two hundred years after the conquest, the Arab scholar Hunayn ibn Ishaq traveled from Baghdad to Alexandria to learn Greek, indicating that Greek scholarship was alive and well as late as the mid–ninth century.[31] The new Arab masters of Egypt quickly fell under the spell of Alexandrian scholarship—especially medicine and physics.

The number of surviving written records in Greek and Arabic from this time is staggering. The National Library in Vienna alone had twenty-two thousand Greek, eleven thousand Coptic, and fifty thousand Arabic papyri in 1933, many of which were lost during World War II.[32] This fortuitous survival of papyri represents the tip of an iceberg of documents recording the multilingual exchanges taking place between

Greek-speaking Egyptian Christians and their Muslim Arab overlords. Friendly relations between Coptic abbots and Arab caliphs were a feature of the time.[33]

The Arab appetite for Greek and Latin knowledge would have created many opportunities for passing on historical and legendary information about Alexander, and possibly the fate of his golden sarcophagus. Somewhere within this vibrant Arab intellectual curiosity about the Greek past may lie the origins of Ma'shar and el-Farghani's story of Alexander's tomb. In this version of events, Daniel was a legendary Alexander-like figure, whose conquests in myth and folklore mirrored those of the historical Alexander.

The Nabi Daniel Mosque is shrouded with legends and stories, including an alternative version of its naming. Sheikh Mohammed Daniel of Mosul spent time in Alexandria during the fifteenth century. While living in the city, he transformed an old mosque—known confusingly as the mosque of Alexander—into an Islamic religious school, or *madrassa*. When he died, the building became his mausoleum, and its name was changed to honor him. The subterranean vault was said to also contain the body of a renowned storyteller, Sidi Lokman.

Both stories have added confusing Alexander elements to the Nabi Daniel Mosque: Alexander's name, his identification with Daniel, the presence of bodies that lie beneath, and its central location near the Kom el Demas—all helped make the mosque an integral part of many nineteenth- and twentieth-century quests for Alexander's tomb.

By the end of the eighteenth century, Alexandria was little more than a village of six thousand souls perched on the old Heptastadion causeway, squatting among the ruins of former glory. In stark contrast to the earliest Muslim impressions, the Arab commentator Yakut observed, "When I visited Alexandria, I went round the city and saw nothing admirable or wonderful except one column."[34]

Despite the sad decline of his city, Alexander's ghost was abroad in Alexandria's streets, inspiring visitors with the prospect of finding his tomb. Islam's transformation of Alexander into Zuqarnein and his inevitable association with Alexandria's mosques gave birth to a new topography of discovery, which fueled the inquisitiveness of Western travelers.

Alexander's tomb was becoming the grail of the as yet unborn science of archaeology. Several locations in the largely empty areas that once had been the Hellenistic, Roman, and Byzantine city held their own promise. The problem was still a matter of where to look and how to recognize the clues.

The catalyst that turned Alexander's tomb from rumor and romance into reality was the same explosive mix of personal ambition, adventurism, and politics that had brought Alexander to Egypt in 332. At the close of the eighteenth century, Alexandria was back on the map of imperialism, and the great conqueror's legacy emerged once more as an inspirational force.

The personalities and the war technologies were different, but in the minds of the new protagonists, Alexander loomed as large as ever, and his tomb transformed into an imperial prize. Perdiccas and Ptolemy would have recognized the scene all too well. A new field, archaeology, in the guise of Egyptology, would be forged in the crucible of the approaching conflict and would in turn revolutionize the search for Alexander's tomb.

NAPOLEON, NELSON,
AND ALEXANDER'S GHOST

NELSON STOOD ON THE QUARTERDECK OF HMS *Vanguard*, his shrapnel-scarred face lit by the flames consuming the French fleet around him. The thick smell of gunpowder and tar mixed with the screams of dying men. At Aboukir Bay on August 1, 1798, Rear Admiral Sir Horatio Nelson made his name with a brilliant naval maneuver, and Napoleon Bonaparte's dreams of Egypt ended in a pyrotechnic display on the dark waters of the Mediterranean. Once again, Alexander had drawn the great men of history to his side.

Nelson watched as the 120-gun French flagship *L'Orient* exploded with such force that its crimson glow lit up the night sky nine miles away in Alexandria. The explosion spewed flaming debris hundreds of feet into the air, only to rain back down on the two entangled fleets. Men on both sides were stunned into silence by the noise. One rumor had it that the *L'Orient* burned so fiercely because it had been fired on with a volatile mixture of phosphorous, known in antiquity as Greek fire, and that the order had been given by Captain Alexander Ball of the HMS *Alexander*.

L'Orient's fiery end sent a splintered chunk of wood from its mainmast hurtling through the air onto the deck of another of Nelson's ships, the *Swiftsure*. The commander, Captain Hallowell, had it fashioned into a coffin and sent it to Nelson with a letter in which he wryly observed, "When you are tired of life you may be buried in one of your own trophies."[1] Nelson kept the coffin propped behind his chair. Seven years later, before setting off for Trafalgar, Nelson had his name engraved on the lid.

Separated by two thousand years, the tombs of two great men had been drawn together by a heady mix of victory and imperialism. As Nelson read Hallowell's message, he had no idea that the Battle of the Nile, which had hewn his coffin, was turning a new page in the story of Alexander's tomb.

Earlier that year, Napoleon had abandoned plans for an invasion across the English Channel, and he renamed his Army of England the Army of Egypt. Europe, he said, was too small for him; he must go east, where all the great men of history had acquired their fame. He read avidly of Alexander's life and achievements, and hungered for glory in Alexander's oriental world. He would conquer Egypt, wresting it from the Mamluk overlords who ruled on behalf of the Ottomans, and emerge as the new Alexander. While Alexandria was a pale shadow of its former self, it still stood between Asia, Africa, and Europe, halfway between history and myth. In Napoleon's hands, it would be the pivot of a new French empire in Asia and a strategic threat to Britain's imperial jewel, India.

In planning the Egyptian campaign, Napoleon emulated his hero, taking not only an army but men of science and art—the savants. This extraordinary group included the father of Ferdinand de Lesseps, who would go on to build the Suez Canal. He recalled in later life how Napoleon had discussed the idea of the canal with him.

It was here that the modern idea of orientalism took root. It viewed the east as comprising backward peoples and inferior cultures to be conquered and dominated by the west.[2] Such ideas may have begun with Alexander himself, arguably the world's earliest colonial conqueror. After all, Alexander had turned the tables on Persia—the great enemy of the west—by defeating the armies of Darius and spreading Hellenism as far as Afghanistan and India.

Some of these ideas must have been in Napoleon's mind as his fleet had earlier evaded Nelson in the waters off Malta and made for the Egyptian coast. For Napoleon, Alexander was the conqueror par excellence, a towering figure who stood at the crossroads of history as he himself aspired to do. Napoleon's private secretary recorded how they would sit on the desert sand surrounded by maps and plans of campaign while Napoleon recalled the triumphs of his childhood hero.[3]

Alexander had walked in the footsteps of Achilles and Dionysus, and Caesar took Alexander as his exemplar. For Napoleon, it was perhaps less imitation than empathy, a mythical identification between men of destiny. Whether Alexander's tomb entered Napoleon's thoughts is unknown, but he likely realized that Alexandria was a funerary monument, a tomb of the mind where memories and myths resided both eternal and unreachable.

Napoleon ignored the reversal that Nelson inflicted on him at Aboukir Bay. Changing gear from military strategist to cultural imperialist, he took a step that forever changed the way the world saw the land of the pharaohs. In Cairo, on August 21, 1798, he created the Egyptian Institute of Arts and Sciences, providing an institution and focus for the 167 scholars he had brought with him.[4] Its remit was ambitious—to investigate, record, and publish everything to do with Egypt, from geography, flora, and fauna, to the country's public health system. It is remembered today for laying the foundations of Egyptology with evocative images of the country's vast store of archaeological monuments, measured, drawn, and painted by the savants.

The monumental *Description de l'Égypte* was a publishing phenomenon. Before 1798, the ancient glories of Egypt were hardly known in northern Europe, and as each volume appeared, people's fascination grew. Alongside colorful images of the Sphinx, the Giza pyramids, and Cleopatra's needle were curious signs known as hieroglyphs, which were displayed in Europe for the first time.

Dominique Vivant Denon was a leading figure among the savants. Draftsman, engraver, and author, he was also a collector and diplomat. He ultimately became director of the Napoleon Museum, now the Louvre. As a young man he was a favorite at the court of Louis XV, where the king entrusted him with Madame de Pompadour's gem collection. He was a frequent guest at the house of Josephine de Beauharnais, where he met Napoleon. The two men appreciated each other's talents, and they journeyed to Egypt together in 1798. By chance, Denon witnessed the *L'Orient*'s fiery end from Rosetta in the western Nile Delta.

Denon and his fellow savants were fascinated by Alexandria's ancient ruins and antiquities. They were intrigued by the Attarine Mosque, said to have been built on the site of the church of St. Athanasius, the fourth-century patriach of the city. In 1802 Denon published *Travels in Upper and Lower Egypt*—an immediate best-seller throughout Europe—in which he described his first impressions of the mosque's ruined courtyard on July 4, 1798.

> Near these baths is one of the principal mosks, formerly a primitive church, under the name of St. Athanasia. This edifice, as much dilapidated as it is superb, may convey a notion of the indolence of the Turks with regard to the objects of which they are most jealous. Before the arrival of the French, they would not suffer a christian to approach it; but they preferred placing a guard at the gates, to giving them any repair. In the state in which the French found them, they would neither close nor turn on their hinges. This mosk has a covered portico . . . which opens into a square court, paved . . . with marble. . . . In the court, plants which have grown into trees, have forced up the marble pavement. In the centre of this court, a little octagon temple incloses a cistern of Egyptian workmanship, and incomparable beauty, both on account of its form, and of the innumerable hieroglyphics with which it is covered, inside and out. This monument, which appears to be a sarcophagus of ancient Egypt, may perhaps be illustrated by volumes of dissertations. It would require a month to draw all its parts. It may be considered a very valuable antique, and one of the more precious spoils of Egypt, with which it is to be wished we could enrich one of our museums. Dolomieux, who was with me when this valuable monument was discovered shared my enthusiasm.[5]

Carved from a block of fine green breccia, the sarcophagus was described as a cistern due to the bore holes around its base designed to let water out. The holes suggested that in the past it had been reused as a bath, perhaps for ritual ablutions.

Given the number of books the savants brought with them, they were likely familiar with the sixteenth-century writings of Leo Africanus, as well as seventeenth-century accounts of European travelers such as the intrepid George Sandys. As they wandered through Alexandria's ancient streets, they may have heard stories concerning the tomb in the Attarine Mosque. Possibly the mosque was off-limits to infidel Christians. Some years previously, a Christian merchant had hatched a plan to steal the sarcophagus, possibly because of its identification with Alexander.

The French considered the sarcophagus a potent symbol of imperial possession, much as Ptolemy had two thousand years before. Acquiring the tomb would ally Napoleon's ambition and achievements with those of Alexander, and all France would bathe in reflected glory. Ignoring local protests, the savants removed the sarcophagus and stowed it aboard a French ship, far from prying eyes.

Napoleon's attentions were elsewhere as these events unfolded. In Constantinople on October 9, 1798, the Ottoman sultan declared holy war against the French. One Turkish army was to move south overland to Egypt from Damascus, while a second force was to be landed on the Egyptian coast aided by the British navy. In January 1799, Napoleon decided on a preemptive strike and marched north toward Syria with an army of 13,000 men. He aimed to intercept the Turkish forces and storm the small but strategic port of Acre—ancient Ptolemais, the stronghold of Djezzar Pasha, nicknamed The Butcher.

The expedition was ill-starred from the first. Small victories at El Arish and Jaffa proved fateful delays. When Napoleon arrived outside Acre, he met the one man besides the Duke of Wellington who had ever defeated him in battle. Sir Sidney Smith was a dashing young captain who had assumed British naval command when Nelson sailed to Sicily after the Battle of the Nile. Strikingly handsome, he inspired loyalty in men and infatuation in women. His adventurous spirit and intimate local knowledge appealed to the Turks, who gave him command of their navy. He arrived in Acre just days before Napoleon and set his men to arm and rebuild its crumbling defenses. Crucially, he captured Napoleon's siege cannons and turned them against the French.

Smith's unpredictable brilliance made him Napoleon's nemesis. He challenged Napoleon to a duel when the latter accused him of being a madman for unsettling his troops with propaganda and bold raids beyond the city walls. In later years, imprisoned on St. Helena, Napoleon recalled, "Had I but captured Acre, I would have . . . changed the face of the world. But that man made me miss my destiny."[6]

Although Napoleon and General Kléber scored a great victory over the Turkish army at Mount Tabor, there was no progress at Acre. Control of the sea was everything. In early June, Napoleon raised the siege and re-turned to Cairo, where he staged a deceitful triumph. Soon after came news that the second Turkish army had disembarked at Aboukir.

While Napoleon considered his options in Cairo, the French in the north were galvanized into action. On July 19, within days of the Turk-ish landing, French soldiers were hastily rebuilding sections of the old Fort Rachid on the outskirts of Rosetta, east of Alexandria. It had been built in the fifteenth century by Sultan Qait Bey, who also erected the fortress at Alexandria, which still bears his name, from the ruins of the city's famous Pharos lighthouse. By 1799 Fort Rachid needed recon-struction and was duly renamed Fort Julien, in memory of one of Napoleon's aides-de-camp.

As the work progressed, Pierre François Xavier Bouchard uncovered a gray stone slab that would change history. The stone was over three feet tall, weighed three-quarters of a ton, and had a polished surface in-scribed with innumerable signs. It was later realized to have come from a temple at nearby Sais, reused as fill by Qait Bey's engineers.

Tall and dark, the twenty-eight-year-old Bouchard was a carpenter's son from the wild country of the Jura mountains.[7] He had served in the new balloon corps under Nicolas Conté, the inventor of the lead pencil and one of Napoleon's savants. Newly arrived at Rosetta, Bouchard was intrigued by his discovery, as the inscriptions seemed to be in three different lan-guages. At the top were fourteen lines of recognizable but undeciphered Egyptian hieroglyphs, below were thirty-two lines in an unknown script, and at the base fifty-four lines written in the familiar Greek alphabet.[8]

The Greek text related to celebrations of Ptolemy V Epiphanes and was dated March 27, 196 B.C.E. What stunned the savants was the last sentence, stating that the decree will be inscribed in "sacred characters, both native and Greek."[9] This was a revelation. What Bouchard and his compatriots were looking at was the same text inscribed in three differ-ent scripts. It held out the tantalizing possibility of deciphering Egypt-ian hieroglyphs.

Bouchard ferried the stone south along the Nile to Cairo, depositing it at the palace of Hasan Kashef, where the Institut d'Égypte held its twice monthly meetings. By lucky coincidence, he arrived just as other good news filtered back from the coast. While the savants had been pondering their discovery at Rosetta, Napoleon had made a lightning march north and routed the Ottoman army at Aboukir on July 25. The French had two rare successes to celebrate, though it was Bouchard's gift that would ultimately prove the greater prize.

Once in Cairo, the stone's inscriptions were copied and studied by scholars, some of whom recognized its importance, but no one could decipher its hieroglyphic message. Years later, it was realized that the stone bore fragments of the same inscription in two languages—Egyptian and Greek—though in three different scripts: formal Egyptian hieroglyphs, the cursive style of Egyptian writing known as Demotic, and Greek. Demotic was the everyday written language of Egypt during Ptolemaic times, and had changed considerably from its hieroglyphic origins. As the Ptolemies spoke Greek but their subjects Demotic, they published their decrees in the three kinds of writing.

Then came another fateful event. While exchanging prisoners after his victory at Aboukir, Napoleon heard that France was in crisis. A Russian army under Field Marshal Suvorov had crossed the Alps and was encamped in Italy while preparing to march on Paris. In the French capital itself, the Directory was falling apart, Royalists were grumbling, and there was talk of counterrevolution.

This was a golden opportunity for Napoleon, for whom the Orient had lost its allure. He abandoned his men for the greater prize and secretly left Alexandria for France on August 23, 1799, never to return. With him went a handful of confidants and savants, including Baron Dominique Vivant Denon. On November 9, Napoleon staged a coup d'état and became first consul, and in 1804 crowned himself emperor. But the dream of emulating Alexander's Asian empire had slipped away.

Back in Egypt, Kléber was furious at his commander in chief. He knew his military situation was hopeless and began secret talks with Sir Sidney Smith. The British government's decision to give Smith political responsibilities as minister plenipotentiary as well as his naval command had proven disastrous. Despite his qualities, Smith had a willful and disobedient streak, and had appointed himself commodore, much to Nelson's chagrin.

Although Smith was not authorized to make a deal with the French, in January 1800 he began negotiations with Kléber onboard his ship the

Tigre, moored at the mouth of the Nile. As soon as the resulting Convention of El Arish was signed, the French began to gather in their ships in Alexandria along with their booty. Some forty savants were aboard the small ship *L'Oiseau,* as was at least one of their prize possessions, the Rosetta Stone. But they went nowhere.

The British government repudiated the arrangement as soon as they heard of it, stating that the French had to surrender as prisoners of war and not be freed to fight another day. The French eventually disembarked and stayed in Egypt for another eighteen months, during which Kléber won an extraordinary victory against the Turks at Heliopolis in March, only to be assassinated in the streets of Cairo three months later.

The stalemate continued. The British controlled the sea, and the French were dug in but trapped on land. On March 22, 1801, events came to a head with the second battle of Aboukir, also known as the Battle of Canope. Under Sir Ralph Abercomby, eighteen thousand British soldiers laid siege to Alexandria. His opponent, General Jacques-François Menou, launched a daring night attack that wasn't repulsed until British reinforcements arrived. The battle was decisive, though Abercomby died of his wounds. The French faced the inevitable denouement. On April 19 at Rosetta, Fort Julien was surrendered by Bouchard, and at the end of June Cairo followed suit.

In a fateful decision, one group of savants left Cairo before its capitulation and headed for Alexandria. While those who stayed behind benefited from generous British terms that allowed them to depart with their possessions, those who escaped were not so fortunate. When they arrived in Alexandria, they found themselves free to sail for France but were ordered to leave their antiquities behind, as Menou deemed them the property of the French Republic and not the Institut d'Égypte.

Menou held out in Alexandria until August 26, when he finally requested an armistice. In article 16 of their draft terms of surrender, the French stipulated they be allowed to keep the artifacts they had collected. The British refused, and there followed an exchange of rancorous letters between Menou and Abercromby's successor Lord Hutchinson, in which the latter countered the French general's increasingly evasive and disingenuous claims as to who owned what artifact, and whether or not each item should be considered of private or public ownership.

The British turned the screw, and matters went from bad to worse. Several savants met with Hutchinson and threatened to destroy their records and artifacts if they were not allowed to retain them or accompany them to London. In the end, both sides compromised. The French could keep their written records, drawings, and floral and faunal collections, but had to surrender the most important antiquities. The British finally got their hands on the Rosetta Stone in the streets of Alexandria, as well as the sarcophagus Denon had removed from the Attarine Mosque three years earlier.

This was an important time for history and archaeology, as well as for the imperial game Britain and France played with regard to the artifacts they both desired. It was full of "if onlys." If the Convention of El Arish had been honored, the sarcophagus and the Rosetta Stone would have ended up in Paris. If all the savants had stayed in Cairo, they would probably have departed with their cherished antiquities. If Menou had let the savants leave with their artifacts before he surrendered Alexandria, the British would never have gained the valuable antiquities. As it was, article 16 of the Treaty of Alexandria ensured that the Alexander sarcophagus, the Rosetta Stone, and a clutch of other important artifacts ended up in London.

After Cairo had been surrendered and before Alexandria fell, a new character appeared. Edward Daniel Clarke was a gentleman scholar and traveler from Cambridge University. A polymath and raconteur, Clarke was on a grand tour of the region. Once described as a nervous, funny little man, the talkative Clarke was known for his imaginative judgments on antiquities. This imagination was about to be tested to the full.

Increasingly frustrated by Menou's decision to hold out in Alexandria, Hutchinson appointed Clarke to find and assess which antiquities the French could keep and what the British should acquire. He furnished Clarke with letters of introduction to various influential people in Cairo, including Signor Rosetti, the imperial consul, and Mr. Hammer, a noted oriental scholar who was lodging with him.[10]

In conversations with these men, Clarke learned more about the famous but undeciphered Rosetta Stone. They also told him that the French possessed a larger object whose importance and whereabouts were a closely guarded secret. His hosts evidently considered it more

important than the Rosetta Stone. This mysterious artifact was a great
stone sarcophagus, hidden somewhere in Alexandria.

Inspired by this news, Clarke left Cairo and set out north along the
Nile, first to Sais and then Rosetta. Approaching Alexandria, he found
the city's surrender under way. Hutchinson, angry at Menou's prevarica-
tions over the antiquities, armed Clarke and his companions with the
necessary papers, food, and horses. According to Clarke, they set out for
the city to find and seize the sarcophagus. He would also take possession
of the Rosetta Stone if possible and make copies of its inscriptions.

Clarke pushed his way through the throng of Arab merchants waiting
outside the city walls for permission to enter and sell food. He noted the
wretchedness of Turkish prisoners freed that morning from French cap-
tivity. Passing through the city gates, he rode into the main square and
then made his way to his new quarters. The group had hardly settled in,
when local merchants arrived at the door to pay their respects and gain
favor with extraordinary news.

The merchants spoke in hushed tones concerning the true nature of
Clarke's mission, which they were clearly familiar with. They asked if
he was looking for the city antiquities acquired by the French. Then
the leader of the merchants astounded the British with the following
question: "Does your Commander in Chief know that they [the
French] have the Tomb of Alexander?"[11]

Cautiously, Clarke asked them to describe it. They responded that it
was a beautiful green stone sarcophagus that the French had stolen from
the St. Athanasius (Attarine) Mosque, which local people had always
considered the tomb of Alexander. Clarke's heart must have pounded as
he listened to these words, for this had to be the object he heard of in
Cairo. The merchant then revealed that they could show him where the
French had hidden it.

The merchant described the secrecy surrounding the tomb's removal.
The tomb was venerated not only by Alexandrians but also by Muslim
pilgrims from as far away as Constantinople, Smyrna, and Aleppo. By
common consent, he whispered, all believed it to be the tomb of the
Prophet Iskander, the founder of Alexandria, whose blessed name was
enshrined in the Qur'an.[12]

Whether this devout association was wishful thinking by Muslim pilgrims or the echo of some lingering folk memory, it is impossible to say. Nevertheless, such a famous identification was as irresistible to Clarke as to Denon. The Arab merchants finally confided that Alexander's sarcophagus was hidden onboard a French hospital ship in Alexandria's harbor, ready to be transported to France.

Clarke's party secured a boat and discovered the sarcophagus onboard the *La Cause* amid the French wounded and dying. Clarke's amazement at finally laying eyes on the prize is captured in his own words:

> Nothing could equal the admiration with which I viewed this beautiful Tomb, having never seen, among the fine works the antients have left us, an instance in which nature as well as art vie with each other to such perfection . . . and strictly does the appearance of it correspond with the description given by Diodorus of the shrine constructed for the body of Alexander.[13]

What follows in Clarke's description of these events remains as murky today as it was at the time. It places the sarcophagus at the center of political intrigue, wild imagination, and character assassination in ways that recall the machinations of Ptolemy and his successors.

Clarke stresses that the French savant did not mention the Muslim tradition of venerating the tomb. Clarke reproduces a drawing based on Denon's original, in which five Muslims are shown worshiping outside an octagonal building and are assumed to be venerating the sarcophagus within. He emphasizes his bewilderment at the discrepancy between Denon's text and image, which he attributes to suspicious motives and French deception. Why Denon would have been silent about the scene in his text—yet go to the trouble of illustrating it—is not explained. And, as it transpired, for good reason.

Clarke admits basing his drawing on Denon's but fails to mention that the original appears in the French edition, not the widely read and easily available 1802 English translation. Also, whereas Denon's caption merely describes his drawing as a view of the interior of St. Athanasius Mosque, Clarke gives his imagination full flight in his caption:

View of the interior of the ruin of the soma in Alexandria; now called the
mosque of St. Athanasius; with the sanctuary enclosing the Tomb of
Alexander, and the manner of worshipping it, as practised before the arrival of the French in Egypt.[14]

Clarke was being economical with the truth. While his drawing and
Denon's original are all but identical, it is not clear that all five figures
are worshiping. Three appear kneeling, one is standing, and the fifth sits
in the shade of a tree. Even more curious is the way the drawing had
been altered by the time it appeared in Book 1 of the French *Description
de l'Égypte*, produced under Denon's direction. There are only two individuals, not five. One is sitting beneath a date palm and the other standing; neither is bowing in worship.

What did Clarke hope to achieve by his imaginative caption and interpretation of the scene? It allowed him to strengthen the case for the
tradition of Muslim worship of the sarcophagus and thus reinforce the
view that this was Alexander's tomb. It also enabled him to highlight
what he saw as Denon's typically French dishonesty by drawing attention
to the discrepancy between what the French savant said and illustrated.

We have no way of knowing whether Denon's drawing represents an
eyewitness scene or was simply an artistic flourish. While Denon knew
of the tomb's popular reputation and coveted it for a Parisian museum,
nothing indicates that he was convinced it was the sarcophagus of
Alexander the Great. The evidence of the later drawing in the *Description de l'Égypte* is ambiguous. It could be Denon's reaction to Clarke's
overly imaginative interpretation, or perhaps an act of pique at the
French losing the tomb to the British. By removing any sign of Muslim
worship, it devalued Clarke's assertions.

Clarke became obsessed at the prospect of having his name associated
with Alexander's for the greater glory of the British empire. In a masterpiece of disingenuous self-justification, Clarke's account casts the British
in the role of the tomb's saviors, whose actions denied Napoleon a
propaganda coup. Clarke argues that the sarcophagus would have been
used to extol the achievements and glory of the French Republic if it
had been taken to France. Just as the readable Greek text of the Rosetta
Stone told of the actions of Ptolemy V Epiphanes, so the still undeci-

phered hieroglyphs on the sarcophagus would eventually relate the conquests of Alexander. Clarke hammered home his point, asserting that a

> prodigious temple would have been erected in the midst of Paris; where, to complete the mockery of Buonoparte's imitation of the son of Philip, the same Tomb that had once inclosed the body of that hero would have been reserved for the bones of his mimic.[15]

Napoleon may have entertained such ideas, especially given the size and pompous splendor of the future emperor's sarcophagus of Finnish red porphyry, which sits today in the Hôtel des Invalides in Paris. If Napoleon did harbor such intentions, it would have been a novel twist. Even in antiquity, no Ptolemy or Roman emperor ever reused the tomb. Alexander's resting place seemed to be inviolate, and its value to rulers in antiquity was as a symbol and metaphor, rather than a recyclable sarcophagus.

The idea of Napoleon being laid to rest in Alexander's tomb was hubris indeed, as Edward Clarke was well aware. In the event, it was not to be. In one of the unacknowledged ironies of history, Napoleon avoided what would have proved to be a humiliation in death equal to those he was to suffer in life at Waterloo and St. Helena.

In the final haul of fifty tons of antiquities seized by the British as victory trophies, the Alexander sarcophagus and the Rosetta Stone took pride of place. They appear to have been shipped to Britain separately, the tomb aboard HMS *Madras* and the Rosetta Stone a little later on a captured French ship renamed HMS *Egyptienne*. On arrival at Portsmouth in February 1802, the Rosetta Stone was taken to the Society of Antiquaries in London, and the rest of the artifacts presented to King George III, who donated them to the British Museum at the end of the year.[16]

Clarke convinced himself that the sarcophagus and other carvings scattered around the Attarine Mosque identified the area as the ancient Soma. In 1805 he published his suitably embroidered magnum opus— *The Tomb of Alexander, a Dissertation on the Sarcophagus from Alexandria and Now in the British Museum*—whose title managed to string together the oldest and newest exemplars of imperialism.

In this book he gave the details mentioned above and explained Denon's supposed deception. If the sarcophagus had been identified with an Egyptian pharaoh rather than Alexander, it seems doubtful that Clarke would have lavished his attention on it.

The sarcophagus was displayed in the British Museum's open fore-court for over twenty years; it excited discussion and curiosity among those who read Clarke's book. At the time, some reviews were favorable, others skeptical. One critic, using the pseudonym Heraclides, identified by some as Dr. Richard Ramsden, published a pamphlet of eight letters in 1806 in which he ridiculed Clarke's ideas with a curious confection of sober argument and pedantry.[17] What basis did Clarke have for writing so imaginative a caption to Denon's drawing? Why was the sarcophagus carved in Egyptian hieroglyphs not Greek? If the Muslims of Alexandria guarded the Attarine Mosque so jealously as Iskander's tomb, where was the lid of the sarcophagus?

On September 28, 1807, Clarke wrote a "A Letter Addressed to the Gentlemen of the British Museum," in which he rehearsed his answers to these and other criticisms.[18] He evidently did not convince them, as between 1808 and 1840, the sarcophagus was described by the museum simply as a "large green breccia sarcophagus."[19] Some suspected Clarke's methods and were frustrated at not being able to read the hieroglyphic inscriptions. Nevertheless, both the sarcophagus and the Rosetta Stone were indisputable trophies of Britain's triumph in Egypt.

Yet this triumph and the assertions that surrounded it were short-lived. It was destroyed by Frenchman Jean-François Champollion, whose inspirational and painstaking scholarship during the early decades of the nineteenth century finally unlocked the secrets of the hieroglyphs. Napoleon's ghost had seemingly reached beyond the grave to reclaim the intellectual treasures lost by Menou to Hutchinson in Alexandria.

Champollion never saw the Rosetta Stone. Only eight years old when Bouchard discovered it, this enigmatic prodigy was an unlikely scholar. A poor student at school, he flourished under private tuition provided by a local priest. He soon mastered Latin and began tackling Greek. He developed a flair for languages, studying Arabic, Syriac, and Chaldean. By 1807, at age sixteen, he decided to decipher Egyptian hieroglyphs and became a member of the Grenoble Society of the Sciences and Arts, whose luminaries believed that his studies would eventually make him famous.[20]

Champollion spent twenty years studying the casts and transcriptions made in Cairo and London. By 1821 he realized the equivalence of signs rendered in Hieratic, Demotic, and hieroglyphs, and believed that the latter followed the same rules as Demotic. On September 27, 1822, he gave a seminal lecture to the Académie des Inscriptions et Belle Lettres in Paris concerning the phonetic nature of hieroglyphs, focusing, ironically, on instances where Greek names like Alexander and Cleopatra had been transcribed into formal hieroglyphs. This was soon published as a pamphlet and became known to history as the *Letter to M. Dacier*, the secretary of the Académie.[21]

For the first time in almost two thousand years, the strange signs could be read. And sometime during the middle to late 1820s, these groundbreaking insights were applied to the inscriptions covering the Alexander sarcophagus.

In a bitter disappointment for many, the royal cartouches yielded the name of Nectanebo II, the Thirtieth Dynasty pharaoh who ruled Egypt between 360 and 342 B.C.E. The other inscriptions, which some had believed would relate Alexander's peerless achievements, were in fact extracts from the funerary text known as the *Amduat*, or "Book of the Underworld."[22] All Clarke's machinations and embroidery had been in vain, and Napoleon had escaped being buried in the wrong tomb.

Champollion's breakthrough was a searchlight on the past, scattering the shadows of conjecture and fantasy, connecting real names to real people, and bringing to life actual historical events. Nowhere in this newly illuminated world was there any indication that Alexander the Great had been laid to rest in someone else's tomb. Yet mystery still clung to Nectanebo II and his great carved stone coffin. The pharaoh's name was linked to Alexander's in the writings of the *Alexander Romance*, and scholars agreed that for reasons still unclear, Nectanebo never occupied the sarcophagus so carefully fashioned to contain his earthly remains.

The drama of these events was played out on an international stage that stretched from London to Paris, and Alexandria to Cairo, and has echoed down to the present. Thousands of visitors daily pass by the green sarcophagus in the Egyptian Hall of the British Museum on their way to stand and stare at the Rosetta Stone. How many know of the intrigues that once raged around these two objects and bound their different fates so closely together?

The idea of orientalism inspired by Napoleon's invasion of Egypt was linked to his imperialistic designs on Asia. The Nectanebo sarcophagus and the Rosetta Stone were at the epicenter of momentous events whose consequences still pulse through the entwined worlds of modern politics and cultural heritage. Yet they were not alone. Other equally notorious objects were caught in the same net.

At the time, Greece, like Egypt, was part of the Ottoman empire, ruled by the sublime porte in Constantinople. During the eighteenth century European society knew little of Egypt but was gaining familiarity with the architecture and sculptures of the classical Greek past, especially those adorning the Acropolis in Athens. Many had begun to covet these embodiments of classical civilization.

The French were the first off the mark. During a tour of Greece in 1780, the comte de Choiseul-Gouffier had teamed up with a fellow countryman, the antiquary and painter Louis-François-Sébastien Fauvel. When the former was appointed French ambassador to the Ottoman porte, he hired Fauvel as his agent to draw and make casts of antique monuments. In the spirit of the times, Fauvel was instructed to take advantage of every opportunity for pillage.[23]

Together, the two Frenchmen carved their names on the monument of Philopappos in Athens and purchased local antiquities. The British ambassador's protests had little effect, and many sculptures were shipped back to Paris. However, when Fauvel requested permission to remove sculptures from the Parthenon, the official document, or *firman,* was not forthcoming.

Almost twenty years later, in November 1799, only three months after Napoleon had left Kléber stranded in Egypt, a new British ambassador presented his credentials to Sultan Selim III. Thomas Bruce, 7th Earl of Elgin, had employed the Italian Giovanni Battista Lusieri to help him acquire Greek artifacts as Fauvel had done for Choiseul-Gouffier. Unlike the French, Elgin's timing was perfect.

Napoleon's invasion of Egypt enraged the Ottoman Turks, who were grateful when the British expelled the French, who had conveniently broken the hold of the independent-minded Mamluks. On June 17, 1801, as Lord Hutchinson received the surrender of French forces in Cairo and Menou forbade the savants from leaving Alexandria with their antiquities, the fortunes of war favored Elgin. Giving a couple of weeks for the news to travel, Elgin received his *firman* almost immediately, on July 5, as one of innumerable gifts the Turks showered on their victorious British allies.[24] While the *firman* made no mention of removing the Parthenon's sculptures, Elgin and Lusieri seized the moment.

As the Alexander sarcophagus and Rosetta Stone made their way back to London, the Turkish authorities turned a blind eye to Elgin's manipulation and corruption of their local officials in Athens. An eyewitness to the removal of the first Parthenon sculptures in October 1801 was Edward Daniel Clarke, newly arrived from Egypt and flush with success over obtaining the sarcophagus. He would soon exercise his imagination in Greece, judging a small slab of marble the work of the great Athenian sculptor Phidias, and a colossal head from Eleusis the bust of Demeter the earth goddess. The treasures that would become known as the Elgin marbles were shipped back to Britain in two lots, the first in 1804, the second in 1812.

These were heady times for the British. The alloy of military victory, political intrigue, and deception that had secured the sarcophagus and Rosetta Stone had been instrumental also in Elgin's acquisition of the Parthenon sculptures. In 1816, the British parliament paid £35,000 for Elgin's marbles, and they were displayed hardly a stone's throw from the Alexander—now Nectanebo—sarcophagus and Rosetta Stone in the British Museum.

A final twist to the affair occurred some sixty years later, on June 1, 1878, when another part of ancient Egypt became an attraction in London. Cleopatra's needle—an obelisk of the pharaoh Sesostris—was erected on the Thames embankment, where it still stands. It had been given to Britain in 1875 by Mohammed Ali, the ruler of Egypt, in belated gratitude for the British expulsion of Napoleon's army almost a century before. In particular, it was meant to commemorate Nelson's victory at Aboukir Bay and the liberation of Alexandria in 1801, which led directly to the acquisition of the Alexander sarcophagus and Rosetta Stone by the British.

The renamed Nectanebo sarcophagus was locked in a curious embrace with the Rosetta Stone and Elgin marbles during the early years of the nineteenth century, blown together by the winds of European imperialism and the entwined fortunes of Napoleon and Nelson. Alexander would surely have approved, and perhaps been wryly amused by, so many ironies—the ones that had already passed and the ones yet to come.

At first, the sarcophagus outstripped the strangely marked Rosetta Stone, but with Champollion's decipherment the roles were reversed. The latter became one of the most famous slabs of stone in the world, and a metaphor of enduring currency. The sarcophagus—the once great imperial prize—ignominiously left the stage. Like its more famous contemporaries, it has remained on public display, but for almost two centuries has endured the humiliation of being invisible in plain view.

While reputations may fade, however, mysteries endure. The failed fortunes of the sarcophagus closed one chapter but opened another: it breathed new life into the quest for Alexander's tomb. As soon as Nectanebo reclaimed his sarcophagus with Champollion's help, Alexander's ghost slipped quietly out of London and back to Egypt. It was not long before the hunt was on again for the final resting place of the son of Zeus Ammon.

Bust of Alexander from Alexandria now in the British Museum. It portrays an idealized Alexander with windswept, tousled hair, fleshy lips and pronounced chin, and dates to around 250 B.C.E.

© Nicholas J. Saunders

(Below) All that remains of the Mausoleum today. It survived largely intact until damaged by earthquakes in the 13th century C.E. In 1494, the Knights of St. John of Malta quarried the site to strengthen the defenses of nearby Bodrum Castle.

© Nicholas J. Saunders

Reconstruction of the Mausoleum at Halicarnassus (modern Bodrum), one of the Seven Wonders of the Ancient World, built around 351 B.C.E. It was seen by Alexander in 334, and may have influenced the funeral pyre he built for Hephaestion as well as his own several tombs in Alexandria.

© Candace Smith

The Oracle Temple of Ammon at the Siwa oasis, where Alexander was allegedly told of his divinity in early 331 B.C.E.

© Nicholas J. Saunders

Reconstruction of Alexander's hearse which was conveying his body to Aegae in Macedonia in the autumn of 321 B.C.E. when it was hijacked by Ptolemy and taken to Memphis in Egypt.

Hadrian's tomb in Rome, begun during the emperor's lifetime around 135 C.E., and completed by his successor Antoninus Pius in 139. It was inspired partly by ancient Etruscan tombs and maybe also by Alexander's second mausoleum in Alexandria.

© livius.org

Diocletian's Column (also called Pompey's Pillar) still stands on top of Alexandria's ruined Serapeum temple. It was built by the Roman emperor Diocletian to mark his successful siege of the city in 298 C.E.

© Nicholas J. Saunders

Alexandria's Serapeum temple was destroyed during the city's Christian riots of 391 C.E., but its subterranean galleries survive. Excavations discovered a large basalt statue of the Apis bull commissioned by the Roman emperor Hadrian.

© Nicholas J. Saunders

Contorniate medallion with bust of Alexander the Great as Heracles, and with the features of Constantine the Great, Rome's first Christian emperor. Photograph

© [June 2006] Museum of Fine Arts, Boston

This 1573 C.E. map of Alexandria by Georg Braun and Frans Hogenberg
was based on the eyewitness account of a traveler, Constantin van
Lyskirchen. It is an impressionistic vista of questionable accuracy, but it
does feature the so-called House of Alexander the Great in its central part.

© A.M. Chugg

Edward Daniel Clarke's 1805 redrawing of Dominique Vivant Denon's
1798 original, showing Muslims in the courtyard of the Attarine mosque
apparently praying before a chapel inside which was Nectanebo II's
greenstone sarcophagus.

© A.M. Chugg

Cyrus the Great's tomb at the old Persian Capital of Pasargadae near Persepolis in Persia (modern Iran). Dated to 530 B.C.E., the tomb was once in the center of a royal park (paradeis) and was visited by Alexander at least once during his Asian campaign.

Profile of Franklin's Fireplace.

The god Serapis was invented by Ptolemy (I Soter) as a Greek style bearded man with a miniature *kalathos* (corn basket) on his head. Ptolemy drew inspiration from the original Egyptian bull deity Osirapis, with whom the new god co-existed.

© Nicholas J. Saunders

Silver tetradrachm coin issued by Lysimachus, one of Alexander's successors, between 298-281 B.C.E. It shows Alexander wearing the royal diadem (ribbon) and Ammon's ram horns emerging from his tousled hair.

© A.M. Chugg

Gold medallion commissioned by Pope Paul III in 1546. It shows Alexander kneeling before the High Priest at Jerusalem, and illustrates how the once great pagan Alexander had been recruited to the medieval Christian cause against Islam.

© Nicholas J. Saunders

The Nectanebo II sarcophagus has sometimes been regarded as used by Ptolemy (I Soter) to bury Alexander in. It was found in Alexandria's Attarine mosque by Dominique Vivant Denon in 1798 and ended up in the British Museum in 1801

© Nicholas J. Saunders

A close up of one of the twelve holes drilled into the Nectanebo II sarcophagus. Were these drainage holes of the Arab period or part of a more sophisticated water fountain display in Ptolemy IV Philopater's Soma funerary park?

© Nicholas J. Saunders

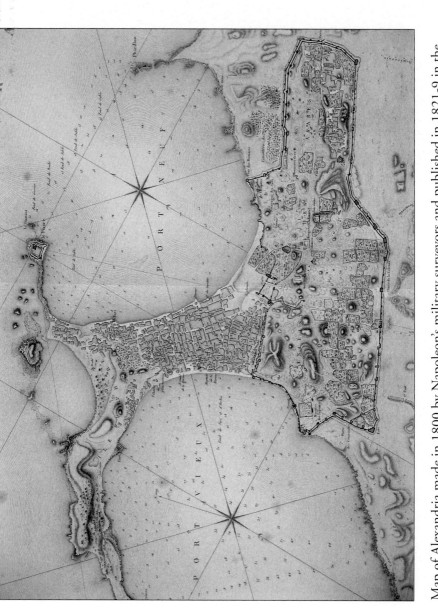

Map of Alexandria made in 1800 by Napoleon's military surveyors and published in 1821-9 in the *Description de l'Égypte*. It is the most accurate map of the city before the 1820s redevelopment altered the urban landscape. The abandoned walled medieval Arabic city and the small 18th century Arabic town on the isthmus are clearly seen. © A.M. Chugg

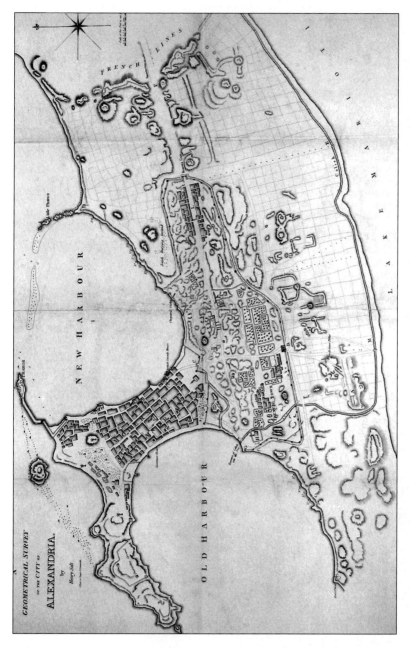

Map of Alexandria by Henry Salt, British Consul General in Egypt, in 1806. It appears to show a faint grid line of streets and indicates the main east-west thoroughfare—the ancient Canopic Way. © A.M. Chugg

The Philosophers Circle at Saqqara in Egypt. Badly damaged today, it originally represented a group of eleven 3rd century B.C.E. statues of famous Greek writers and philosophers. Alexander's Memphite tomb may be nearby.

© Nicholas J. Saunders

The entrance to the subterranean galleries of the Serapeum at Saqqara in Egypt. Large buildings surrounded the entrance tin Alexander's time, all of which have disappeared and their foundations covered by sand.

© Nicholas J. Saunders

Sarcophagus of King Abdalonymus discovered near Sidon in what is now Lebanon in 1887. It was briefly and erroneously identified as Alexander's tomb, though it does feature images of him on its decorative panels. It is now in Istanbul.

© Sabine Gevaert and livius.org

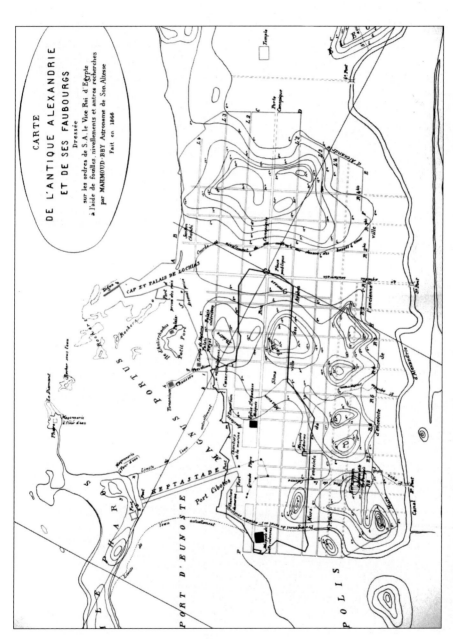

Mahmoud Bey's map of ancient Alexandria made in 1866 and published in 1872. It shows the Greco-Roman street grid, the much larger Lochias peninsula, and the problematic line of the eastern walls.

© A.M. Chugg

The Nabi Daniel mosque was founded possibly in the 15th century C.E. but completely rebuilt on the same spot in the early 19th century. This ca. 1900 view shows the new mosque before Alexandria's redevelopment obscured it.

© Nicholas J. Saunders

The Alabaster Tomb in the Latin Cemeteries area of Alexandra. A Mecedonian style sepulcher, it was reconstructed by Achille Adriani in 1936, and is dated to the 3rd century B.C.E.

© Nicholas J. Saunders

The last surviving section of the Ptolemy I Soter's eastern city wall in Alexandria's Shallalat Gardens. It was later altered and incorporated into the new walls built by Sultan Ahmed-Ibn-Tulun in the late 9th century C.E. as the Arabic city shrank in size from its previous larger Roman extent.

© Nicholas J. Saunders

(Center) The scattered remains of the Doric Temple at Bilad ed-Rum in the Siwa oasis. Long recognized as a 1st century C.E. Greco-Roman temple, it was identified as part of a 3rd century B.C.E. Macedonian mausoleum for Alexander by Liana Souvaltzi.

© Nicholas J. Saunders

The grilled entrance to Alexander's tomb at Bilad el-Rum in the Siwa oasis according to Liana Souvaltzi.

© Nicholas J. Saunders

The well-preserved subterranean necropolis of Mustapha Pasha in eastern Alexandria dates to the 3rd century B.C.E. Its columns, courtyards, and colorful murals indicate it was a high-class burial ground where the living banqueted among the dead as a way of paying respect to their ancestors.

© Nicholas J. Saunders

Alexandria today looking east across the harbor and its submerged ruins to the Lochias peninsula (now the Silsileh promontory) and the area of the Ptolemaic Inner Palaces.

© Nicholas J. Saunders

ARCHAEOLOGISTS, MAPS, AND TOMBS

IN 1803 AN ORTHODOX PRIEST FROM KIEV named Konstantinos journeyed to Alexandria in search of Alexander's tomb. He looked in vain, seemingly unaware of Alexander's connections with the Attarine and Nabi Daniel Mosques, and oblivious to the tale of Nectanebo's sarcophagus now reposing in London. Konstantinos concluded only that Alexander's mausoleum was known until the fifteenth century, and then was lost.[1]

During the eighteenth century, other travelers such as the Danish Captain Norden and a Russian monk named Vassili Barskij also searched without success. Times were changing, and the past was becoming the domain of a new breed of tomb searchers, caught between the pull of antiquarianism, the lure of lucrative and sensational discoveries, and the intellectual gravity of the new discipline of archaeology.

The nineteenth century brought the dawn of archaeology and a fledgling scientific rigor to probing the complex and elusive meanings of the ancient world. Archaeologists could never escape their antiquarian beginnings, and they often peopled imposing ruins with the great names and heroes of antiquity. Irrefutably, archaeology was rooted in and fueled by rampant imperialism and nationalism. Troy, Mycenae, Athens, Nineveh, and Memphis-Saqqara were all reclaimed from obscurity at this time, revitalized and reborn into a world hungry for knowledge of the past.

Romanticism bathed ancient ruins in a rose-tinted glow, yet beneath sand and soil a legacy lay waiting. Across the untouched ruin field of the

Middle East, the remains of a thousand years of pagan classical civilization and several millennia of earlier (and almost unknown) civilized life were frozen in time. Greece, Turkey, Egypt, Syria, Palestine, Mesopotamia (Iraq), and Persia (Iran) had seen their clocks reset by first Christ and then Mohammed.

As Konstantinos brushed off his failed quest in Alexandria, the prospect for archaeology was stunning and seductive. Abandoned cities, ruined temples, fortresses, cemeteries, and entire libraries of papyri and sun-baked clay tablets lay just beneath the surface. This was the blind heart of orientalism—an exquisite confection of past glories jutting from the ruination of a decaying Ottoman empire, captured forever in the paintings of David Roberts and Frederick Catherwood. The empty suburbs of Alexandria were like this, and Alexander's tomb a waiting prize.

Ambroise Schilizzi, a Greek-born dragoman, was working for the Russian consulate in Alexandria in the middle years of the century. In 1850 he shocked the city by announcing his discovery of a secret chamber beneath the Nabi Daniel Mosque. Peeking through a narrow hole in a wooden door, he spied a mummified body encased in a crystal sarcophagus. It wore a golden crown and was surrounded by ancient papyri scattered on the floor. Schilizzi's remarkable acuity—discerning so much while standing outside the chamber holding a candle—was undermined by a single crucial error.[2]

Much of our knowledge of Hellenistic, Roman, and Arab Egypt comes from caches of fragmentary papyri. But these priceless scraps survive only where climate and geology conspire to preserve them. Unfortunately no papyri have ever been found in Alexandria due to the combined effects of land subsidence, a high water table, and rising damp. All papyrus evidence concerning the city has been found outside Alexandria. Schilizzi's papyri were impossible, and his claim an elaborate hoax.

Subsequent investigations found nothing but debris in the subterranean chambers. Schilizzi supplemented his income by collecting and dealing in antiquities and would have kept any genuine discovery to himself.[3] Furthermore, he added to his earnings by escorting tourists around the city's ancient sites, and his concocted story enhanced his commercial activities.

Mahmoud Bey el-Falaki was officially the court astronomer to the Ottoman viceroy of Egypt, the Khedive Ismail Pasha. He had recently returned to Alexandria after spending seven years studying engineering and cartography at the Ecole des Artes et Métiers in Paris.[4]

Napoleon III, emperor of France, wanted to write a biography of Julius Caesar. He turned to his friend Khedive Ismail for assistance with information about Caesar's Alexandrine War. What he needed, Napoleon wrote, was an accurate map of ancient Alexandria at the time of Caesar's triumph. As the most accomplished man on the Khedive's staff, and with French credentials and connections of his own, Mahmoud Bey was the logical adviser. He quickly discovered that there were no ancient maps of the city, only short and ambiguous descriptions preserved in the ancient (mainly Roman) sources. And maps made since the fifteenth century were, for the main part, impressionistic and wildly inaccurate.

Mahmoud Bey had to begin afresh by conducting his own investigations among the ruins of the city. As a preliminary step toward creating a map of ancient Alexandria, Mahmoud Bey and five engineers surveyed the city as they found it. Tramping the streets and alleyways with theodolites in hand, they made an accurate, beautiful map of contemporary Alexandria in 1865, of which only a few examples survive.[5] The map enabled Mahmoud Bey to start tracing the antique city, tying in wherever possible what survived above with what he discovered below.

After centuries of neglect, Alexandria was changing fast. During the 1820s, Egypt's ruler, Mohammed Ali, initiated a policy of modernization and repopulation for Alexandria, and the city grew from around 12,000 inhabitants in 1821 to around 200,000 by the late 1860s. Now, under Khedive Ismail, the population was burgeoning, houses and businesses were appearing, and large sectors of the city were being redeveloped and recolonized, especially along the shoreline that would become Alexandria's famous corniche.

For three hundred years, ever since the Ottomans had avoided the old Tulunnid city and settled instead on the promontory between

Pharos island and the mainland, ancient Alexandria had been left undisturbed. Great swathes of the Ptolemaic, Roman, and Byzantine city lay beyond the eastern Tulunnid walls, abandoned to desolation and treasure hunters beneath vast tracts of drifting sand dunes.[6] As Mahmoud Bey planned his work, developers were plowing through the city, giving little thought to the ancient splendors that lay beneath. Every day, some irreplaceable gem of Alexandria's two-thousand-year history was being lost.

In 1866, armed with the Khedive's authority and his newly completed map of the modern city, Mahmoud Bey began his explorations. Employing a small army of workmen, he dug down into the city two hundred times, reassembling the jigsaw of Alexandria's history. Marshaling the scattered evidence produced by his investigations, Mahmoud Bey estimated where the ancient city walls had stood and calculated the course of two major roads—the Canopic Way, running east–west, and a grand avenue beginning in the north by the Lochias peninsula (now the Silsileh promontory), running south to cross Canopic Way, and on to the shores of inland Lake Mareotis.

Napoleon III was defeated by the Prussians at the Battle of Sedan in 1870 during the Franco–Prussian War. He never finished his volume on Caesar, and he had no use for Mahmoud Bey's painstakingly researched map. Mahmoud Bey self-published his findings in 1872 under the title *Mémoire sur l'antique Alexandrie, ses faubourgs et environs découverts*. The map and descriptions brought antique Alexandria back to life, yet would Strabo have recognized the city that Mahmoud Bey conjured up? And what influence would it have on those trying to locate Alexander's tomb? Modern opinions are divided between those who are critical (if not dismissive)[7] and those who think Mahmoud Bey was basically correct.[8]

Mahmoud Bey called on his engineering and mapmaking skills to draft his plan, but they could only be stretched so far. Archaeology is a different skill, requiring knowledge of artifacts, a geologist's eye in recognizing stratigraphy, and interpretive abilities to recognize the implications of what was found where. Mahmoud Bey's mission to trace the outlines of the ancient city depended not only on engineering and cartography, but also on skills he lacked. He had to dig down through two millennia of confusing layers of civilization that still test modern-day archaeologists.

Mahmoud Bey's neat and tidy map captures his excitement and frustration, not least in his projection of where Alexandria's eastern walls lay—a crucial issue in searching for Alexander's Soma. Exploring east of the Lochias peninsula, Mahmoud Bey traced a section of wall several kilometers long, digging where possible and using hearsay to fill in the gaps. His map confidently depicts a long, impressive wall dominated by the great Canopic gate, but in fact it is based on ambiguous remains and guesswork.

Mahmoud Bey traced the ancient city's street grid as well, uncovering the vestiges and plotting the course of eleven north–south roads and seven east–west ones. Crucially important for locating the Soma was his identification of the main east–west avenue called the Canopic Way (today's Sharia Horriya Street), which he called L1, and the major north–south road from the Lochias peninsula to Lake Mareotis, which he labeled R1 (modern Fuad Street). He reported finding columns, the remains of fine houses, and an underground aqueduct—all of which he judged as evidence that R1 was a fine dual carriageway intersecting with the Canopic Way at the center of the city.

Mahmoud Bey's meager archaeological experience was balanced by professionalism and honesty. His findings, he admitted, were only six to ten feet down, thus Roman and not Ptolemaic. Ptolemy's city, he guessed, lay far deeper—between twenty-three and sixty-five feet below ground level.[9] Mahmoud Bey had uncovered two main roads of the late Roman city whose association with the Alexandria of the Ptolemies was unproven. He may not even have reached the city seen by Strabo in 25 B.C.E.

Mahmoud Bey's lack of archaeological credentials, haphazard diggings, and shaky conclusions attracted justifiable criticism from some archaeologists. Excavations by David George Hogarth in 1895, for example, threw doubt on Mahmoud Bey's identification of the Canopic Way, partly because of the shallowness of the digs.[10] Although the eastern wall problem remains unresolved, Mahmoud Bey's orientation of the street grid seems to be correct, albeit refined by recent investigations.[11] Alexandria, it seems, was undergoing constant renewal, with new streets built and others retaining their original course for centuries, and being resurfaced on many occasions.[12]

The layout of Alexandria's ancient streets and their relationship to the modern city is crucial to locating Alexander's tomb. In the area of the Soma—the old Palaces District—Polish archaeologists revealed streets with a different and older orientation than that shown on Mahmoud Bey's map.[13] This may have been a sign of affluence and power adopted by the Ptolemies for their high-status neighborhood, or it may indicate that Mahmoud Bey's grid is mainly Roman and overlies a different set of earlier alignments.[14]

Mahmoud Bey's seductive image of ancient Alexandria continues to shape modern views of the city. Napoleon III requested a plan of the city as it was during Caesar's time in 47 B.C.E., when it was Ptolemaic and not Roman, and much smaller than it was after Octavian's arrival in 30 B.C.E. Mahmoud Bey was looking to resurrect the golden city of the Ptolemies, and his map is widely and erroneously regarded as being exactly that.

The obvious and fatal flaw in Mahmoud Bey's map is that he did not find a city frozen in time around 47 B.C.E. The term "ancient Alexandria" disguises the fact that there were at least three cities to be identified and mapped: Ptolemy's original, the larger and later Roman one, and the medieval Arab city nestling behind Ahmed ibn Tulun's ninth-century C.E. walls. Possibly during late Roman/Byzantine times another city wall was built somewhere between the Ptolemaic and Roman ones.

These three cities were not superimposed in neat archaeological levels but were churned, moved, and altered over two thousand years. They are superimposed one on another, each recycling parts of its predecessor and each a composite entity. Ancient Alexandria is a palimpsest—each layer needing to be identified and then lifted like overlays in a book. Mahmoud Bey achieved a great deal under challenging conditions, but did he conflate three cities into one? Experts are divided, and questions remain as to whether Mahmoud Bey actually uncovered any of the walls, still less Ptolemy's originals.[15]

Despite his education, intellect, and honesty, Mahmoud Bey lacked modern techniques for analyzing what belonged where. The crucial issue, as he recognized, was that more often than not he was only un-covering late Roman/Byzantine remains. Despite this, the eastern walls on his map continue to be interpreted as enclosing Ptolemy's city rather than the much larger Roman one they clearly define.[16]

Mahmoud Bey dug two hundred times across Alexandria, reconstruct-ing a city that mainly belonged to the period 150 C.E.–600 C.E. In the years following 400 C.E. Alexandria was drastically refurbished as a Christian city. Searching for the city of the Ptolemies, he created a plan of late Roman Alexandria. The crucial questions remain unanswered: Did Roman Alexandria sit on top of the earlier Ptolemaic city, replicat-ing its alignments and street orientations? Did the subsequent Byzantine Christian city simply lie on top of the pagan Roman one? If so, then Mahmoud Bey's map is an accurate guide to the Hellenistic city (as long as one dug deep enough). In its fundamentals of shape and street layout, archaeological investigations suggest that this was indeed the case.

Mahmoud Bey could not resist the lure of Alexander's tomb. He breathed new life into the idea, so scandalously distorted by Ambroise Schilizzi a decade before, that the great conqueror lay beneath the Nabi Daniel Mosque. Mahmoud Bey's error of judgment emerged from his own street plan, in which he brought tradition and rumor together in published form.[17]

In drafting his map, Mahmoud Bey identified the intersection of the Canopic Way and Street R5 as a major crossroads in the ancient city. The Nabi Daniel Mosque is located on street R5 not far from the Canopic Way, the proximity suggesting that the Soma was somewhere nearby. It was a short leap of imagination to join old rumors to new ev-idence and suggest that the Nabi Daniel Mosque was, in ancient tradi-tion and archaeological reality, the long-lost site of Alexander's tomb.

Mahmoud Bey made his way down into the subterranean world of the Nabi Daniel Mosque, discovering well-made passages that he felt sure led to Alexander's tomb. Influenced by old legends about the site and stories he heard at the time, he lapsed into the fantastic world of Alexandrian urban myths that surrounded Alexander's tomb, convinc-ing himself that here was the lost sepulchre.

The tenacious story, buttressed by Mahmoud Bey's conviction, swayed later investigators as well, including Evaristo Breccia of the

Graeco–Roman Museum.[18] Breccia's own excavations, however, found no evidence of the royal burial and revealed that Mahmoud Bey's passages were water conduits associated with Roman cisterns.[19]

The identification of the Nabi Daniel Mosque with Alexander's tomb took on a life of its own during the late nineteenth century. It was given unexpected momentum sixteen years after Mahmoud Bey's diggings when one of the great names of archaeology arrived in Alexandria determined to discover the Soma beneath its well-trodden floor.

It was 1888, and Heinrich Schliemann was waiting impatiently in Alexandria for official permission to dig in and around the Nabi Daniel Mosque. In the meantime, Schliemann busied himself by exploring and digging nearer to the coast in the part of the city known as Ramleh, where he discovered a cemetery belonging to the time of the Ptolemies.

Despite this success, he was adamant that the Soma had to be located in the vicinity of the Nabi Daniel Mosque. Schliemann never got permission from the authorities and left the city for a cruise on the Nile. He died just two years later. Schliemann's undeniable intuition or luck—his nose for a find—and his astounding earlier successes raise the question, Would he have made a breakthrough no less astonishing than his discoveries at Mycenae and Troy? Schliemann's inability to dig burnished the Nabi Daniel legend.

In 1898 Alexei Ramonsky, an official at the Russian embassy in Alexandria, befriended the caretaker of the Nabi Daniel Mosque. Creeping into the vaults one night, Ramonsky encountered a black basalt block in the middle of a room on which was perched a glass cage covered with a three-inch layer of dust. Wiping it clean, Ramonsky saw a mummified figure sitting on a throne. Papyri were scattered everywhere, as were vases, Macedonian weapons, and even a Roman standard. On the base of the basalt block was inscribed the name "King Alexander" in Greek.[20] Ramonsky echoes Schilizzi's earlier fantasy, demonstrating the chameleon-like persistence of a good yarn.

Wary of the wild publicity generated by investigations, mosque authorities refused to grant further permission, and for a time even forbade Christians from setting foot inside the mosque.[21] This heightened the mystery, giving rise to suspicions that mosque authorities were hiding something.

So persistent is the identification of the Nabi Daniel Mosque and Alexander's tomb that the mosque is still marked and described as the Soma on many modern maps of Alexandria. Even during the 1990s, city authorities were receiving applications to dig for Alexander's tomb beneath Nabi Daniel.

Legend outstrips reality, and the archaeological truth is that the Nabi Daniel Mosque has never produced evidence of being an ancient tomb during Hellenistic or Roman times. Evaristo Breccia finally came to the same conclusion as Achille Adriani—his successor at the Graeco–Roman Museum—that any hope of finding Alexander's remains at the Nabi Daniel Mosque should be abandoned.

As in life so in death, Alexander would not be tied down to one particular time and place. During the late nineteenth century, as Alexandria was buzzing with endless rumors and clandestine diggings, other contenders for Alexander's tomb were beckoning.

In 1887, a year before Schliemann arrived in Alexandria, the Turkish antiquarian and painter Osman Hamdi Bey was digging the remains of the old royal cemetery in the hills behind Sidon in what is today southern Lebanon. At the time, this part of the Levant, along with Egypt, was still part of the Ottoman empire. To his astonishment, he stumbled across a set of elegant marble sarcophagi belonging to great figures of Sidon during Alexander's time.[22]

Hamdi Bey arranged to have the tombs ferried by boat across the Aegean to Istanbul, where they were put on public display. He founded the Ottoman Imperial Museum in the same year in order to display them in appropriate surroundings.

One of the stone coffins caught Hamdi Bey's eye and struck a chord in his imagination. It became known as the Alexander sarcophagus and drew countless visitors to Istanbul.[23] One early pilgrim was the intrepid multilingual traveler, archaeologist, and author Gertrude Bell. In June 1898, Bell visited the museum to see what she believed was the tomb of Alexander the Great.

Bell set down her impressions in her diary, describing how the setting sun accented the delicate color of the sarcophagus, and how the battle scenes were so realistic that she expected to hear the din of war. She marveled at Alexander's finely wrought image and mused that a skull found in the tomb and also on display belonged to the great man himself.[24]

When Bell identified the Sidon sarcophagus as Alexander's tomb, she reflected the general fascination with discovering the conqueror's last resting place. Bell herself had excavated across the Middle East, read Greek and Latin, and eventually drew the post–1918 boundaries of Mesopotamia that created the modern nation of Iraq. Alexander's pull, even on Bell, would not be denied.

Despite the initial euphoria, archaeologists soon realized that the enigmatic tomb was not Alexander's. Its design, shape, and intriguing decorative friezes nevertheless offered clues concerning Alexander's life and his postmortem adventures. Alexander was present at the tomb, not as a corpse but as a decoration and an inspiration.

The Alexander sarcophagus was carved at great expense and with extraordinary craftsmanship from two great blocks of pentelic marble weighing some fifteen tons. This is a fine white stone that ages to a golden tint. It was (and still is) quarried from the flanks of Mount Pentelikon northeast of Athens, and it is used only for the most important buildings and sculptures. Its use in the Sidonian sarcophagi indicates the power and wealth of the original occupants.

Gazing at the distinctive shape and design of the Alexander sarcophagus, the viewer is drawn into another world. Its unusual form suggests that the sarcophagus was inspired by eyewitness familiarity with Alexander's funeral hearse, which passed close by Sidon in late 321 B.C.E. on its way from Babylon to Memphis under Ptolemy's armed escort.[25] But Alexander's funerary car carried only his golden mummy case, assorted royal paraphernalia, and paintings. Possibly the Alexander sarcophagus was an artistic transformation of Alexander's own overelaborate catafalque in sarcophagus form. But who would have been so concerned to emulate Alexander's hearse and spend vast sums on realizing his ambition?

Abdalonymous, the last native Phoenician king of Sidon, is the most likely candidate. This might explain why, in purely artistic terms, the Alexander sarcophagus is adorned with the style of carvings found on all the sarcophagi discovered by Osman Hamdi Bey.[26]

Abdalonymous owed his crown to Alexander. Hephaestion found him living on the outskirts of Sidon and realized he was a perfect choice for a new king. Alexander was suspicious of the current king, Straton, who was an ally of the Persians. Sidon had long been famous for its shipbuilding, made possible by the proximity of the extensive forests of Lebanese cedar in the hills behind the city. Straton's contribution to the Persian war effort was not soldiers, but warships to be used against Alexander.

Abdalonymous was a distant and impoverished member of the Sidonian royal family and thus had the right kinship ties, but was in no way associated with Straton's actions. Hephaestion presented Abdalonymous personally to Alexander, who immediately deposed Straton and installed Abdalonymous. Apart from this dramatic elevation to kingship, Abdalonymous is a shadowy figure; even his death is disputed, 312 B.C.E. and 306–305 B.C.E. being equally possible.[27]

Little is known about Abdalonymous, but his marble tomb speaks of opulent and fevered times. Abdalonymous commissioned dramatic action scenes for two sides of the sarcophagus, and a carefully orchestrated royal hunt of lions and panthers for the third. The swords and spears wielded by the figures were originally fashioned of gold and silver, but looters had stolen them before Hamdi arrived. All except one, a miniature silver ax, as Gertrude Bell noticed in a display case during her visit in 1898. Bell also observed traces of paint that would have brought the scenes to life.

The main battle scene, carved on one long side, shows Macedonians fighting Persians, with Alexander in a fantastic lion-head helmet. He spears a Persian cavalryman in a scene apparently immortalizing the Battle of Issus.[28] Alexander appears on the other long side in the lion hunt. He is depicted wearing a distinctive (and unusual) blend of Macedonian and Persian dress—the tight-fitting Persian chiton. Alexander's sartorial detail may help date the sarcophagus, as he adopted this style after the murder of Darius in 330 B.C.E. Only Hephaestion, as Alexander's alter ego, wears similar attire.

Abdalonymous's sarcophagus, like Alexander's own tomb in Alexandria, was always a political monument, tying the Phoenician king to the lord of Asia in a three-dimensional marble celebration of royal associations. But it is also difficult to decipher, as there is no clear or coherent artistic program—no underlying structure—that links the four friezes. Abdalonymous appears in the lion hunt frieze riding a horse in front of Alexander and being attacked by a lion while Hephaestion gallops forward from the other direction. Alexander is not the central figure, which prompts the question, What is Abdalonymus trying to tell us?

Perhaps it is a mythical event or maybe it depicts Alexander hunting lions in one of the royal game parks established by the Persians in Syria.[29] Abdalonymous's prominence at the center of the action emphasizes his regal status and suggests that the sarcophagus was commissioned during his own lifetime, as was common practice.[30] If finished before Abdalonymous died, it may have been displayed in a royal palace, which would make it a precursor to Alexander's Soma in Alexandria—a tourist magnet designed to impress the dignitaries who visited Sidon during and after Abdalonymous's life.[31]

The two long sides and their painted carved-relief panels show Alexander pursuing his two favorite pastimes—fighting Persians and hunting lions. Abdalonymous may have been inspired by Alexander's passion for lion hunts, but such imagery was also part of a long Asian tradition, as shown by alabaster reliefs at Nineveh depicting Ashurbanipal stabbing lions more than three hundred years earlier, around 650 B.C.E.

The Alexander sarcophagus is so called because of its magnificent representations of Alexander, not because it ever held the god-king's body. It raises the question of what Alexander's actual sarcophagus looked like. Ptolemy directed Alexander's burial in Memphis and reburial in Alexandria, but we do not know if he ever saw Abdalonymous's tomb.

Possibly Ptolemy caught a glimpse of the actual tomb in the first few months of 311 B.C.E., when he temporarily controlled Sidon in the wake of his victory at the Battle of Gaza. If he did, it may have influenced his mortuary arrangements for Alexander, whose body was probably still in Memphis. It is tempting to speculate on the irony of Ptolemy gazing on a royal tomb whose design was influenced by Alexander's funerary car, which he had hijacked a decade previously. If Perdiccas's probable aim of burying Alexander in Macedonia had succeeded, the elaborate catafalque would have taken a different route and not passed

Sidon at all. Abdalonymous's marble tomb, perhaps, would have looked quite different.

Although the misnamed Alexander sarcophagus never held Alexander's mummy, it is associated with it in a surprising way. The fourth and most intriguing frieze carved on Abdalonymous's tomb shows Macedonians killing an unarmed Macedonian. This may portray the assassination of Perdiccas in his royal tent during his disastrous invasion of Egypt in 320 B.C.E.

Abdalonymous's impulse for commissioning this scene is unclear, though he may simply have been currying favor with his new political masters—the assassins and those who inherited power once Perdiccas was dead. To be anti-Perdiccan after 320 B.C.E. was probably a good thing. Perdiccas invaded Egypt to take Alexander's body from Ptolemy and may have ended up with his murder immortalized on a Phoenician king's tomb, itself inspired by Alexander's passing cortege.

Auguste Mariette (1821–1881) was born into the cold, salty winds that whip through the channel port of Boulogne in northern France. As a young man he lived in England for a while before returning home and inheriting drawings made by a cousin who had accompanied Champollion to Egypt in 1828. Mariette was mesmerized by the images, which triggered an obsessive and lifelong passion for Egypt. He taught himself hieroglyphics and Coptic, eventually finding employment at the Louvre in Paris, where he inventoried the museum's ancient Egyptian inscriptions. His moment came in 1850, when his employers sent him to Egypt to purchase ancient papyri for the Louvre's collections.

Mariette soon launched into the exploration and excavation of the great Serapeum temple at Memphis-Saqqara. He later dug at Giza, Thebes, Karnak, and Abydos, and he became the first director of the Egyptian Antiquities Service in 1858. He was showered with honors over the years, being elevated to the rank of bey and then pasha. His early discoveries at Saqqara added a new twist to the search for Alexander's tomb.[32]

The great Serapeum temple, dedicated to the cult of the Apis bull and founded during the Eighteenth Dynasty (1550–1295 B.C.E.), was a lodestone to early Egyptologists. Napoleon's savants and others had searched in vain for this famous temple mausoleum, but Mariette's keen eye and inspired guesswork found it. He began excavating in 1851.

Clearing the sand from the Serapeum Way, which led from the Nile up to the Saqqara plateau, Mariette uncovered the row of sphinxes encountered by Strabo two thousand years before. At the end of the ritual path, where it enters the inner sanctum, he stood amazed as eleven statues emerged from the desert sand. These were not stylized figures of pharaohs or animal gods, but lifelike images of Greek poets and philosophers. In the middle of Egypt's most sacred burial ground, consecrated by millennia of pharaonic mythology and cosmology, were the most famous figures of an alien religious and philosophical tradition.

The style of the figures dated them to the third century B.C.E., perhaps to the reign of Ptolemy himself, and so coincided with the time when Alexander lay in Memphis. Among the well-known faces that greeted Mariette were Homer, Plato, Pindar, Hesiod, and Thales of Miletus—now known collectively as the Philosophers Circle.[33] Mariette's subsequent discovery of giant Apis bull sarcophagi in the subterranean depths of the Serapeum stole the headlines, but the Philosophers Circle posed intriguing questions for those interested in Alexander. When exactly were they made? Who commissioned them? Why were they in the middle of an Egyptian necropolis that was ancient when Alexander invaded Egypt in 332 B.C.E.?

By Mariette's time, it was known that Alexander had three Egyptian tombs, the first located somewhere beneath the vast tracts of desert that covered Memphis-Saqqara. Mariette's discovery of the Philosophers Circle aroused suspicions in the minds of those primarily interested in Hellenistic Egypt.

Mariette continued digging at the Serapeum. Near the Philosophers Circle he uncovered other typically Greek sculptures carved in local limestone and representing scenes from the life and times of mythical Dionysus. He found a panther, a lion being ridden by a young Dionysus, and several peacocks also being ridden by the god. Two chapels—one Greek, the other Egyptian—were located nearby, attesting to the popularity of the cult of Osiris/Apis among the Macedonians who, at Ptolemy's direction, had renamed it Serapis.

Mariette was uncovering a strange confection of images and styles representing the hybrid Greco–Egyptian fusion of religion that Ptolemy pursued in the volatile years following Alexander's death. Here was archaeological proof of the relationship between Alexander, Ptolemy, and Serapis—all appropriately focused on the Serapeum.

Alexander followed in the footsteps of Dionysus's mythical wanderings in Asia and became forever linked to the god. Mariette's peacock statues were particularly intriguing in this respect. The peacock, later a symbol of Christian resurrection, was unknown in Egypt before Alexander's time. The Roman author Aelian, writing some five hundred years after Alexander's death, recorded a story originating in modern-day Pakistan that the peacock enjoyed a special relationship with Alexander.[34] He was astonished and entranced by the peacocks' beauty and placed them under royal protection.

Following Alexander's death, the peacock acquired religious importance among the Ptolemies. In the grand procession of Ptolemy II Philadelphus in 275–274 B.C.E., the colorful birds were paraded in cages and may have been worshiped, perhaps dedicated to Zeus. Alexander's association with peacocks, Dionysus, and India, and Mariette's discovery of peacock statues adjacent to the Philosophers Circle at Saqqara, suggested that an important tomb was nearby, presumably of Greco–Macedonian origin. Alexander is the only obvious candidate.

Were the unexpected Greek statues and sculptures the remains (or perhaps a commemoration of) Alexander's brief rest in Memphis? Did Alexander's first tomb lie somewhere in the vast burial field of Saqqara?

New evidence brings Alexander tantalizingly close. Polish and Egyptian archaeologists excavating a couple hundred yards south of the Philosophers Circle uncovered a cemetery from the time of the Ptolemies—with mummies and skeletons lying just below the sun-baked surface.[35] Investigators were surprised to find nothing below these remains except an Old Kingdom rock-cut mastaba tomb with superb paintings and reliefs of an Egyptian vizier named Meref-nebef.

For a period of almost two thousand years—between the end of the Old Kingdom (2686–2181 B.C.E.) and Ptolemy's establishment of Macedonian rule in 332 B.C.E.—archaeologists found no human remains. The location had been deliberately kept empty, perhaps as a sacred place not to be ritually violated by other burials. But something dramatic occurred around 332 B.C.E. to make it a popular burial spot.[36]

If Alexander was buried nearby, even for a short time, then the area might have had its status redefined. Alexander's fame and godlike status would have made it a desirable burial ground for Greco–Macedonians and others long after his remains were moved to Alexandria. The area between the Philosophers Circle and the tomb of Vizier Meref-nebef intrigued the Polish excavator, who said that "it may still prove to be a theater of sensational discoveries."[37]

A final twist to the story of Alexander's tomb at Memphis-Saqqara begun by Mariette's discoveries lies with the enigmatic pharaoh Nectanebo II. He built the small temple near the Serapeum, immediately adjacent to where the Philosophers Circle would later be erected. Ptolemy, eager to foster Alexander's legendary parentage by Nectanebo II, perhaps buried his king nearby in a still undiscovered tomb or maybe laid him to rest temporarily in the cool depths of the Serapeum's vaults. Somewhere on the Saqqara plateau, at the edge of the Western Desert, clues to the strange relationship between Alexander, Ptolemy, and Nectanebo II still wait to be found.

The nineteenth century transformed the search for Alexander's tomb. At the beginning, it was likely that Alexander lay in the British Museum in the green sarcophagus taken from the Attarine Mosque in Alexandria. Champollion dissolved this illusion, and soon archaeologists, antiquarians, mapmakers, and treasure seekers joined in the hunt.[38]

Alexandria was still the most likely location, but Memphis-Saqqara also staked a claim, and even Istanbul could boast its own Alexander sarcophagus found at Sidon. Clearly future quests would be in the hands of archaeologists. Less clear was what they would find and where they should look. Would Mahmoud Bey's beautiful map guide them or lead them astray?

ALABASTER, FANTASY, AND ANCIENT WALLS

EVARISTO BRECCIA WAS THE SECOND OF THREE Italian directors of Alexandria's Graeco–Roman Museum. His predecessor, Giuseppe Botti, founded the museum in 1892, and Achille Adriani would succeed Breccia in 1932. In this first golden age of Alexandrian archaeology, the pace of urban renewal pushed excavators away from the city center and toward the outskirts that are now Alexandria's modern suburbs. What Botti, Breccia, and Adriani found were the ancient cities of the dead, the old burial grounds of Anfushi, Chatby, el-Shuqafa, Hadra, and Mustapha Pasha. Alexandria's great tombs—Alexander's Soma and the sepulchres of the Ptolemies—were lost, but their magnificence was hinted at by these lesser, though spectacular burials at the city's edge.

Breccia made the breakthrough, discovering a tomb for Alexander whose story spans the entire twentieth century. Breccia began exploring various cemeteries of the Ptolemaic era scattered along the eastern limits of Alexandria, near the line of Ptolemy's original city walls. Between 1907 and 1910, he was investigating the famous Chatby burial ground and exploring a quarter of the city known as El Ibrahimeyah. He was drawn intuitively to the Roman Catholic Terra Santa cemetery (part of the so-called Latin Cemeteries), which lay on top of deeply buried Greek and Roman remains.

Early photographs show a tantalizing scene. Among the Catholic graves Breccia found a chaotic tumble of alabaster blocks lying in a heap like a mound of debris. Unusual as this was (in fact it was unique),

Breccia was not unduly impressed. He made this discovery in 1907[1] but did not announce it until 1914 in a French edition of his guidebook to the city's antiquities—*Alexandrea ad Aegyptum*.[2] Ironically this disassembled monument—later regarded as Alexander's tomb—appeared as a tourist attraction in the two-thousand-year tradition that began when the original Soma drew visitors to Alexandria.

Breccia did not consider the pile of alabaster slabs a possible tomb for Alexander, but his successor at the Graeco–Roman Museum was of a different opinion. Achille Adriani became increasingly disenchanted with the endless and fruitless identifications of the Nabi Daniel Mosque as the site of the Soma. Its empty vaults convinced him there was nothing to find, and he decided to look again at Breccia's shiny white blocks in the Latin Cemeteries. These unusual slabs had drawn Adriani's attention from the moment he arrived in Alexandria, their polished beauty contrasting with the rest of the city's often drab ruins.[3]

Adriani's timing was perfect. In 1936 cemetery authorities decided to clear the area of its old graves, offering a unique opportunity to make small excavations on the west side of the monument. He uncovered a deep rectangular well cut into the bedrock that connected to an underground channel, but elsewhere found little despite digging down thirteen feet.[4] Excavations north, south, and east of the monument were impossible due to the presence of other structures, and nothing had ever been found there. The alabaster slabs seemed nothing more than a pile of up-market debris with no identifiable archaeological context.

But Adriani was unsatisfied and began reconstructing the monument, fitting the alabaster blocks onto a huge slab that had evidently been the floor of the sepulchre. As the tomb took shape, it became apparent to Adriani that the superbly (and expensively) polished interior contrasted dramatically with the rough and battered exterior, suggesting to him that the outside face of the tomb was never intended to be seen by the public. He calculated that the rough outer casing either was covered by lost architectural features or originally had an earthen mound or tumulus heaped up on top, in typical Macedonian style.

Adriani reassembled a traditional Macedonian tomb on what, in Ptolemy's time, was an area just within, or more likely just outside, Alexandria's eastern walls. Its shape and style date it to the time of

Ptolemy or perhaps his son Philadelphus, meaning the very beginnings of the city. The extraordinary Alabaster Tomb is still unique in Alexandria.

As a professional archaeologist, Adriani was cautious in his interpretations of the tomb's original appearance, changing his mind several times. Eventually he decided that it was a simple two-room tomb with a templelike facade, not dissimilar to the large tumulus tombs excavated by Manolis Andronikos at Vergina in northern Greece in the 1970s.[5]

Breccia had found the tomb in pieces on the surface, but there was no indication of how it came to be in that condition. Had it been shaken down by an earthquake, or perhaps dismantled as a source of marble for other buildings? The appearance of the Alabaster Tomb is as stunning as it is misleading. As no further evidence has yet come to light, it is impossible to know what other structures or features were originally associated with it. The Alabaster Tomb may have been a tumulus, or perhaps it once supported a grand temple or pyramid-shaped roof, the remains of which were taken away to embellish later Byzantine or Arab buildings.

Adriani's reconstruction makes clear that the tomb's unique style signifies the burial of a wealthy and important person during early Ptolemaic times. Whether this was Alexander the Great or a lesser member of the Ptolemaic dynasty is impossible to say. Nevertheless, whoever was interred here possessed strong Macedonian connections, and the tomb itself might preserve a sense of what Alexander's first and perhaps more Macedonian-style tomb looked like.[6]

Adriani was alive to the knotty archaeological problems of identifying the Alabaster Tomb as Alexander's. During the 1960s he was cautious, but in the 1970s he became more convinced. After his death his students Nicola Bonacasa and Patrizia Minà gathered his private notes and publications to publish a definitive account of his most recent convictions in the Italian book *La tomba di Alessandro* (2000).

The Alabaster Tomb gathered international renown and support as Alexander's sepulchre in the final decades of the twentieth century. Those who jettisoned the Nabi Daniel Mosque usually turned to Adriani's reconstructed tomb. In 1992 Egyptian archaeologists excavated 330 feet east of the tomb, but the curious dearth of any archaeological remains continued.[7] Did this emptiness indicate an area deliberately kept free of buildings and occupation during Ptolemaic times? Was it perhaps a royal garden or a royal cemetery—maybe even the lost royal enclosure of the Soma built by Philopater?

Adriani's belief that the Alabaster Tomb is part of the Soma raises another intractable issue. Ptolemy's first tomb for Alexander survived for about a century before Philopater replaced it with the grander Soma enclosure, during which time Alexandria developed its own unique mortuary styles. By 215 B.C.E., the Alabaster Tomb's Macedonian appearance would have been a deliberate anachronism. How likely is it that Philopater would have known or cared what an authentic royal Macedonian tomb looked like a hundred years before?

The simplest answer is that the Alabaster Tomb was Ptolemy's original construction and was disassembled and moved along with Alexander's body from its original location and reassembled in the Soma enclosure. Alternatively it may have been a copy. Perhaps Adriani was not the first person to reconstruct the tomb. Credible but unlikely, this idea brings us no closer to explaining why Philopater might have wanted to recreate an old-style tomb, though it does highlight the inventive explanations that can be invoked to fill the void created by a lack of solid archaeological and historical evidence.

The Alabaster Tomb's growing fame attracted a host of strange admirers seeking proof of its newfound status as the Soma. In 1979 Stephan Schwartz led a bizarre expedition to Alexandria in search of the city's antiquities. Schwartz and his team were remote viewers—people with a psychic ability to see and experience the past as if they were actually present.[8]

In March of that year, these searchers gathered at the Alabaster Tomb. One of them, a photographer named Hella Hammid, had a special talent—a sharp psychic sense that could penetrate the earth and discern long-buried archaeological objects. Standing inside the tomb, Hella slipped into a trance like a Victorian spirit medium. As her body began to quiver, she described a great plaza, a tall beacon by the sea, and a grand tomb strewn with debris. Schwartz was recording her séance when suddenly the tape recorder failed. Clearly moved by this encounter with the numinous, it refused to record Hella's voice and played back a mysterious hissing noise.[9]

The team of psychics failed to identify who had discovered the Alabaster Tomb just seventy years earlier. Schwartz's account of this dodgy day's work reverently credited the tomb's discovery to "the great Italian archaeologist Adriani in 1907."[10] Evaristo Breccia probably turned in his own grave, while the mature Adriani was transformed into a child prodigy working wonders from across the sea in Italy. Remote viewing had uncovered an astonishing instance of remote control.

Twenty years later, a more scientific type of remote sensing found its way to the Latin Cemeteries. In 1998 an international team of geophysicists conducted a survey of the area surrounding the Alabaster Tomb.[11] Their nondestructive techniques identified and located buried objects and guided excavations by the Egyptian scholar Fawzi Fakharani, who found large limestone blocks buried ten feet below the surface.[12]

This success prompted a more ambitious survey by Greek geophysicists in 1999, aiming to identify other sections of the tomb as well as more deeply buried structures nearby.[13] The results suggested buried metals and stone structures at various locations, especially beneath a garden nursery east of the tomb and the Greek Orthodox cemetery to the north.[14] Fakharani dug again, this time down to twenty-six feet below the surface, but found nothing.[15] In 2002 a follow-up excavation by the French Centre d'Études Alexandrines (CEA) investigated the anomalies identified by the Greek team but found nothing of importance.

Time and again, archaeologists probed the earth around the Alabaster Tomb but failed to find support for its interpretation as Alexander's Soma. The most intriguing discovery was that there were no discoveries. How did the original Alabster Tomb meet its fate? If Breccia found the pile of collapsed blocks in its original location, then the tomb had stood in magnificent (and suggestive) isolation. Either that, or the area had been stripped bare by centuries of pillage for building materials. Perhaps the tomb was found—intact or collapsed—by Arab laborers searching for materials to build Sultan Ahmed ibn Tulun's new walls around the shrinking medieval town in 870 C.E. The tomb lay outside these walls, which incorporated stone blocks scavenged from the Greco–Roman city and made use of the only surviving section of Ptolemaic walls at the modern city's Shallalat gardens.[16]

Perhaps the alabaster blocks were dragged to the Latin Cemetery from the Jewish cemetery during the nineteenth century, when moving and recycling ancient tombs was fashionable among Alexandria's upper classes.[17] Giuseppe Botti lies inside an ancient sarcophagus of Aswan granite not far from the Alabaster Tomb.[18] Archaeology has not yet resolved the problems surrounding the Alabaster Tomb, but there are other clues to its identification with Alexander.

Mahmoud Bey reaches beyond the grave to influence all who search for Alexander's tomb. While his map accurately portrays the shape of the city and the orientation of its streets, the course and location of Alexandria's eastern walls remain in contention.

Alexander's two tombs must lie within the boundaries of Ptolemy's original city. The first may have been built near the city center, and the second closer to the royal palaces clustering around the base of the Lochias peninsula. While all the ancient sources indicate that Alexander lay inside the perimeter walls, is it possible that the Alabaster Tomb is telling a different story?

For the Greeks, the living were polluted by contact with the dead, and so cemeteries were built beyond the city walls. This was as true for the Alexandria of the Ptolemies as it was for Athens, Thebes, or Corinth. When Ptolemy and his son Philadelphus built, beautified, and fortified Alexandria, they placed the city's first cemeteries outside the grand encircling ramparts. For Greeks and Macedonians, walls were spiritual boundaries as well as physical barriers.

In the northeast part of the city, the burial ground known today as Chatby begins just east of the Lochias peninsula. It came to light at the end of the nineteenth century, as building work spread the modernizing city eastward across the churned ruin field of the ancient city.

Chatby exploded onto the public arena in 1893 when a Greek named Ioannides discovered a stunning tomb while searching for Alexander's mausoleum.[19] Digging down nearly forty feet, Ioannides insisted that the burial chambers he found were the unlooted tombs of Alexander the Great and Cleopatra VII. Both tombs, he said, had bronze doors inscribed in Greek, with the names of their royal occupants sculpted over the entrance. Ioannides peered through a hole in the door with the aid of a magnesium light, spying marble sarcophagi resting on feet carved as lion paws. He also saw papyri or parchments in the gloom and claimed to recover jewelry and beautiful Greek vases.[20] Many who read the account of Ioannides's escapades in the *Egyptian Gazette* on the morning of June 20 were reminded of the exploits of Ambroise Schilizzi almost fifty years before.

The Chatby tomb was real, but Ioannides's identification of it as Alexander's Soma was a hoax. Ioannides, unlike others, was at least looking in the right part of Alexandria. The burials at Chatby date mainly to the early Ptolemaic times of the third century B.C.E., and so the cemetery must have been established just beyond the eastern walls and then spread out over time.[21] Chatby was part of a funerary landscape in which commoners and the well-to-do were buried in close proximity. Philadelphus erected a (now disappeared) mausoleum to his mistress Stratonike by the sea just beyond Chatby.[22] Farther east lay the beautifully preserved high-class tombs of the Mustapha Pasha cemetery. It appears like a semisubterranean city of the dead, with tombs having staircases, fluted columns, courtyards, elaborate facades, and doorways, in addition to well-preserved paintings.[23] Some tombs appear like houses, and their facades allow us to glimpse the theatricality of death rites during this time. Stratonike's mausoleum and the Mustapha Pasha tombs also belong to the third century B.C.E., indicating that there is no problem with identifying the Alabaster Tomb's wealthy occupant lying outside rather than inside the city.

Startling to modern eyes but commonplace in antiquity, the walls of Alexandria were ringed by monuments to the dead. Approaching Alexandria from the east, ancient visitors passed through a cordon of tombs—a vast city of the dead—flanking the living community. It seems to have stretched from Chatby in the north to another burial ground known as Hadra in the south.[24] Coins belonging to Alexander's lifetime and Ptolemy's reign have been recovered from both cemeteries, indicating overlap in time as well as space.[25]

Chatby and Hadra lay just outside Ptolemy's original walls, and the wall line itself was slightly west of the burial grounds. Yet this line has nothing in common with that drawn by Mahmoud Bey. He drafted his perimeter wall far to the east, enclosing the much larger Roman period city and leaving Chatby and Hadra stranded in the center of the expanded city.[26]

Ptolemy's eastern ramparts were breached by early Roman times. Alexandria's Jewish community burgeoned, spilling out over the walls and building houses and living in between the now mainly abandoned Chatby tombs and graveyards.[27] These neighborhoods of the dead became suburbs for the living, a process that continued throughout the Roman period and led eventually to a new line of walls built far to the east.

Almost three hundred years after Ptolemy designated Chatby as the city cemetery, it was falling into disuse while retaining some of its sacred and symbolic importance. Stratonike's tomb probably still stood overlooking the sea, and the Alabaster Tomb—so close to the Canopic Gate—probably also was intact. It was likely the lingering attraction of the Chatby area that made it the ideal place for perhaps the last high-profile, particularly grisly burial there in 48 B.C.E. When Caesar was presented with Pompey's decapitated head, he buried it with due ceremony and respect in a shrine dedicated to Nemesis just north of the Alabaster Tomb.[28]

By 24 B.C.E., Strabo was wandering around Alexandria's streets, eyes alert and stylus in hand. The city had changed greatly since Ptolemy's day. Gazing east, Strabo saw a Jewish residential district, not a pagan cemetery.[29] This may explain his silence concerning the eastern burial grounds and his comments on the great cemetery outside the city's western walls. Sections of the eastern walls probably still stood. Under Roman rule, Alexandria was growing, and to the east it was the Jewish population that was colonizing the area beyond the wall. The emperor Antoninus Pius formalized the new walls between 138 and 161 C.E., when he built the great Sun Gate as the city's main eastern entrance.

The Alabaster Tomb lies south of the Chatby necropolis and west of the Hadra cemetery. Its position is ambiguous, fertile ground for imaginative interpretations: was the tomb just inside or just outside Ptolemy's original city walls?

A line drawn south from Chatby cemetery runs straight through the Alabaster Tomb, suggesting that both lay outside the original city walls. The Alabaster Tomb could not belong to Alexander, though it would be in good company with other high-status sepulchres east of the city. If the Alabaster Tomb was somehow inside the walls, then it was only by a whisker. A location so close to the wall's interior could not be Alexander's centrally placed first tomb.

Philopater built the Soma enclosure around 215 B.C.E., when Alexandria was still inside its original perimeter walls. High-class residences with beautiful, expensive mosaics lay just inside the eastern walls.[30] The Soma enclosure was the collective burial ground for Alexander and the Ptolemies, and it could not have occupied the same area as the up-market villas. If the Albaster Tomb was just inside the walls, then it was unlikely to have been part of the Soma and could not belong to Alexander. Strabo stresses the opulence of the Palaces District—with its parks, gardens, statues, temples, and groves. It is difficult to see why the Soma would be built in an eastern suburb next to a boundary wall rather than in the center of all this luxury.

Outside or inside, the Alabaster Tomb hugged the eastern walls that Ptolemy built. Caracalla enclosed the royal palaces with his own ramparts—the area known as the Brucheum—as a defensive tactic. A glance at any map of ancient Alexandria shows how far out on a limb the Alabaster Tomb is in this respect. Caracalla worshiped Alexander as a hero and would not have left the Soma outside his new defenses, but it is difficult to imagine him extending them to encircle such an isolated spot.

The Alabaster Tomb is a stunningly beautiful enigma, with powerful arguments for its identification as one of Alexander's tombs matched by equally convincing arguments against it. With the North African sun glinting off its translucent alabaster, it is easily imagined as a grander mausoleum that once held the body of Alexander the Great. Yet the logic of history and archaeology makes for an awkward fit. What would either tomb of the city's founder be doing on the eastern boundary of Ptolemy's city, so far from the political and dynastic center of power? Strabo says the Soma lay within the Royal Palaces District and makes no reference to the eastern walls, suburbs, or Canopic Gate. If the tomb was there, he surely would have told us.

Alexander's replacement sarcophagus may lie somewhere beneath Adriani's reassembled splendor of the Alabaster Tomb. The problem of Alexandria's original eastern walls is critical; the written sources take us no further, and only archaeology can resolve the issue. The case for the

Alabaster Tomb remains seductive but unproven. Almost certainly it is neither of Alexander's tombs.

Tutankhamun's golden treasures made Howard Carter the most famous archaeologist in the world when he discovered them in 1922. Having survived the media-driven myth of King Tut's curse, Carter fell for the lure of Alexander's tomb. In 1936, while escorting the future King Farouk on a private tour of the Valley of the Kings, he let slip that he knew where Alexander was buried but would never breathe a word. He kept his word, dying three years later without saying anything to anyone.[31]

Carter was probably playing to the gallery with Farouk, and there is no evidence that he had the time or inclination to become seriously interested in searching for the Soma. Others, however, did, and often in bizarre fashion. During the mid–twentieth century the population of Alexandria was a vibrant cosmopolitan mix of Arabs and Europeans, a melting pot of languages and customs that retained its strategic importance during World War I and World War II because of its proximity to the Suez Canal. Its artistic and cultural life was dominated by the poet Constantine Cavafy, as well as the novelists E. M. Forster and Lawrence Durrell.[32] While these eminent writers mined the city's historical legacy and created Alexandria as the "city of memory," many ordinary citizens dreamed of finding Alexander's tomb.

Stelios Koumatsos, a Greek café waiter, was the most colorful among those who searched for Alexander's mausoleum. His job was a perfect foil for his fantasies—retailing gossip, overhearing rumors, and avidly examining items shown to him by customers. Koumatsos became entangled in a succession of extraordinary and often clandestine digs across the city. Every penny he earned he saved, pouring it into the ground in a curious reversal of what he hoped to achieve—the wealth of Alexander's Soma. Ignorant of Alexandria's archaeology or history, Koumatsos began his adventures in the mid-1950s, somehow managing to obtain official permission for several of his digs. Official records show that he applied 322 times for excavation reports and permissions to dig during more than thirty years of searching.[33]

Koumatsos, driven by some inner demon, was unable to restrict himself to officially sanctioned excavations. He dug secretly and at night in the courtyard of St. Saba monastery, uncovering old masonry and announcing to the press that he had finally discovered Alexander's lost tomb.[34] Some escapades were more embarrassing than worrying, as when he insisted on digging trenches in areas that had been underwater until the previous century.[35] Koumatsos's activities ended abruptly when the authorities denied him further permission to dig. Subsequently he perpetrated several hoaxes in a curious and desperate attempt to persuade them to reverse their decision.[36]

Koumatsos's notoriety was international. In June 1961, an unlikely summit took place between the extremes of fakery and respectability on matters of ancient Alexandria. In the faded splendor of the city's Athenaion patisserie, haunted by the ghosts of Cavafy and Durrell, Koumatsos sat down for tea with Professor Peter Fraser of Oxford University—the greatest living authority on Ptolemaic Alexandria.[37]

What brought Fraser face-to-face with a character who was his polar opposite was the opportunity to see what Koumatsos jealously guarded and portentously called the "Alexander Book." Its ancient pages contained irrefutable evidence supporting his various searches for the long-lost tomb. Fraser may have been expecting to examine the volume at leisure, but he was soon disappointed. Koumatsos allowed only the briefest of inspections, but it was enough. Fraser immediately saw that the Alexander Book was no proof at all, except perhaps of Koumatsos's gullibility. The Oxford don recalls, "To my astonished—almost incredulous—eyes there were presented page after page of crude and erroneous copies . . . [in addition to] . . . childishly drawn façades of Greek temples and tombs with meaningless inscriptions."[38]

The Greek inscriptions, he continues, were mixed with Coptic letters; badly executed sphinxes stood shoulder to shoulder with poorly drawn churches. When Koumatsos pointed out an inscription he thought was a hymn to Alexander, Fraser did not have "the heart to tell him the truth. . . . It is almost incredible that any person should be the victim of such delusions when the evidence to refute them lies before his eyes written in his own language, but such are the facts."[39]

The inscriptions, Fraser realized, were shoddy copies of genuine ones displayed in the Graeco–Roman Museum, which had been acquired from a dealer by Evaristo Breccia in 1912. The originals, and probably also the fakes, had come from the village of Abu el-Matamir in the western Nile Delta, and in Fraser's opinion both had been made by the dealer himself.[40] Koumatsos's holy grail was not the unique ancient document he believed but a fanciful mishmash of images artificially aged in an oven.

Koumatsos was not daunted and continued his quest for the Soma. As the years and the money disappeared, his hoaxes became increasingly desperate, as when he forged an ancient map whose occult symbols purported to show the exact location of the tomb. Eventually he fell back on a tried and tested formula—spying a glass coffin through a hole in the wall of a subterranean passage inscribed with Alexander's name.[41] The shades of Schilizzi and Ioannides nodded their approval from the other side.

Toward the end of his life, Koumatsos offered to exchange all his data with a patron for a pension and a Mercedes—a small deal for what would have been a gold mine if he had ever struck lucky.[42] This colorful character finally joined his ancestors in 1991. For better or worse, Koumatsos presumably has the answer in death that eluded him in life: chatting with Alexander about the tomb, joking with Achille Adriani, and looking forward to having the upper hand when Peter Fraser arrives.

Stelios Koumatsos was not alone in his exploits. During the 1960s and 1970s, the so-called fools of Alexander included office workers, laborers, a nurse, and many other ordinary citizens of Alexandria.[43] All display the easy logic of the nonexpert—a wistful confection of hope, desire, misguided intuition, and fantasy that draws inspiration from dreams, hunches, and unlikely kinds of proof.

One hopeful Alexandrian found the Soma, logically enough, beneath Sharia Iskender el-Akhbar (Alexander the Great Street), while another reported it lying alongside the tombs of Ptolemy and Nectanebo II in a part of the city that lay beneath the waters of the eastern harbor in Ptolemy's time.[44] Another claim surfaced when a man reported a cavity in his father-in-law's house leading to a marble-faced tunnel that was undeniably part of Alexander's tomb. The house, unfortunately, lay beyond the eastern walls of the Ptolemaic city.[45]

Alexander's tomb became a fetish during the twentieth century. Stimulated and provoked by rumors, hoaxes, and archaeological discoveries during the nineteenth century, Alexandria's inhabitants joined the free-for-all, hoping to find riches akin to those of Schliemann at Troy and Carter in the Valley of the Kings. Everyone had a theory and all knew where the tomb lay, but none could make that final step to discovery. It was time to look elsewhere.

POLITICS OF THE DEAD

ALEXANDER AND HIS COMPANIONS HAD TO RIDE their horses for more than a week to reach the Siwa oasis; today the journey is a jolting nine-hour bus ride from Alexandria. Alexander's route now travels past the bloody World War II battlefield of El Alamein, abandoned military outposts, and oil rigs toward the endless horizon. The visitor who arrives at nightfall can understand how Siwa's lushness attracted people from the earliest times. The stone tool traces of Paleolithic hunters and Neolithic farmers reveal how the palm groves, freshwater springs, and salt pan lakes must have been as attractive in prehistory as they are now.[1]

Siwa announced itself to the world around 500 B.C.E., as the site of an oracle to the Egyptian god Ammon, who soon forged links with the Greek Zeus. The oracle of Zeus Ammon at Siwa became one of the most famous in the ancient world, although confusingly (for us), sometimes the two deities were joined as one, at other times recognized as separate gods.[2] Alexander, prompted by Siwa's renown, remoteness, and sense of mystery, arrived in the spring of 331 B.C.E., adding the luster of his name to the oasis at the edge of the world.

Alexander's journey was difficult and ill-timed. Darius was massing a second grand army in Persia behind him. When Alexander and his entourage became lost and disoriented among the dunes, two talking serpents appeared and guided them to safety. The god Ammon was associated with snakes, probably accounting for this story. According to a variation, the expedition was saved by following two crows as they flew. Bird divination, in Siwa as in Babylon, was a favorite device for discerning the wishes of the gods. These supernatural signs show the real purpose of Alexander's visit to Siwa—to seek an encounter with the gods and tap into a powerful propaganda source.

In the Oracle Temple Alexander met alone with the high priest, who told him for the first time that he was not the earthly son of Philip but the divine offspring of Zeus Ammon. This dazzling and unprecedented revelation powerfully confirmed his unique status in a world where myth, religion, and politics exerted a persuasive force lost on the modern mind. Although the ancient writers tell different versions of what passed between Alexander and the priest, only the two men knew what was said. Alexander made great propaganda use of this confidentiality for the rest of his life.[3] As the stories grew in the telling, so did Alexander's desire to be buried with his true father, Ammon, among the date palms and freshwater springs of Siwa.

The stone-built Oracle Temple stands today amid the eroding ruins of the fortified mud-brick town of Aghurmi, which grew up around it during the thirteenth century C.E. and remained inhabited until the 1920s. The sun beats down fiercely, forcing the visitor to move into the shade of the medieval entrance. Ancient benches sculpted from mud evoke the long-departed elders who once passed the hours keeping an eye on all who came and went.[4]

The Oracle Temple dominates the citadel's raised interior, while all around anonymous structures crumble into dust. The temple's cladding of sun-baked mud buildings was removed during the 1970s, a clear indication of which of Siwa's many pasts was thought to be of greatest interest to tourists, the majority of whom were foreign and came to see the site of Alexander's visit. The temple is a curious hybrid—built by Pharaoh Amasis of the Twenty-Sixth Dynasty, then enlarged during Ptolemaic times to give the semblance of a Greek temple. Pausing on the threshold of the inner sanctuary, the visitor reflects on one of the few spots we are sure that Alexander also stood on.

From the highest point of the ruins the visitor sees a second Temple of Ammon, now called Umm 'Ubaydah. Only one solitary and scaffolded section still stands above the green mat of date palms. It was mentioned in the accounts of Alexander's visit, and surely he saw it in all its multicolored hieroglyphic splendor. It survived largely intact until an earthquake struck in 1811. A local official finished the demolition with gunpowder in 1897 to obtain building stone for his house.

In 1820, Heinrich von Minutoli, the German consul in Cairo, came to Siwa and sketched the temple before its demise. These now priceless drawings preserve a trace of the royal cartouche of its builder—the Thirtieth Dynasty pharaoh Nectanebo II.[5] Perhaps Alexander first encountered the dead pharaoh in Siwa, beginning the long and mysterious relationship which, with Ptolemy's intercession, lasted for two millennia. The intoxicating stories of Alexander's brush with immortality—whatever their political or psychological motivations—fueled a new theory: Alexander's tomb was not in Alexandria but at Siwa.

In 1989 Greek archaeologist Liana Souvaltzi was digging at Siwa and had an encounter that changed her life and caused an international sensation. Cassandra Vivian, an American author, visited Souvaltzi's excavations while researching a guidebook to the oases of Egypt's Western Desert.[6] Vivian recalls that Souvaltzi was digging a Doric-style temple in hopes of finding Alexander's remains among the debris. Souvaltzi explained to her, "The hypothesis is that Alexander is buried in Siwa, and the temple, being the only existing Greek structure, will offer clues to support the theory. To date no inscriptions or artifacts have been found."[7] A year later, Souvaltzi went public at an Egyptology conference in Turin, Italy, giving an intriguingly and provocatively titled lecture, "Discovering a Macedonian Tomb in Siwa Oasis."[8]

Souvaltzi was in fact excavating a temple at Bilad el-Rum (Town of the Romans), long recognized as a first-century C.E. Greco–Roman site.[9] The temple was still standing during the nineteenth century, when it was described and drawn by several European travelers, including Frederic Caillaud in 1819, Heinrich von Minutoli in 1820, and Gerhard Rohlfs in 1869, who commented on its unusual five-room plan.[10] In 1938 the Egyptian archaeologist Ahmed Fakhry probed the temple again, publishing his results and a sketch plan in 1944.[11] Souvaltzi's critics accused her of using Fakhry's information in her 2002 book *The Tomb of Alexander the Great at the Oasis of Siwa* without acknowledging it.

The Turin lecture was not well received, and in 1992 she went to the Greek and Egyptian press; once again her ideas made little impact. Three years later, Souvaltzi's claim to have discovered Alexander the

Great's tomb was splashed across the world's front pages. She insisted that the oasis of Zeus Ammon had been hiding Alexander's body for more than two thousand years. The ancient sources and all those searching in Alexandria, she said, were wrong. Alexander was in Siwa.

Unable to ignore the growing furor, the general secretary of the Egyptian Association of Antiquities led a group of experts to Siwa in January 1995, who confirmed her claims. Politicians followed their lead, and within a few weeks the Egyptian minister of culture was announcing the discovery to the world's press and media, who flocked to interview Souvaltzi. She announced, "We are sure. We have a unique monument. There is no such monument in all of Egypt, not even Greece. It is royalty, it is really Macedonian."[12]

As proof, Souvaltzi said she had discovered carved images of oak leaves worn in the crowns of Macedonian kings and an eight-pointed star—the symbol adopted by Alexander—carved on a piece of limestone.[13] This royal insignia, she added, survived in folklore as a decorative motif used in the traditional dress of Siwa women.[14]

The key to the identification, in Souvaltzi's mind, was three damaged limestone tablets inscribed in Greek and found buried by the tomb's entrance. Souvaltzi translated one as having been written by Alexander's general Ptolemy, recounting that Alexander had been poisoned and how he (Ptolemy) had brought the "light" (i.e., mummified) body to Siwa. The second tablet was dedicated by the Roman emperor Trajan, who, Souvaltzi believed, visited the sepulchre some four hundred years later, and the third was by an unknown individual.

In the rough and tumble of media questioning, Souvaltzi expressed surprise at discovering the tablets. She added a public relations flourish by saying that excavation had been halted for the holy Muslim month of Ramadan and then said, "Of course we'll find the body. In what condition we'll find the body after so many thousands of years, I cannot say."

Souvaltzi's investigations were far from complete, yet she was inspired by an almost messianic sense of certainty over what her team was about to discover. There were, she confidently asserted, two tombs some 165 feet apart—a large, ornate chamber meant to be a decoy and a smaller one that had two rooms and was built of large stones. She fleshed out her theory with implausible details, saying that when

Alexander was buried, Siwa had 400,000 inhabitants, compared with Alexandria's 300,000 around the same time and the modern village total of about 10,000. Imagination was swamping common sense as well as the logic of history and archaeology.

Ever mindful of supporting her ideas with photogenic and headline-grabbing objects, Souvaltzi produced an unusual item—a carved-stone head of a pharaoh whose appearance recalled Hellenistic or Roman facial characteristics rather than stylized Egyptian ones. Souvaltzi claimed to have found it in one of the sacred rooms of the tomb. After cleaning it, she recognized it as a stone representation of Alexander's mummified head, originally part of a statue to which offerings were made.[15]

International scholars responded swiftly to Souvaltzi's growing list of discoveries and her radical interpretations. Archaeologists were astonished by her bold claims, not least because this was the second time in five years that the same husband-and-wife team announced finding Alexander's tomb in the same location.[16] The Greek expert Olga Palagia took exception to Ptolemy's putative inscription, calling it a fraud. Greek delegates from the Ministry of Culture in Athens visited the site, examined a dedication inscribed on a building from Trajan's reign, and left unconvinced. Souvaltzi was dismissive, saying their visit had been brief and illegal.[17] The flurry of activity and acrimonious edge unsettled the Egyptian Supreme Council of Antiquities, which quickly convened a second press conference, distancing themselves from this embarrassing media circus.

Responding to criticism with increasingly lurid stories, Souvaltzi blurred serious archaeological arguments with images tailored for media exploitation. The *New York Times* reported that Souvaltzi was receiving mystical guidance from snakes in the area. She later claimed she had been misquoted and had really meant "saints."[18] Later, however, she described a miracle she experienced while walking in the desert, when "two of the most dangerous snakes in the area slithered between my feet."[19] The parallels and the symbolism were clear. Ammon was associated with serpents, as was Alexander's mother, Olympias; and Alexander had been guided to safety by two talking snakes, according to some.

Souvaltzi's credibility was crumbling. Her professionalism was questioned, and she was accused of obsessing over Alexander's tomb.[20] Her

excavations at Siwa were called lamentable, and Egypt's Supreme Council of Antiquities described them as the worst they had ever seen.[21] Even
worse, she was alleged to have misled the authorities and the media by
describing the well-known Doric temple as a newly discovered Macedonian tomb.[22]

Souvaltzi shocked her detractors again when she presented a mummified head to a Greek newspaper and identified it as one of the Macedonian warriors guarding Alexander's tomb. The grisly skull had a
Ptolemaic coin pressed into its mouth, and its henna-colored hair was
described as belonging to a blond Macedonian.[23]

Specialists exploded her story of the Greek inscriptions by showing that
the three tablets were a single dedication from Trajan's reign extolling the
emperor's good fortune. The translators did not confirm a single word of
Souvaltzi's readings. A smaller inscription, translated by Souvaltzi as Siwa
having a population of 110,000 soldiers of which 30,000 were an elite
tomb guard, was revealed as a date of the dedication.[24]

Because of the international scandal, Egyptian authorities refused to
renew Souvaltzi's work permit at the end of 1996. Her supporters
pointed the finger of suspicion at Costas Simitis, the Greek prime minister, whom they accused of intervening in the affair.[25]

Souvaltzi's discoveries unleashed a media feeding frenzy and bitter attacks by archaeologists eager to debunk her claims. But Alexander had
been used as a political tool from the moment he died. Souvaltzi was
convinced that she was the victim of an anti-Greek conspiracy by the
Greek government. On the Internet Greek politicians were accused of
undermining Greek Orthodox religion and Greek culture, language,
and values.[26] Paranoia gripped those who accused the "bureaucratic bottom feeders" and "clock watchers" in Greece's Central Archaeological
Council of simultaneously denying Souvaltzi's claims and attempting to
hijack the excavation for themselves.[27] Souvaltzi's supporters memo-
rably described one political figure as "that paradigm of political fart-
smellers and parasitical hangers-on."[28]

Souvaltzi was accused of harboring extreme nationalist political sym-
pathies in an article in the Cairo newspaper *Le progrès égyptien*. She was
alleged to believe the prophecy of Alexander's Greek seer, Aristander, that
whoever possessed the conquerer's body would rule over a prosperous

realm. This assertion had always been interpreted as Ptolemaic propaganda attempting to explain why Macedonia's fortunes declined after Alexander was buried in Egypt rather than Aegae.

But times were different now, and dangerous too. In the early 1990s, this politically charged outburst plugged into a Balkan imbroglio hurtling toward war and genocide. The breakup of Yugoslavia, the Bosnian conflict, and the emergence of the Former Yugoslav Republic of Macedonia (FYROM) as a sovereign nation culminated in Serbia's bloody invasion of Kosovo and defeat by NATO in 1999.

Souvaltzi was playing on an international stage. Her belief in Aristander's prophecy was interpreted as meaning that if a Greek possessed Alexander's body, then the Greek nation would gain control of the province of Macedonia where he was born. Souvaltzi's discovery at Siwa was widely believed to be a well-orchestrated political maneuver, implying that Greece would not have to share the name Macedonia with FYROM.[29] Souvaltzi was that Greek—Alexander's remains were almost within her grasp—and she had been thwarted by the Greek-hating politicians in Athens.

Wittingly or not, Souvaltzi had been drawn into a wider political conflict in which Greece's sovereignty and identity were at stake. She saw parallels between herself and Manolis Andronikos—the hero of Greek archaeology who excavated the royal Macedonian tombs at Vergina (Aegae) during the 1970s.[30] She quoted the answers that Andronikos gave to those who doubted his identification of the tomb of Philip, Alexander's father: the size of the tomb, the architectural sophistication, lion imagery (emblematic of Macedonian royalty), the rich finds within, and the royal Macedonian star. All of these features, Souvaltzi announced, were present also in her desert tomb.[31]

To her supporters, Liana Souvaltzi is the heroine who made the "greatest archaeological discovery in history" when she uncovered Alexander's tomb among the shifting sands of the Siwa oasis.[32] Denied the honor and status due to her, as well as banned from further digging, she is rumored to speak regularly with Alexander in dreams.

This extraordinary episode, with its arguments over Greek cultural identity, Alexander's Greekness, racist conspiracies, and the name "Macedonia," reveals that Alexander and his tomb remain a political and volatile subject after two millennia. To this day, access to the ruined Doric temple of Bilad el-Rum is restricted, the excavations stopped in their tracks by the Egyptian authorities.

In late afternoon, the fading light throws a luminous glow over dozens of stone blocks scattered in the sand. Some are fallen lintels covered with beautiful decorative friezes, and a few retain their white Roman paint. A cover is lifted, revealing a carved-stone sun disk flanked by two cobras—the symbol of Ammon. But nothing is standing, despite the fact that the Doric temple was intact when Rohlfs visited in 1869; fifty years before that, Caillaud described it as the most beautiful monument in the oasis.[33] The last rays of the sun pick out an incongruous wooden grill that blocks the small entrance to the flooded chamber where Souvaltzi is convinced Alexander awaits her.

The wind picks up at Bilad el-Rum. The local children crowd around the jeep, smiling and shouting "haylo" at the unexpected visitors. Beyond the village, rows of Roman tombs are carved high into the face of a vast wind-sculpted hill, bathed in orange light. All are empty now, their entrances in shadow, staring out over the oasis—confused by how the temple they knew for two thousand years has suddenly become a scandal-ridden tomb.[34]

This is a timeless place, where archaeology has become a battleground—a landscape of claim, counterclaim, and missing bodies. Here the past is inscribed in the present, its ever changing shape revealing more of the modern world than the ancient one. As if making the point, the children shout and follow; for an instant, they appear framed like a photograph in the rearview mirror and then—like Alexander—disappear.

The farcical Souvaltzi affair highlights deeper issues involving Macedonia and Alexander's role in the politics of modern Greece, Europe, and even the international Greek diaspora. Geography and history confront each other in the Balkans, as both Greece and FYROM lay claim to Alexander, his legacy, and the places and symbols of his reign.[35] Extreme FYROM nationalists have even identified themselves as the direct descendants of Alexander the Great.[36]

The royal Macedonian star is center stage in these bitter arguments. Unknown before Andronikos discovered it embossed on the golden larnax of Tomb II at Vergina, FYROM emblazoned it on its new flag and Greece adopted it as an official symbol. The royal emblem of the Argead dynasty was soon adorning T-shirts, key rings, postage stamps, and coins.[37]

Greeks believe that in modern times the name "Macedonia" has only geographical significance. There is no Macedonian ethnicity, and thus there can be no Macedonian nation-state. The ancestors of the Slavic people who live in FYROM only arrived in the region during the sixth and seventh centuries C.E. and consequently cannot claim any identity or continuity with Alexander's world of the third century B.C.E.[38] Greek newspapers began referring to the new state as the Republic of Skopje, while the international community preferred FYROM.[39]

Alexander's role in the modern world lies at the heart of this issue. Alexander—the Greek hero who spread Hellenism across the ancient world—is a role model, a national hero, and an inspiration for modern Greek politicians, soldiers, and civilians. Of all the Greek figures from classical antiquity, only Alexander survived in medieval Greek folk memory, becoming the rallying symbol in the run-up to the Greek war of independence (1821–1830).[40]

An alternative view points out that Alexander distrusted the Greeks as much as they detested him. These ancient attitudes were partly due to the difference between the Athenian devotion to democratic ideals and fear of tyranny, and the monarchical absolutism of Macedonian kingship.[41]

In fact Macedonian-born Alexander was a Hellenophile in a Mediterranean world that was largely Hellenic. In Alexander's time, as today, politics, identity, and self-interest were the prime motivators. Alexander fought against Greek cities, but the Greeks also fought among themselves, notably in the disastrous Peloponnesian War between Athens and Sparta. The Athenians, once rampant imperialists themselves, hated Macedonian imperialism. Whatever the Greeks and Alexander thought about each other, and whatever insults and barbs were thrown, it was Greek language and culture that Alexander spread across Asia, albeit in a monarchical format.

These issues cut to the heart of the modern quest for Alexander's tomb and possession of his memory. This is clearly illustrated in ancient burials of Alexander's age in Macedonia itself.

In 1977 Manolis Andronikos discovered the royal Macedonian tombs at Vergina in Macedonia. He singlehandedly revitalized Macedonia's archaeological heritage, converting the tombs into symbolic weapons for Greek national identity. Andronikos's discoveries reignited Greek politicians' interest in Alexander as they realized there was political capital to be made from the unexpectedly lavish tombs.[42] As gold, silver, and royal bones tumbled out of the Vergina tombs, Macedonia came into the public eye in Greece and across the world. Greek archaeology aimed to prove the ancient Hellenic origins of Greek national culture, as well as all of Western civilization.[43] As he did two thousand years before, when he conveyed the Athenian war dead home after Chaeronea, and later enraged the city's leaders by his claims to divinity, Alexander was once again reaching to the top of Greek politics in Athens.

Constantine Karamanlis, then Greek prime minister, supported the Vergina excavations, stating that Alexander symbolized national unity and continuity between the ancient and modern Greek worlds.[44] Alexander, Karamanlis said, represented all Greeks and spread Hellenism beyond the ancient Greek world. Politics penetrated archaeology with allegations that public pressure forced Andronikos to identify Tomb II with the formidable Philip II and not the weak-minded King Philip Arrhidaois.[45] The latter was an embarrassment and a useless symbol; Philip II was a great warrior king and father of Alexander the Great.

Andronikos understood how Tomb II could generate and focus Greek emotions on the subject of Greece's Macedonian heritage. In a 1988 interview, he expressed hope that Philip's skeleton would be displayed inside or in front of the tomb and become the object of "truly pious pilgrimage."[46]

Tying together the nationalist dimension of Greek Orthodox religion and archaeological sites by labeling visits as pilgrimages was an adroit move, reminiscent of Ptolemy's use of Alexander's mausoleum as a focus for cult activity. The previous year, Andronikos revealed that his discovery of Tomb II occurred on November 8, when the Greek Orthodox Church celebrates the archangels Michael and Gabriel—implying perhaps that the saints themselves guided his discovery.[47] The identities of the remains in Tomb II are sharply splintered bones of contention to this day.

Alexander's ghost was now hovering over modern Macedonia—transforming the search for his tomb into a quest for national identity, geographical integrity, political expediency, and cultural and religious purity. Ptolemy had wrestled with the same issues as he sought to create a political talisman out of Alexander that would establish his Greco–Macedonian–Egyptian kingdom in Alexandria.

Perhaps inevitably, Alexander's own tomb soon moved into the picture, and Macedonia became the latest location of the great conqueror's final resting place. The farthest thing from the minds of those who were arguing over the human remains in Tomb II was the thought that the body might be Alexander himself.

Triantafyllos Papazois is a retired major general of the Greek army. During the early 1990s he began reexamining the evidence of Tomb II. He came to the startling conclusion that neither Philip Arrhidaios nor Philip II was buried beneath Vergina's earthen tumulus, but rather Alexander and his wife Roxanne.[48]

Papazois reinterpreted known facts, spinning them in a distinctive way. In 274 B.C.E., Pyrrhus, the king of nearby Epirus, invaded Macedonia and defeated King Antigonus Gonatas. Pyrrhus's Gallic mercenaries ran riot, despoiling the royal tombs of Aegae (Vergina)—an act enshrined in the name he subsequently acquired, Pyrrhus the tomb robber.[49] Andronikos believed that Tombs II and III had escaped this vandalism, but Papazois was not convinced. He considered that when Antigonus Gonatas eventually regained the upper hand and threw Pyrrhus's forces back over the border, he reburied Alexander together with his queen and resealed the tomb, disguising the fact that it had been ransacked.[50]

Papazois's theory has a basis in scientific fact. Initially a team of British experts examined the bones from Tomb II and agreed with Andronikos that they belonged to Philip II. A later, more detailed forensic examination cast doubt on this view. The new study found no evidence of the extensive but healed battle wounds that Philip suffered earlier in life, and no trace either of the well-documented eye wound that the British team had identified.[51]

More convincing still, the bones were more or less complete. When a complete body is cremated (i.e., flesh and bones), the bones splinter. Only when a fleshless skeleton is cremated do bones remain intact. Alexander cremated Philip II according to traditional Macedonian rites, and Papazois concluded that these complete and unfractured remains could not possibly belong to Philip. But who did they belong to?

A likely candidate was Philip Arrhidaios, whom Olympias murdered and buried in 317 B.C.E. It was suggested that Cassander, Olympias's sworn enemy, dug up Arrhidaois's remains and gave them an honorable cremation within a year of the murder, when the flesh would have long since rotted away. The bone evidence, it was argued, fits Arrhidaios and his wife Eurydice, but not Philip II and his spouse Cleopatra.

Papazois accepted the science but interpreted it in a radically different way. Alexander, he says, was brought from Egypt and entombed in the main burial chamber at Vergina. The bones in the smaller antechamber belong to Roxanne, retrieved from the unknown grave near Amphipolis where she had been hidden by her murderer Cassander in 309.

Papazois rejected evidence from ancient sources saying that Alexander had been mummified, buried at Memphis-Saqqara, and then moved by Ptolemy to Alexandria. Ingeniously, Papazois suggested that Ptolemy cremated Alexander at Memphis, and wily Egyptian embalmers fashioned a lifelike effigy that was later transported to Alexandria. Alexander's remains were secretly brought back to Macedonia, and an uncanny facsimile was put on show in the Soma that fooled everyone, including the Roman emperors who came to visit.[52]

Even the weapons found in Tomb II, Papazois says, support this theory. Andronikos believed they were Philip's weapons, but their style in fact belongs to Alexander's reign.[53] Papazois believes they were taken from Alexander's tomb at Memphis along with his remains and brought to Vergina. It is possible that the shield, helmet, and iron breastplate (cuirass) were Alexander's, but if so they are more likely to have been royal heirlooms placed there at a later date.[54] The breastplate is similar, some say identical, to the one Alexander wears in the so-called Alexander mosaic discovered in Pompeii in 1831.[55] The idea that Alexander himself lies in Tomb II is unproven, though the tomb was probably accessible until the great earthen tumulus was heaped up over it around 310 B.C.E.[56]

Papazois's theory is inventive but implausible. It is better understood in light of arguments concerning the use of the name "Macedonia." As a senior Greek soldier born in Greek Macedonia, Papazois spoke out at the height of the Macedonia affair with FYROM. What more powerful way to excite and rally support for Greek claims to the name and royal star of Macedonia than to identify at Vergina the remains of Alexander the Great inside the very larnax that publicized the star for the first time in two thousand years?

Alexander's tomb became a political football in the closing decade of the twentieth century. It rapidly regained its place as a powerful idea, recalling its origin with Ptolemy and subsequently Philopater. Claiming Alexander was a political act burnished with an ideological luster, a touchstone of legitimacy for all who sought to possess it.

Alexander's tomb was never a single idea or a discrete historical place. Its elusiveness preyed on the imagination of those caught in the web of fascination and power it projected. Released from the chains that bound him briefly to Siwa and Vergina, Alexander was again on the move as the new century beckoned.

THE ETERNAL QUEST

EACH NEW REVELATION CONCERNING THE SOMA'S whereabouts is driven by an idea or an obsession—a longing to connect with one of history's most illustrious figures. But Alexander's elusive spirit stays just out of reach, and his tomb just one step ahead of those who seek it. In 2002, after two thousand years, a group of Greek Americans sought to have a huge head of Alexander carved into Mount Kerdylia in Macedonia. Resurrecting Stasikrates's original conceit, Alexander would tower 230 feet over the landscape, gazing out across the Aegean Sea.[1] This was a headline-grabbing move in light of the bitter dispute with FYROM, but times had already changed.

Greek archaeologists called it a monstrous proposal, pointing out that the carving would threaten an ancient theater and a Byzantine church. Supporters countered with the undeniable truth that it would boost the local tourist economy. The whole idea, so preposterous to many, sounded like something from the pages of *The Alexander Romance*. And in the same year Alexander threatened to reappear larger than life, a long-forgotten tomb made a new bid for fame.

The Egyptian pharaoh Nectanebo II died around 342 B.C.E. His tomb was carried to England in 1802 in the mistaken belief that it had once contained Alexander. Its true owner was finally identified when Champollion deciphered Egyptian hieroglyphs, but Nectanebo's beautiful green sarcophagus went on to have an afterlife of its own.

In 2002, Andrew Chugg, an English aerospace expert, resurrected the idea that Alexander had indeed been interred in the pharaoh's sarcophagus.[2] The argument was based on old ideas suggesting that in the rush to bury Alexander, Ptolemy had placed the royal mummy in the empty sarcophagus made for, but never occupied by, Nectanebo II. This event, it was said, may have inspired the confused legend enshrined in *The Alexander Romance* that Nectanebo II was Alexander's real father, making Alexander the legitimate pharaoh of Egypt.[3]

Chugg's enthusiasm breathed new life into old ideas. Once again, the scattered, ambiguous evidence from the ancient writers Pausanius, Curtius, Strabo, and Diodorus was combed for clues and reinforced by the findings of Auguste Mariette at Memphis-Saqqara. Alexander, it was suggested, had lain in Nectanebo II's stone casket in a small room of the temple adjacent to the entrance of the Serapeum, virtually alongside the Greek statues of the Philosophers Circle.[4] When Ptolemy's son and heir Philadelphus moved the body to Alexandria, he took the sarcophagus along.

The theory is as intriguing today as it was fifty years ago, but not watertight. No one knows where Nectanebo II's father—Pharaoh Nectanebo I—is buried, though it may be near the Serapeum at Saqqara. Fragments from his gray stone sarcophagus have been found in Cairo, and a *ushabti* funerary figurine was discovered in Memphis.[5] Nectanebo I was devoted to the Osirapis cult, and he built or greatly extended the Serapeum temple.[6]

If the sands of Saqqara are hiding Nectanebo I's remains, then his son may not be far away, though tradition says he fled south to Ethiopia when the Persians invaded in 343 B.C.E. and abandoned his magnificent sarcophagus.[7] Ptolemy had the perfect location for Alexander's hurried burial if this was the case—an empty mausoleum and a vacant sarcophagus near the tomb of Nectanebo I, within the sacred precincts of Saqqara.

Reviving the fortunes of Nectanebo II's sarcophagus turns partly on whether or not the pharoah ever returned to Memphis, alive or dead. Nectanebo II's one-way flight to the southern marches of Egypt is often asserted, but the archaeology is ambiguous. Does an *ushabti* figure of Nectanebo II found at Memphis suggest that although he died in Upper

Egypt his body may have returned to Memphis and been buried at Saqqara?[8] *Ushabtis* are miniature figures in the shape of a mummy that accompanied the dead pharaoh to the afterworld, doing menial work on his behalf. However, they are made before as well as immediately after death, and consequently the discovery of one of Nectanebo II's post-mortem helpers does not necessarily indicate a burial and a body.

The possibility that Ptolemy reused Nectanebo II's sarcophagus to bury Alexander is attractive but can never be proved. It is, however, only one of several possibilities; changing the perspective reveals a different explanation.

The Roman author Pliny provides a glimpse into the sumptuous (some would say effete and incestuous) royal court at Alexandria in the years after Ptolemy's death. Pliny says that Philadelphus brought an obelisk of Nectanebo II from Heliopolis to Alexandria, reerecting it in the temple dedicated to his sister-wife—the Arsinoeion, which also housed her iron statue, floating in midair through the artful use of magnets. Recycling old monuments was a habit of the Ptolemies, who used the abandoned site of Heliopolis as a quarry, removing its statues, obelisks, and sphinxes to adorn Alexandria's streets and temples. Pliny's observation prompts the question, How did Philadelphus and his successors see their relationship with Nectanebo II, and how many of his monuments did they move?[9]

After Vivant Denon ordered the sarcophagus removed from the Attarine Mosque and after its true identity was discovered, it was assumed that Nectanebo II's stone casket was taken from Memphis to Alexandria. In fact, the home of the Thirtieth Dynasty pharaohs to which Nectanebo's royal family belonged was not Memphis or Thebes, but Sebennytos in the Nile Delta.[10] Sebennytos enjoyed a special relationship with Memphis because of this royal connection.

Traces of this relationship survive engraved and painted on ostraca—fragments of pottery or limestone—that tell of a priest named Hor who came from Sebennytos to work at the Serapeum temple at Saqqara, and another, named Teos, who had two jobs, working as an army scribe at Sebennytos and a priest in Memphis.[11] Perhaps most significantly, the Egyptian high priest Manetho, whose advice to Ptolemy on Egyptian history and religion helped fashion legendary connections between Nectanebo II and Alexander, was also a native of Sebennytos. Perhaps Nectanebo II was planning to be entombed in his ancestral city rather than Memphis, and perhaps it was at Sebennytos rather than Memphis that Ptolemy or Philadelphus discovered the sarcophagus and took it to Alexandria.

Archaeological evidence does not contradict this possibility. Just north of Sebennytos, at Behbeit el-Hagar, Nectanebo II began building a new temple to Isis and Osiris, the so-called Iseum. This was one of six large construction projects, one of which may have been intended as a royal mausoleum. The Persian invasion of 343 B.C.E. halted building work, but it was completed by Philadelphus decades later.[12] Royal cartouches engraved into its gray granite blocks record the names of Nectanebo II, who began the building, and Philadelphus, who completed it.[13]

At Sebennytos, stone blocks proclaim the relationship between Nectanebo II and the Ptolemies in cartouches carved with the names of the pharaoh, the two kings Philip Arrhidaios and the young Alexander IV, Philadelphus, and Ptolemy XI.[14] This royal connection spans several hundred years, suggesting that the Sebennytos temple begun by Nectanebo II was restarted during the reign of the twin kings and completed, perhaps extended, during the reigns of the later Ptolemies.[15]

The Ptolemies patronized Nectanebo's home city. Their willingness to build demonstrated the important role Egypt's last native pharaoh played in the legitimization of Greco–Macedonian rule. Bringing Nectanebo's monuments to Alexandria was part of the glorification of this royal relationship, and transferring the sarcophagus would have been a stunning propaganda coup.

Egyptian sarcophagi were crafted at the site of an intended burial. Thus Nectanebo II's empty tomb may have been decorated and inscribed at Sebennytos and later moved to Alexandria. While it is impossible to know for sure where the sarcophagus was before it was taken to Alexandria, it seems equally likely that it was Sebennytos as Memphis-Saqqara. The possibility that the empty sarcophagus was never at Saqqara undermines the idea that Alexander's body ever lay inside it.

Philadelphus obsessively displayed his connections with Nectanebo II, whether at Alexandria, Sebennytos, or Memphis-Saqqara.[16] Eager to prove a dynastic kinship with an Alexander he never knew, Philadelphus manipulated the monuments and cultic rites associated with Alexander. Philadelphus deified his father in the temples of the dead at Saqqara, including in the small temple built by Nectanebo II adjacent to the Serapeum.[17] His close relationship with the Egyptian priesthood and his fictional links to Nectanebo II may have inspired Philadelphus to bring the sarcophagus to Alexandria during the great Ptolemaia festival of 275–274 B.C.E.

The Ptolemies overemphasized their associations with Nectanebo II, decorating Alexandria with recycled monuments from the pharaoh's reign. Philopater, who built the Soma enclosure in around 215 B.C.E., may have had a particular interest in Nectanebo II's sarcophagus suggesting a dramatic new interpretation of how the stone coffin was used.

A long overlooked clue to Philopater's concern with the sarcophagus is revealed by the strange shape of the holes drilled around its base, which have been ignored or viewed as drainage holes from the much later Arab reuse of the tomb as a bath for Islamic purification in the Attarine Mosque.

Islam did not have a monopoly on ritual cleanliness, which played an important role also in Hellenistic/Ptolemaic, Roman, and Byzantine Christian rituals. Holy water was a feature of all the religions that shaped Alexandria's history. No evidence supports the traditional assumption that Alexandria's Muslims invested the time and effort necessary to drill twelve small holes through seven tons of breccia when two or three larger ones would have sufficed to drain away polluted water.

European travelers of the sixteenth and seventeenth centuries saw Muslims revering the sarcophagus but never mentioned its use in ritual ablutions. The Muslim traveler Evilya Çelebi infers as much but does not say he saw such use or that Muslims made the holes.[18] By the 1500s, Muslims from all over the Islamic world were venerating the sarcophagus as belonging to the Qur'anic prophet Zulqarnein (Alexander), and it seems unlikely they would pollute such a sacred object by washing in it or deface it by boring holes through its sides. If Muslims did not drill the holes, who did?

Beneath the streets of modern Alexandria lies an extraordinary world of subterranean tombs from Ptolemaic and Roman times. Many Ptolemaic sepulchres were supplied with flowing water that played an important role in funerary rites.[19] For the city's Greco–Macedonian inhabitants, as elsewhere in the Hellenistic world, contact with the dead polluted the living, and ritual washing was an integral part of removing contamination caused by handling the dead or being in proximity to them. Across Alexandria— from the tombs of Gabbari on the western outskirts, to Anfushy in the north and Mustapha Pasha in the east, are the remains of ancient cisterns that once supplied water for these ritual ablutions.[20]

The sight and sound of running water evokes a world of sensuality, combining cleanliness and purity in relationships that the living once enjoyed with the dead. Nowhere is this more evident than at Tomb I at Mustapha Pasha, whose elaborate hydraulics siphoned off water from one basin to another like a fountain, suggesting it was as much for display as for hygienic and ritual purposes.[21] What was true for Mustapha Pasha must have been far more pronounced at the royal sepulchres within the Soma enclosure, and especially for Alexander's heavily visited mausoleum that dominated it.

A closer look at Nectanebo II's sarcophagus in the British Museum reveals how it may have been part of the Ptolemaic concern with water displays and rituals. From the outside, the so-called drainage holes are evenly spaced, and of uniform width and depth. They were evidently drilled with precision, presenting an attractive face to the onlooker. Each long side has four identical holes, the outward-curving front has three, and the rear end has one. Strangely, these well-rounded holes only penetrate two-thirds of the way through the sarcophagus wall. Peering inside the sarcophagus reveals the holes to be roughly made pinpricks by comparison.[22]

At least eleven of the twelve holes were made at the same time; the design makes little sense if only for drainage. The idea that these holes were quickly punctured through by Arab workmen begins to lose its force, and an extraordinary alternative explanation emerges.

The carefully carved outer holes, standard in width and spacing, were drilled only partway through, concealing the point at which the inside holes connected with them. If the large exterior holes were drilled all the way through, the water would gush out, emptying the sarcophagus almost as rapidly as it could be filled. If the holes on the inside were small, the sarcophagus would take much longer to empty. Interestingly, the internal water pressure would force the water out through the small interior holes to emerge in the middle of the wider outer holes—producing an attractive spouting flow, akin to a water fountain. It could easily be regulated by closing off the miniature holes from the inside.[23]

Philopater, when building the Soma enclosure, could have brought Nectanebo II's sarcophagus to Alexandria to adorn his funerary park with a dazzling water display—part of the elaborate decoration of the Soma adorned with sacred groves, marble statues, fountains, and recycled pharaonic monuments. Perhaps it was associated with Alexander's tomb itself. This seductive image is in keeping with the extravagance of Ptolemaic Alexandria, the symbolic emphasis placed on water in structures known as nymphaeums, and the sumptuousness of the Palaces District where the Soma was located.

A poem in praise of the Ptolemies written on papyrus lends fascinating support to this view. It belongs to the late third century B.C.E., when Philopater was building the new urban cemetery. It describes a water fountain (nymphaeum) dedicated to Philopater's wife, Queen Arsinoe III, with Ionic columns, marble fittings, and carved reliefs of water nymphs in the middle of which is Arsinoe herself, all resting on a glistening base of speckled granite.[24]

This unusual edifice blends the marble and limestone favored by the Greeks with the native Egyptian preference for granite and diorite. This fusion of styles began during Philopater's reign, reflecting his passion for hybrid design. An unknown member of Philopater's court dedicated the Arsinoe fountain in honor of the royal family—a modest example of grander dedications that Strabo says filled the Palaces District.[25]

Philopater, surrounded by fountains and recycled pharaonic monuments, may have decided to convert the empty sarcophagus of his official ancestor into a grand nymphaeum. Sacred water spouting from the sparkling green tomb of a deified predecessor adjacent to statues of Alexander and the Ptolemies has an undeniable power. Erected in the Soma enclosure, where ancestor worship and legitimacy were publicly displayed to greatest effect, the sarcophagus fountain would have been a stunning visual metaphor, playing equally to the religious and political sensibilities of the Greco–Macedonian court and the powerful Egyptian priesthood.

This interpretation is unprovable conjecture but appears more likely than the sarcophagus being a recycled tomb for Alexander. The royal associations (hieroglyphs were still understood at the time) with the sarcophagus suggest that only a Ptolemy could authorize moving and remodeling such an important object. It could have been placed anywhere in Alexandria to beautify the city, but as the tomb of Alexander's legendary Egyptian father, it was more likely placed in the Soma enclosure.

During later Arab times, Muslim authorities in the Attarine Mosque might simply have been taking advantage of a ready-made cleansing bath, perhaps found in the debris of the unrecognized Soma. By this time, hieroglyphs were a dead and silent script, and the sarcophagus an anonymous object. Does the British Museum possess the only surviving object from the Soma?

Alexander spent most of his life on the move, and death did not end his wandering. His identity changed dramatically over two thousand years, not least as a religious icon. In life he was a royal hero in the Homeric tradition and may have seen himself as divine. Later, Alexander became the ultimate pagan in the eyes of zealous Christians, and later still he was the two-horned Muslim prophet Zulqarnein. Most recently he has morphed from John Chrysostom's "devil" to a famous Christian saint.

If Alexander was not smuggled away by devout pagans or pocketed in pieces by souvenir hunters when the Soma was pillaged around 391, then what became of him? In 2004 Andrew Chugg announced that Alexander's body lay beneath the high altar in St. Mark's Basilica in Venice and had been there for almost twelve hundred years.[26]

This ingenious theory was inspired by —a fourth-century account of the martyrdom of the saint in Alexandria during the first century after Christ. According to the story, pagans tried but failed to burn the murdered saint's body. Local Christians spirited it away, burying it in a church in the eastern part of the city. In 828 two Venetian merchants, Buono of Malamocco and Rustico of Torcello, stole the body and took it to Venice. A grand basilica was erected to house the holy relic, and the story of the abduction was depicted in a beautiful mosaic.

Chugg grafted an imaginative sequence of conjectures onto these historical facts. Assuming that St. Mark's tomb and Alexander's ruined

mausoleum lay near each other and close to the ancient central crossroads of Alexandria, Chugg suggests a daring body snatch took place
during the Christian riots of 391. An unknown church official, concerned for the safety of Alexander's body, moved it from the ruined
Soma to the saint's conveniently empty tomb nearby. When Buono and
Rustico stole the body, they unwittingly acquired Alexander's remains,
not St. Mark's.[27]

The prospect of finding Alexander in Venice is too seductive to ignore but is built on the shifting sands of ambiguous evidence and wishful thinking. Strabo, our most reliable eyewitness, infers that while the
Palaces District may have extended to the crossroads, the Soma was
likely close to the inner palaces in the northeastern part of the city.
There is no convincing argument why the Soma enclosure, and Alexander's mausoleum within it, would be at the southern boundary of the
Palaces District, so far away from the royal palaces.

The Roman period St. Mark church was damaged and rebuilt several
times and its exact location is unknown. Alculfus, a Christian pilgrim visiting Alexandria between 670 and 680, saw St. Mark's, which contained
the martyr's bones, just inside the eastern city walls. Two centuries later, in
870, another Christian visitor named Bernard the Wise commented that
St. Mark's monastery and church lay outside the eastern walls.

This discrepancy between two eyewitnesses is easily explained. Alculfus visited within a few decades of the Muslim takeover of Alexandria in
642, at which time the eastern boundary walls enclosed the larger late
Roman–Byzantine city. By 870, when Bernard arrived, Alexandria had
shrunk behind the walls built by Sultan Ahmed ibn Tulun, leaving
St. Mark's Church stranded beyond the new perimeter. The Venetian
theft of 828 took place at the church that Alculfus saw, located just inside the Roman–Byzantine walls farther east and nowhere near the area
of the crossroads.

The early European maps, based on hearsay and not firsthand observation, are beautiful but misleading. By the fifteenth century, Alexandria
had long been the small town nestling inside the Tulunnid walls. Yet,
while Ugo Comminelli's 1472 map correctly shows St. Mark's Church
outside the Arab walls, Braun and Hogenberg's 1573 map locates it
inside their highly inaccurate wall line.[28] The location of Alexander's

mausoleum and St. Mark's sepulchre is unknown, and their association with the crossroads speculative and unproven. Whoever Buono and Rustico snatched in 828 for the greater glory of the Serene Republic of Venice, it was not Alexander.

The final flourish of the new theory concerns the discovery of a funerary monument beneath the main apse of St. Mark's basilica in Venice.[29] Carved on a large stone slab is what appears to be a shield decorated with the royal star of Vergina.[30] While not a perfect likeness, it is an intriguing, if ultimately unconvincing, coincidence. A simple archaeological truth sinks the theory.

Manolis Andronikos was astonished when he saw the glittering golden larnax inside Tomb II at Vergina in 1977. He was the first person to see the royal star probably since early Roman times. It is unlikely that the unknown Christian official who decided to save Alexander's body would have recognized (or cared about) the star's significance or arranged for it to accompany Alexander's body to its new home in St. Mark's Church. Even more unlikely is that the two Italian body snatchers of 828 would have understood the symbol's importance and then laboriously smuggled it aboard their ship alongside the reeking mummy.

The royal Macedonian star became redundant when the Romans defeated Perseus, the last Macedonian king, in 168 B.C.E. In Alexandria, any royal aura the symbol retained was lost when Octavian conquered the city for Rome in 30 B.C.E., and Cleopatra's suicide ended the Ptolemaic line. By 828, no one had seen or understood the star's significance for almost a thousand years.

The fascination that Alexander's tomb excites is tenacious. The logic of history and archaeology cannot weaken its grip on the imagination. If Alexander is impersonating St. Mark in Venice, it would be a remarkable transformation and an astonishing coincidence—the tallest of tall stories to add to the roll call of mysteries and enigmas surrounding the Soma.

AFTERLIFE

THE WORLD IS FILLED WITH THE DEAD. They follow us everywhere, constant companions in the slipstream of life. We sense them in places where they may linger on the threshold between our world and theirs. And so it is with Alexander. Historians, archaeologists, politicians and generals, hoaxers and dreamers have sought to understand the man and the legend, to find proof of mortality in the tomb that once existed.

Alexander's tomb may yet be found beneath Alexandria's urban sprawl, though not in the vaults of the Nabi Daniel Mosque or adjacent to the Alabaster Tomb. It lies west, not east, of Ptolemy's original eastern boundary wall, and nowhere near the center of the larger and later Roman city.

The Soma lies deep beneath Alexandria's streets, just south of the old Lochias peninsula, today's much smaller Silsileh promontory. This is the edge of the old inner palaces in the modern district known as Mazarita, bounded by Sharia Iskender el-Akhbar (Alexander the Great Street) and Sharia Sultan Abdul Aziz (Sultan Abdul Aziz Street)—just a few minutes' walk from the sea. Many maps have conjured up the ancient city, but only the German scholar Günter Grimm locates the tomb here, and he is probably right.[1]

Fired by antipagan rage, rioting Christians of 391 may have burned the pagan mummy. Although we can trace in detail the desecration of the Serapeum and its idols, there is not even a whisper about the Soma or its famous occupant. Given the reverence that Alexander inspired in Christians who wore his amuletic image, utter destruction of his remains is not the only fate that could have befallen them. And if the

body had been destroyed, we would expect to hear how Christ conquered the ultimate pagan. The silence is more in keeping with Alexander's body being hidden or perhaps carved into talismanic souvenirs for
pagans and Christians alike.

If the mummy was removed intact, where would it have been taken?
Pockets of paganism survived the tumultuous fourth century. Pagans
were caught and executed across the eastern Mediterranean for centuries
after Theodosius I's imperial edict ordering all temples closed in 392;
the last Egyptian temple of Isis at Philae shut it doors permanently only
in 537. Paganism survived in its influence on ordinary Egyptians who
became Coptic Christians, particularly in their saint cults, amulets,
dreams, oracles, and magical papyri. (Alexander himself survived on
Coptic religious tapestries.) It all became part of the new spiritual age.[2]
Is it possible that Alexander's mummy was spirited away to some remote
place in this new world of rituals and beliefs?

Perhaps it was taken back to Memphis, hidden in its original Saqqara
tomb and forgotten. Maybe it was disguised as a Christian saint and
buried in one of the remote religious communities springing up across
Egypt. Maybe it was returned to the Siwa oasis, where it lies in the arms
of Zeus Ammon, untroubled by Liana Souvaltzi? Perhaps it made the
short canal journey to Canopus near Alexandria, where pagan rites and
Christian–pagan practices lingered until the Arab conquest in 642.

No evidence supports these suggestions. When talk turns to Alexander's tomb, though, hope and speculation are always rife, especially if
something is discovered that seems to fit the requirements. The Bahariya
oasis, halfway between Memphis and Siwa, is such a place.

Alexander's journey to Siwa in 331 B.C.E. is shrouded in mystery.
Alexander's purpose, and what he was told by the priests of Zeus Ammon, is unknown apart from rumor. Even his route is disputed; perhaps
he returned via Alexandria, or maybe his trip back took him straight to
Memphis across the desert, stopping briefly at the oasis at Bahariya. His
coming this way would explain a dramatic discovery.

In 1938 the Egyptian archaeologist Ahmed Fakhry stumbled across a
temple of Alexander the Great at Bahariya. Fakhry uncovered a red
granite altar inscribed with Alexander's name at the temple entrance
and, on an outside wall, a royal cartouche (now worn away) engraved

with Alexander's hieroglyphic name. When he went inside the temple's inner sanctuary, Fakhry found images of Alexander and the town's governor offering incense to Ammon and his wife—the goddess Mut. Fakhry calculated that the temple was built in Alexander's lifetime, and so these images may record historical fact or may be simply an artistic flourish.

Fakhry's excavations revealed why the Bahariya oasis would have been an ideal place for pagans or even Alexander-friendly Christians to hide the royal mummy. The oasis (and most likely Alexander's temple) flourished during Ptolemaic, Roman, and Byzantine times, perhaps up to the twelfth century C.E. Greek, late Roman, and Coptic Christian remains have been found in and around the temple. Pottery, lamps, amulets, and coins all attest to a thriving settlement in the fifth and sixth centuries after Christ.

In this remote place, far from prying eyes, pagans became Christians in the shadow of Alexander's temple. They surely mixed together the two religions as others were doing across the late Roman–Byzantine empire. Unlike many other desert settlements, Bahariya has no church. Perhaps Alexander's temple served this purpose, seamlessly linking the transition from pagan to Christian beliefs—a unique place of worship for those caught between two worlds. All that was missing from the desert village Fakhry investigated was a cemetery—somewhere perhaps to hide Alexander's remains.

In 1996 a drama unfolded when a cemetery appeared from the desert sands. A donkey fell into a hole and made the most extraordinary discovery since Howard Carter entered Tutankhamun's tomb in 1922. The Valley of the Golden Mummies, as the discovery became known, was excavated by Zahi Hawass, the general secretary of the Supreme Council of Antiquities. He estimates that perhaps ten thousand bodies from the Greco–Roman period lie buried beneath two and a half square miles of Bahariya's sand and soil.[3]

The gilded mummies lie only half a mile from Alexander's temple, convincing Hawass that the burials began here so the dead could lie near Alexander. A similar motive may explain the Ptolemaic burials near the Philosophers Circle at Memphis-Saqqara, in the area suspected of housing Alexander's first tomb. Hawass's digging at the Bahariya cemetery recovered a wealth of items, from Ptolemaic pottery to amulets and coins, one belonging to Cleopatra VII.

No trace of Alexander has been found in Bahariya's subterranean world of the dead. Yet it is precisely the kind of place that fourth-century devotees might have taken the mummy. Archaeologists have only scratched the surface of this vast cemetery: what better place to hide one royal mummy than among ten thousand others?

Where do we look and how do we recognize what we see? These are the timeless dilemmas for those who seek Alexander's Soma. However romantic or "connected" we feel as we gaze on the Alabaster Tomb, Nectanebo's sarcophagus, or the windblown sands of Saqqara or Siwa, we perceive only ghosts raised by the books we read or the stories we hear. Memory and imagination are equal partners in the conspiracy to recapture what is forever lost.

Museums guide us, striving to reassemble the past, stimulate our senses, and engage us with objects pulled from the earth. Archaeologists know there is no single unimpeachable past. There are only imagined pasts, written in the present and rewritten in the future.

Knowing this, our ability to make pictures move connects us to a living and breathing world of Alexander and his times. Cinemas, like tombs, are dark theaters of the imagination, where fantasy and spectacle conjure spectral figures on a gigantic scale. We can never know what Alexander or Ptolemy might think about Hollywood's attempts to portray them. But from the corner of half-closed eyes we sense something ineffable—a brush with time, a touch from the past. Horses against elephants, murder and succession, alien moralities, inconceivable wealth, unbounded power, excruciating deaths, and the sheer luck of surviving in such a violent and uncompromising world. Searchers for the tomb dream of time travel, but the world they would find would shock them.

Whether Alexander's tomb lies beneath desert sands or Alexandria's bustling streets, it will hold no dazzling treasures. Unlike the sealed chamber of Tutankhamun, there will be no masterpieces of ancient art, no golden hoards of immeasurable wealth. The ravages and ruptures of time, human greed, and changing faiths have long since stripped it bare. The richest treasures are those we create in our minds, where they endure untarnished and immutable. Once reduced to physical form, Alexander's old bones would lose their grip on our imagination, though we may gaze in wonder at their survival.

As long as Alexander exists somewhere within the physical world but beyond our grasp, he remains a timeless symbol, constantly recast as hero or villain for an ever changing present. As long as his sepulchre lies undiscovered (or unrecognized), Alexander is guaranteed eternal life. Like Jason's golden fleece, the Soma is a grail—a unique expression of immortality standing against the transience of life. More than a place, Alexander's tomb is an enduring and priceless idea, and we, like the ghosts of the future that we are, scan every horizon hoping to glimpse his return. In death as in life, Alexander defines the restlessness of the human spirit.

The Greeks have a saying, a two-thousand-year-old question: "Does Alexander live?" they ask, to which the reply is, "He lives and rules and governs the world." An alternative response captures a deeper philosophy: "He lives and rules and may you also have life."[4]

At the heart of the quest are two other questions. Can we afford the sense of disappointment and loss that discovering the tomb might bring? Do we really want to discover the mortal remains of history's most immortal son?

DRAMATIS PERSONAE

Abdalonymus An obscure member of the royal family of Phoenicia (Lebanon) until Alexander appointed him to the throne of Sidon in 332 B.C.E. Commonly identified as the occupant of the magnificent Alexander Sarcophagus discovered near Sidon in 1887 by Osman Hamdi Bey.

Achille Adriani Italian archaeologist who became the third director of Alexandria's Graeco-Roman Museum, succeeding Evaristo Breccia in 1932. Adriani excavated beneath the Nabi Daniel Mosque but became convinced it was not Alexander's tomb. During the 1930s, he reassembled the giant slabs found by Breccia, creating the Alabaster Tomb seen today. Professionally cautious in identifying the tomb with Alexander, his increasingly optimistic views were published posthumously in 2000 as *La Tomba di Alessandro* by his student Nicola Bonacasa.

Achilles Tatius Greek novelist probably of the third century C.E., said to be a native of Alexandria. His famous novel *Leucippe and Cleitophon* supposedly uses Tatius's eyewitness account of a walk through Alexandria, observing the walled enclosure of Alexander's second tomb, the Soma. In fact, Tatius doesn't mention the Soma by name, and it may be that this description arises from secondhand accounts, not firsthand acquaintance.

Ahura Mazda "Wise Lord" of the Zoroastrian religion of the Persian empire. Zoroaster (Zarathustra) was his prophet, and taught that there was always a battle between the forces of morality and immorality, and that believers should practice good thoughts, good words, and good deeds. As a single deity, Ahura Mazda and Zoroastrianism may have influenced other monotheistic religions such as Judaism and Christianity. Fire temples were an important feature of religious rituals, as the light of fire was the light of god. The link between Persian kings and Ahura Mazda is made explicit in the inscriptions at Behiston that Alexander saw in 324 B.C.E. Today Zoroastrians are called Parsis (Parsees).

Alexander III of Macedon (Alexander the Great) Born in July 356 B.C.E. to King Philip II and Queen Olympias at Pella. He was tutored by Aristotle in his youth, and became king on the assassination of his father, Philip II, in 336. He left Macedonia to conquer the Persian empire in 334, never to return. Over the next ten years he created the largest empire of the ancient world, spreading Hellenism from Egypt to Persia, and from Afghanistan to India. En route, he created a semi-divine status for himself through his reputation as an invincible conqueror. He died unexpectedly in Babylon in 323 at the age of thirty-two. He would probably have been buried at Aegae in Macedonia if Ptolemy had not intervened and taken his mummified corpse to Egypt, where it began its long and equally adventurous afterlife.

Alexander IV Only legitimate son of Alexander the Great and his wife Roxanne. He was born in Babylon after Alexander's death in 323 B.C.E., and was always a pawn in the hands of others, such as Perdiccas, Olympias, and Cassander. He was acclaimed co-king by the Macedonian army in Babylon in 322 along with Alexander's half brother Philip III Arrhidaios. He and his mother were used by Olympias to further her political ends, and then kept under house arrest in Amphipolis by Cassander, who finally murdered them both in 309.

Ammianus Marcellinus A pagan from a noble family of Antioch, he lived between c. 325 and c. 391 C.E. He served in the army of the pagan Roman emperor Julian the Apostate. In his *Res Gestae*–an account of events between 353 and 378–he tells the story of Bishop Georgias of Alexandria who was murdered by the city's population when he appeared to threaten to destroy Alexander's tomb. Ammianus also left a record of the effects of an earthquake and tidal wave that struck Alexandria in 365.

Ammon Greek form of the Libyan-Egyptian god Amun, identified by the Greeks since Herodotus's time with Zeus, king of the Olympian gods of Greece. Ammon's sacred oracle was at the Siwa oasis in the western Egyptian desert, which Alexander visited in 332–331 B.C.E. Alexander identified himself as the divine son of Ammon, and in later images, was shown with the ram horns of Ammon emerging from his curly locks.

Amr-ibn-al-As Arab general who conquered Egypt for Islam in 641 C.E., and took Alexandria the following year. He records how the city made a stunning impression on himself and his desert warriors, especially the brilliant white marble streets and buildings.

Manolis Andronikos Greek archaeologist born in 1919, he excavated the unplundered tombs at Vergina (ancient Aegae) in western Macedonia from 1977 to 1982. The discovery of burned human bones led to his interpretation that Tomb II held the remains of Alexander's father, King Philip II. This sensational (and not uncontested) claim put Macedonia on the world archaeological map, as did the discovery of the golden funerary box (larnax) in which the bones were found, and a set of miniature ivory sculptures that he regarded as representations of Philip II, Olympias, and Alexander himself. He vigorously defended his identification of Philip II's remains until his death in 1992.

Antipater Born in 399 B.C.E., the son of a Macedonian general called Iolaus, he served under three Macedonian kings–Perdiccas III, Philip II, and Alexander the Great. He was instrumental in getting Alexander crowned as king after his father's assassination. Rewarded by Alexander with control of Europe during the king's absence in Asia, he argued continually with Olympias. His son, Iolaus, was accused of poisoning Alexander, and Olympias later desecrated Iolaus's grave. Antipater played a key role in the wars of the Successors, and became protector of Alexander's wife Roxanne, and heir, Alexander IV, in Macedonia. He died in 319, was briefly succeeded by Polyperchon, then Cassander.

Apis bull Regarded as the sacred reincarnation of the Egyptian creator deity Ptah, whose cult center was at Memphis where the bulls were kept, pampered, and worshiped during life. At death they were mummified and buried in huge stone (sometimes wood) sarcophagi in the subterranean galleries of the Serapeum temple on the Saqqara plateau nearby. Egyptians believed that the dead bull's immortal soul joined those of its mummified predecessors, that were collectively worshiped as Osiris-Apis or Oserapis, a name shortened by the Greeks to Serapis. Serapis was redesigned by Ptolemy (I Soter) to be a hybrid Greek-Egyptian god in the form of a bearded man.

Aristotle Greek philosopher (384–322 B.C.E.) whose father had been the royal doctor to Philip II's father, King Amyntas III. He tutored the young Alexander and his peers at Mieza in western Macedonia between 343 and 340. According to tradition, Aristotle gave Alexander an annotated copy of Homer's *Iliad*, which the conqueror carried with him all his life. Alexander sent Aristotle specimens of plants and animals from his Asian campaign. Aristotle was spuriously implicated in the rumors of poisoning that surrounded Alexander's early death in Babylon in 323.

Arrian Greek politician and military commander from Nicomedeia (Asia Minor), born in late 80s C.E. He worked mainly during the reign of the Roman emperor Hadrian (117–138) and was known by his Latin name Lucius Flavius Arrianus Xenophon. His books the *Anabasis* and *Indica* are two major (and widely regarded as the best) sources on Alexander's life and exploits. He avoided hero worship and scandal in favor of factual detail, and based his work on the now lost histories of Aristobulous and Ptolemy.

Barsine Persian noblewoman, daughter of Artabazus, born in 363 B.C.E. She was rumored to be Alexander's mistress before he met and married Roxanne, whereupon she was sent back to Asia Minor. She gave birth to an illegitimate son, Heracles, who was widely regarded as Alexander's. She lived at Pergamum until taken along (with Heracles) by Polyperchon on his invasion of Macedonia in 309, with the idea of putting the eighteen-year-old boy on the throne as a puppet ruler. When Polyperchon changed his mind, Barsine and Heracles were murdered.

Gertrude Bell Born in 1868, an intrepid British archaeologist and traveler, heir to a wealthy British family of industrialists. She visited Istanbul in 1898 to see the Alexander Sarcophagus recently found near Sidon in what is today Lebanon. She was convinced that this was Alexander's tomb, and her account of her visit is full of imaginative speculations about what she saw. She later played a prominent role in drawing the boundaries of modern Iraq. She died in 1926.

Mahmoud Bey (el-Falaki) Officially the court astronomer (el-Falaki) to the Ottoman viceroy of Egypt, Khedive Ismail Pasha, Mahmoud Bey was an engineer who trained in Paris as a cartographer. He was appointed by Ismail Pasha to produce a map of ancient Alexandria for the French emperor Napoleon III. In 1865 he produced a map of contemporary Alexandria as a basis for archaeological excavations that began the following year. In 1872, he published his plan of the ancient city along with descriptions of his investigations in his *Mémoire sur l'antique Alexandrie, ses faubourgs et environs découverts.* The map has been influential in many of the searches for Alexander's tomb ever since, though scholars are divided as to its accuracy.

Osman Hamdi Bey An Ottoman Turk who was a renowned artist, antiquarian, and archaeologist (1868–1926). He excavated the Royal Necropolis at Sidon in modern Lebanon in 1887, and found several beautifully carved sarcophagi—one of which came to be called the "Alexander Sarcophagus." He established the Ottoman Imperial Museum (now the National Museum) in Istanbul to display them.

Napoleon Bonaparte Born in Ajaccio, Corsica, in 1769 to a family of minor Italian nobility. A French revolutionary general and brilliant military commander. In 1798, he invaded Egypt but was cut off when his fleet was destroyed by Nelson at the Battle of Aboukir Bay. Long an admirer of Alexander, he was inspired to emulate his hero's successes in Asia but failed. He, or others on his behalf, may have entertained the idea of his being buried in the greenstone sarcophagus found in Alexandria's Attarine Mosque and which some regarded as Alexander's tomb. He sailed for France in 1799, became First Consul the same year, then emperor in 1804. Defeated at Waterloo in 1815, he was exiled to St. Helena and died there in 1821. His monumental tomb is on display in Les Invalides in Paris.

Evaristo Breccia Italian archaeologist who was the second director of Alexandria's Graeco-Roman Museum, succeeding the museum's founder Giuseppe Botti. Breccia excavated in the depths of the Nabi Daniel Mosque but became convinced that this was not Alexander's tomb. By chance, he discovered a pile of alabaster slabs in the city's Latin Cemetery while excavating nearby in 1907, though he never considered it a possible site for Alexander's tomb. Photographs of the unassembled slabs appeared in his 1914 guidebook *Alexandrea ad Aegyptum.*

Calanus A Brahmin priest–one of the so-called Gymnosophists (naked philosophers)–who joined Alexander's army at Taxila in the modern Punjab. In 324 B.C.E., at Persepolis, after falling ill during the crossing of the Gedrosian desert, he decided to commit suicide by fire in the traditional manner and persuaded Alexander to agree to it. The Macedonians were astonished as he climbed the funeral pyre and lay motionless as he was consumed by the flames.

Caligula (Roman Emperor Gaius) Son of the Roman general Germanicus and Agrippina, Gaius's nickname Caligula (Latin for "little boots") came from his parents' habit of dressing him in army uniform. He became emperor after murdering Tiberius in 37 C.E. Caligula was obsessed with Alexander, and regarded himself as a reincarnation of the Macedonian conqueror. He visited Alexander's tomb and took his breastplate, which he then wore around Rome. He was murdered by his own Praetorian Guards in 41 C.E.

Caracalla (Roman Emperor Marcus Aurelius Antoninus Caracallus) Born in 188 C.E., in Lyon, eldest son of Emperor Septimus Severus. After his father died he murdered his younger brother Geta and became emperor in 193. He had a lifelong fascination with Alexander, and was welcomed by Alexandria's population when he visited the city in 215. He visited Alexander's tomb and left his purple cloak and rings, an act of hero worship that became megalomaniac obsession. He believed Alexander had entered his body, and he ordered statues of the dead king set up across the empire. When the Alexandrians ridiculed his behavior he slaughtered thousands, and then marched east to emulate Alexander's Asian victories. In 217 at Carrhae in Syria, he was murdered by one of his own centurions.

Cassander Son of Antipater. Treated with contempt by Alexander in Babylon in 323 B.C.E., he later played a bloody role in the wars of the Successors after Alexander's death. He infamously organized the public stoning to death of Alexander's mother, Olympias, in 316, and murdered Alexander's wife and child, Roxanne and Alexander IV, at Amphipolis in 309. He convinced the aged general Polyperchon to kill Alexander's Persian mistress, Barsine, and their illegitimate son

Heracles, in exhange for the return of his country estates, also in 309. He was probably behind the killing of Alexander's sister Cleopatra, again in 309. He was said, perhaps unsurprisingly, to be haunted by nightmares of Alexander, and died in 297.

Evilya Çelebi Born in Istanbul in 1611, the son of a jeweler at the sultan's court, his name is unknown, and Çelebi a pseudonym. Educated at a Qur'anic school, he spent forty years travelling across the Ottoman empire. He visited Alexandria somewhere between 1670 and 1682, and visited the Attarine Mosque. There he saw the greenstone sarcophagus later attributed to Alexander, and described its elaborate decoration of (the then unreadable) hieroglyphs and figures. He was the first to mention its use as a water container for ritual cleansing.

Jean-François Champollion Born in 1790 in Figeac, France, he early exhibited an extraordinary linguistic talent, teaching himself Latin, Greek, Arabic, Coptic, and Chaldean. In 1809 he became professor of history at Grenoble. Believing that ancient Egyptian hieroglyphs followed the same rules as demotic (the everyday written language, and the basis of Coptic), he spent twenty years cracking the hieroglyphic code by studying the texts on the Rosetta Stone. In 1822, he announced his decipherment in Paris to an astonished audience. The lecture was published soon afterward as *Lettre à M. Dacier, secrétaire perpétuel de l'Académie royale des inscriptions et belles-lettres.* He died in 1832. Champollion's decipherment identified the greenstone sarcophagus in the British Museum as belonging to Nectanebo II, not Alexander.

St. John Chrysostom Born around 347 C.E. into a noble Christian family in Antioch, Syria, he became a deacon in 381, and bishop of Constantinople in 398. He preached against extravagance in the church hierarchy and royal court, for which he was banished several times. A prodigious writer, his sixteenth homily on St. Paul's 2 Corinthians scorned Alexander, rhetorically asking who knew where his tomb was, and querying the value of his earthly conquests compared to the spiritual ones of Christ. His gift of eloquence led him to be named Chrysostom (golden-mouthed) after his death in 407.

Andrew Chugg British aerospace expert whose fascination with the fate of Alexander's mausoleum began in 1998 and resulted in the publication of *The Lost Tomb of Alexander the Great* in 2004. He published several academic articles on his research, including resurrecting and refining the theory that Nectanebo II's sarcophagus was used by Ptolemy to inter Alexander's body and, more speculatively, that Alexander's remains may lie in the Basilica of St. Mark in Venice. His work comprehensively reviews ancient sources on the tomb, and highlights the existence and value of many historical maps of Alexandria.

Edward Daniel Clarke A British gentleman scholar (1769–1822), who became professor of mineralogy at Cambridge University in 1808, cofounded the Cambridge Philosophical Society, and traveled widely in Scandinavia and the Middle East. While in Egypt, Clarke tracked down the greenstone sarcophagus taken by Vivant Denon from the Attarine Mosque, and hidden on a French ship in Alexandria harbor. After the sarcophagus arrived in the British Museum, the imaginative and publicity-seeking Clarke wrote his magnum opus, *The Tomb of Alexander the Great* (1805), in which he gave his interpretation of the great stone sepulchre.

Cleopatra VII Philopater Born in the year 70–69 B.C.E., the daughter of Ptolemy XII and Cleopatra V. She famously seduced Julius Caesar in 48 and bore him a son, Caesarion, a year later; he made her queen of Egypt. She was not the stunning beauty of popular imagination. Her attraction was irresistible charm, persuasive character, a magnetic presence, and the skill to speak well on many topics in several languages. Her subsequent romance with the Roman general Mark Antony brought war and defeat at the hands of Octavian (the future emperor Augustus) in 31. She raided Alexander's tomb for gold to pay her army, but in 30, Octavian conquered Alexandria and Cleopatra committed suicide as the last Ptolemaic ruler of Egypt.

Constantine I (the Great) Born a pagan in what is now Serbia, between 271 and 273 C.E., Constantine converted to Christianity in 312, supposedly on the night before the Battle of the Milvian Bridge, which saw him become joint emperor. He announced Christianity as the empire's religion later that year, and became sole emperor in 324 after defeating Licinius at Chrysopolis. He refounded the old Greek city of Byzantium as Constantinople in the same year, attended the

Council of Nicaea in 325, and announced the discovery of Christ's tomb in Jerusalem later that year. He died in 337.

Craterus Son of a Macedonian nobleman from Orestis, and son-in-law of Antipater. One of Alexander's childhood friends. A tough and brave soldier, and a brilliant commander in Alexander's army, he was also an ultratraditionalist in affairs of state. He despised Hephaestion, and Alexander's adoption of Persian habits. He became a marshal of the empire and was taking 10,000 veterans back to Macedonia when Alexander died. In the Wars of the Successors, he was killed fighting Eumenes in 321 B.C.E.

Cyrus II (the Great) Founder of the Achaemenid dynasty and Persian empire (c. 559–530 B.C.E.) who died fighting to expand his realm near the Caspian Sea. He was buried at his capital Pasargadae, near Persepolis, and his tomb was visited by Alexander at least once.

Darius III Persian king who confronted Alexander. He had assassinated his predecessor Artaxerxes IV, and is often regarded as incompetent and cowardly in his dealings with Alexander. He ruled from 336 B.C.E. until defeated (for the second time) by Alexander at the Battle of Gaugamela in 331. He fled the battlefield and was murdered by the pretender Bessus the following year.

Dominique Vivant Denon A leading member of the French savants (scholars) whom Napoleon took to Egypt in 1798. Draftsman, engraver, collector, author, and diplomat, Denon (1747–1825) was fascinated by Egypt's antiquities. He was drawn to the Attarine Mosque in Alexandria where he found the highly decorated greenstone sarcophagus later to be called "Alexander's Sarcophagus," though whether he believed it to be so is debatable. He removed it to a French ship in the city's harbor intending to transport it to Paris. He publicized the event in his 1802 book, *Travels in Upper and Lower Egypt*.

Diocletian (Roman Emperor) Of humble birth on the Dalmatian coast, Diocletian (236–316 C.E.) was a gifted military commander, and was acclaimed emperor in 284 by his legions. He besieged a rebellious Alexandria in the year 299–298, and wrought great destruction on the city's Brucheum district where Alexander's Soma tomb enclosure was located. In 298, he erected a victory column (later erroneously known as Pompey's Pillar) that became and remains a landmark (*see glossary*, Diocletian's Column). In 303, he issued harsh anti-Christian edicts compelling the worship of Rome's pagan gods. He retired to his villa in Split in 305 and died in 316.

Diodorus Siculus Greek historian born in Sicily ca. 90 B.C.E., whose forty-book *Bibliotheca historia* (Historical Library) preserves an incomplete account of Alexander's life and exploits. His work drew on the (now mainly lost) work of other authors such as Hieronymus of Cardia–whose description of Alexander's hearse Diodorus has preserved. He traveled to Alexandria before his death in 30 B.C.E. and probably visited Alexander's tomb.

Dionysus Greek God of wine and excess, as well as disguise. Alexander and his mother Olympias were keen followers of Dionysus's religious cult. Dionysus's mythical adventures in India inspired Alexander to outdo him. This connection inspired much of the symbolism and pageantry of the Ptolemies during later Hellenistic times in Alexandria.

Jean-Yves Empereur Founder and Director of the French Centre d'études Alexandrines (CEA) in Alexandria, established in 1990. He is also a director of research at the French National Center for Scientific research (CNRS), and the foremost archaeologist working in Alexandria. He has conducted underwater investigations, notably at the site of the Pharos lighthouse, and many land-based excavations in and around Alexandria. In 1997, he published *The Tombs of Alexander the Great* (in Greek), and probably has a better idea than anyone alive today of where to look for Alexander's tomb.

Eumenes A Greek born in 362 B.C.E. in the area of the Hellespont (Dardanelles). He became chief secretary to Alexander during the campaign in Asia. Despite his talent for bureaucracy, he also had military gifts, and allied himself with Perdiccas in the war of succession that followed Alexander's death in 323. He famously inspired his army by placing Alexander's scepter and weapons on the dead king's empty throne and claiming to talk to him in dreams. He was captured and executed by another of Alexander's generals, Antigonus One-Eye, in 316.

Ahmed Fakhry Born in 1905 in Egypt's Fayum region, he was one of the country's first and most professional archaeologists, becoming professor of ancient Egyptian history at Cairo University. During the 1930s he visited the western desert oases of Siwa and Bahariya, and made detailed drawings and plans of the then much better preserved remains. He discovered the so-called Alexander Temple at Bahariya and noted its depictions of the Macedonian conqueror. He also made a plan of the Doric Temple at Siwa, interpreted as Alexander's tomb by Liana Souvaltzi in 1995. He retired in 1965, and died in 1973. Several of his important books are still in print.

Alessandro Farnese *See* Pope Paul III.

Peter Fraser Retired professor at Oxford University, and the most renowned modern historian of Alexandria during the Hellenistic period. His magisterial, three-volume *Ptolemaic Alexandria* was published in 1972, and remains an extraordinary scholarly achievement and a mine of erudite knowledge and insight.

Hadrian (Roman Emperor) Hadrian (76–138 C.E.) was a Hellenophile and a great admirer of Alexander. He undoubtedly visited (and perhaps renovated) Alexander's tomb on a visit to Alexandria in 130, during which he also commissioned coins showing himself being welcomed by Alexander. He ordered a city built on the spot where his lover Antinous drowned during a trip up the Nile, in a sense outdoing even Alexander's grief for his beloved Hephaestion. Hadrian spent most of his life touring his eastern empire. His circular drumlike mausoleum in Rome was similar to that of Augustus, and is thought by some to imitate Alexander's tomb in Alexandria.

Zawi Hawass Egyptian archaeologist, born in 1947, who became secretary-general of Egypt's Supreme Council of Antiquities in 2002. He excavated a small part of the spectacular Valley of the Golden Mummies at Bahariya oasis from 1999. He estimates the cemetery contains ten thousand bodies from the Greco-Roman period, buried in proximity to the Alexander Temple nearby.

Hephaestion Amyntoros Born in 357 B.C.E., the son of the Greek mercenary general Amyntor at the court of Philip II at Pella. He was the most intimate friend of Alexander from childhood to death. The two men were lovers, and likened to the two Homeric heroes Achilles and Patroclus in the *Iliad*. Hephaestion was appointed grand vizier of the empire before his unexpected and unexplained death at Ecbatana in October 324. Alexander ordered a hugely expensive funeral for him in Babylon in 323, just weeks before his own equally unexpected death.

Heracles (Alexander's son) Born in 327 B.C.E., he was the illegitimate first son of Alexander and his Persian mistress Barsine, herself of noble Persian descent. He spent his life in Asia Minor, probably Pergamum. After Alexander's death, Heracles's position in the wars of succession was championed by Alexander's former admiral, Nearchus, but to no avail. From Pergamum he and his mother were taken by Polyperchon when the latter invaded Macedonia with the aim of placing the eighteen-year-old Heracles on the throne as a puppet ruler. He was murdered along with his mother by Polyperchon in 309 when the old general changed his plans.

Heracles (Greek hero) Greek hero, son of Zeus, famed for his superhuman strength, and shown in art as wearing the skin of the Nemean lion, which he slew, and carrying an oversize olive wood club. Alexander identified Heracles as one of his mythical ancestors and often was shown wearing the hero's costume in coins and medals. Alexander famously impersonated Heracles during the banquets that took place en route to Ecbatana in 324 B.C.E.

David George Hogarth Born in 1862, English archaeologist who became keeper at the Ashmolean Museum in Oxford in 1909. He excavated several locations in Alexandria in 1895, was scathing about Mahmoud Bey's lack of archaeological skills, and questioned his interpretations. He died in 1927.

Iolaus Son of Antipater, who was accused of poisoning Alexander's wine in Babylon in 323 B.C.E. Rumors were rife and nothing proved, but Alexander's mother Olympias was convinced of Iolaus's guilt and later desecrated his grave.

Julian the Apostate (Roman Emperor) Born in 331 C.E., the son of Julius Constantius, half brother of Constantine the Great. His name refers to the fact that he renounced Christianity on becoming emperor in 361, and reinstated paganism as the imperial religion. He was also a Hellenophile and an admirer of Alexander, believing himself to be a reincarnation of the Macedonian conqueror. Despite this, there is no record he ever visited Alexandria, though he died in 363, trying to emulate Alexander's success against the Persians.

Stelios Koumatsos Greek café waiter in Alexandria who became obsessed with finding Alexander's tomb beginning in the mid-1950s. Retailing gossip and rumors from his day job, Koumatsos dug legally and illegally for decades across the city, making one sensational claim and hoax after another and gaining international notoriety. He met Professor Peter Fraser in 1961, briefly showing him a document he called the Alexander Book, which guided his searches, but which Fraser immediately identified as a potpourri of badly faked inscriptions and images. During the 1980s, he offered to sell his lifetime's work for a pension and a Mercedes. He died in 1991.

Leo Africanus Born Al Wezaz al-Fasi, in Fez, Morocco, in 1495, he was a Muslim traveler who visited Alexandria between 1515 and 1517. Captured by Spanish pirates, he was taken to Rome and became a Christian, baptized as Giovanni Leone. Better known as Leo Africanus, he was a prolific writer and in 1526 wrote his *Description of Africa*, in which he mentions his viewing in Alexandria's Attarine Mosque of the greenstone sarcophagus that would later become known erroneously as Alexander's Sarcophagus. He died in 1552.

Libanius Born in Antioch in 314 C.E. to a cultured pagan family, he dedicated himself to the study of rhetoric at age 14. He studied in Athens, began his career in Constantinople, but was exiled after accusations of sorcery. He became a friend of the future emperor Julian the Apostate and, ironically, taught both the pagan Ammianus Marcellinus and the future scourge of pagans, John Chrysostom. He moved between the pagan and Christian worlds, and was a prodigious writer. In his most famous work, *Pro Templis*, he complains of the desecration of pagan temples by Christians during the fourth century. Around 390, in another work, he seemed to suggest that Alexander's body was on public display in Alexandria. About 1500 of Libanius's letters and various other works have survived. He died in 393.

Lucan (Marcus Annaeus Lucanus) Born in 36 C.E. into a prominent Roman family, Seneca the Elder was his grandfather, and Seneca the Younger his uncle. He had strong Republican sentiments, which

colored his epic (and unfinished) poem, the *Pharsalia* (composed between 61 and 65), an account of the war between Julius Caesar and
Pompey the Great that took place a century before. The poem,
named after the Battle of Pharsalus, offers a unique insight into
Alexander's tomb as it describes Caesar descending into a subterranean grotto or cavelike sepulchre, while the Ptolemies were interred
in built mausoleums. Lucan committed suicide in 65, after being implicated in a failed assassination attempt on the emperor Nero.

Auguste Mariette Born in 1821, in Boulogne, France, he early developed a lifelong fascination for Egypt. He taught himself hieroglyphics
and Coptic, and found employment at the Louvre in Paris. In 1850,
he went to Egypt to buy papyri, but in 1851 began excavating the
Serapeum temple at Memphis-Saqqara. He uncovered a sphinx-lined
avenue and the group of Greek-style statues known as the Philosophers Circle, whose discovery suggested to some that Alexander's
temporary Memphite tomb was nearby. He excavated the depths of
the Serapeum, finding huge sarcophagi of the mummified Apis bulls.
In 1858 he founded and became the first director of the Egyptian
Antiquities Service. He excavated also at Thebes and Karnak, and accompanied the French Empress Eugenie at the celebrations of the
opening of the Suez Canal in 1869. He died in 1881.

Nectanebo II (Nakhthoreb) Belonging to the Thirtieth Dynasty, he
was the last indigenous pharaoh of Egypt, and reigned from 360 to
343 B.C.E., ultimately losing his kingdom to the Persian king Artaxerxes III. He fled to Nubia, perhaps to the Kushite court, and was
never buried in the greenstone sarcophagus made for him. The
Ptolemies made him a mythical (and politically useful) forebear, and
the *Alexander Romance* tells how, as a great sorcerer, he fathered
Alexander on Olympias. This complex relationship has inspired the
idea that his empty sarcophagus was used by Ptolemy I to hold
Alexander's corpse.

Octavian (Emperor Augustus) Born in 63 B.C.E., he was a distant relative of Julius Caesar, who adopted him as his son and heir in his will
published after his assassination in 44. Octavian joined forces with
Mark Antony to defeat the tyrannicides Brutus and Cassius at
Philippi, then fell out with him when the latter started a politically

dangerous romance with Cleopatra. Octavian defeated the combined forces of Mark Antony and Cleopatra at Actium in 31, and took Alexandria a year later. He visited Alexander's tomb, and famously refused to visit the mausoleums of the Ptolemies, whom he despised. Tradition tells how Octavian placed a golden crown on Alexander's body and showered it with flowers. He may also have broken the dead king's mummified nose. He returned to Rome, adopted Caesar's name as a title, and called himself Augustus. He died in 14 C.E.

Olympias Born in 375 B.C.E., she was the daughter of Neoptolemus, king of the Molossian tribe of Epirus, and thus a royal princess. She married Philip II in 357, and gave birth to Alexander a year later. Energetic and spiteful, she was implicated in Philip's assassination and despised Hephaestion's influence on her son. She plotted incessantly during Alexander's absence, and after his death murdered his mentally impaired half brother King Philip III Arrhidaios in 317. She was killed by her archenemy Cassander in 316 at Pydna near Mount Olympus.

Bishop Ossius Born in Cordova, Spain, probably in 257 C.E., he became the most influential religious advisor to Constantine I (the Great), especially in matters concerning the so-called Arian heresy. Constantine sent him to Alexandria in 325, where he may have seen Alexander's mausoleum. Soon afterward, he presided over the Council of Nicaea in northern Turkey. He played a probably crucial but unrecorded role in persuading Constantine and Bishop Makarios of Jerusalem to "discover" Christ's tomb in the city. He died around 356.

Triantafyllos Papazois Retired major general of the Greek army who reinterpreted the burial evidence discovered by Manolis Andronikos at Vergina. Papazois believes that Alexander himself, as well as his wife Roxanne, are the principal burials at the site. He argues that Alexander was cremated by Ptolemy I at Memphis and his ashes eventually transported back to Macedonia for interment at Aegae (Vergina). History, he maintains, was fooled by a lifelike dummy made by Egyptian embalmers and placed in Alexander's several tombs at Memphis and Alexandria.

Pope Paul III (Alessandro Farnese) Born in 1468 into the ancient Roman Farnese family, his privileged upbringing eased his church career. He was an expert in Latin and a true Renaissance scholar who transformed Rome's buildings and roads. He was elected pope in 1534, and refurbished Hadrian's mausoleum (the Castel Sant' Angelo) as his private rooms, the Sala Paolina. A fervent admirer of Alexander, partly because of his own name but especially because he saw him as a heroic role model for fighting the heathen of the east, who in his time were Muslims. He decorated the rooms with paintings of scenes from Alexander's life, though was probably not aware that the architecture of Hadrian's tomb may have been influenced by Alexander's. A beautiful gold medallion made for him showed Alexander kneeling in worship at the gates of Jerusalem, implying that even Alexander bowed before the Christian god. He died in 1549.

Perdiccas Born around 360 B.C.E., son of a Macedonian nobleman called Orestes from the highland region of Macedonia known as Orestis. He was one of Alexander's childhood friends, and became one of his seven bodyguards in 330. After Hephaestion's death in 324, Alexander appointed him grand vizier of the empire, and tradition has it that he received Alexander's signet ring when the king was on his deathbed. In the War of the Successors he was initially preeminent, but lost control of Alexander's sacred body when his rival Ptolemy hijacked it near Damascus in 321. He compounded this mistake in 320 by invading Egypt to regain Alexander's body and being defeated twice by Ptolemy. He was murdered by his lieutenants on the banks of the Nile the same year.

Philip II Son of King Amyntas III, he became king in 359 B.C.E. A gifted, energetic soldier whose army reforms and string of victories transformed Macedon into the most powerful state in Greece. He married the Epirote Princess Olympias in 357, and his son Alexander was born in 356. He campaigned ceaselessly, and at the Battle of Chaeronea in 338, became effective ruler of all Greece. A womanizer and a wily political operator, he was nevertheless assassinated at Aegae in 336, perhaps with the connivance of Olympias and Alexander—who in any event succeeded him.

Philip III Arrhidaios Born in 357 B.C.E., he was the illegitimate son of Philip II and a Thessalian dancer named Philinna. His mental deficiencies and possible epilepsy have been explained as the result of an only partially successful poisoning by Olympias, Alexander's mother. He was acclaimed co-king with Alexander's newborn son Alexander IV at Babylon in 322. He was murdered in 317 by Olympias. It has been suggested that his is one of the bodies buried at Vergina.

Plutarch Greek philosopher and biographer born in Chaeronea in 46 C.E. His famous *Parallel Lives* is a pairing of twenty-three Greek and Roman figures. Alexander's pairing with Julius Caesar preserves most of our information about Alexander's first twenty years. He died in 120.

Polyperchon Born in 394 B.C.E., the son of a Macedonian nobleman named Simmias from the region of Tymphaea. In the wars of the succession after Alexander's death, he was made regent and commander of Macedonia by Antipater on the latter's death in 319, though he was quickly replaced by Antipater's son, Cassander. He took Alexander's mistress, Barsine, and her son, Heracles, along when he invaded Macedonia in 309, but was persuaded by Cassander to murder them in exchange for having his Macedonian estates restored. He died in the Peloponnese in 303.

Ptolemy (I Soter) Born around 367 B.C.E., son of a nobleman named Lagus and a mother Arsinoe. He was a childhood friend of Alexander who accompanied him across Asia and was rewarded for his loyalty and martial skill by being made a marshal of the empire. After Alexander's death, he wisely chose to keep control of Egypt rather than compete with the other Successors for the whole empire. He hijacked Alexander's body in 321 near Damascus in Syria and buried it in Memphis. He became king-pharaoh in 305, established his own (Ptolemaic) dynasty, devised a state cult for Alexander, and may have transferred the mummified body to a grand tomb in Alexandria that he also made Egypt's new capital.

Ptolemy II Philadelphus Son of Ptolemy I Soter and Berenice I, born in the year 309–308 B.C.E. He was co-regent with his father between 284 and 282, when he became king. He first married Arsinoe I with whom he had a son who became his successor as Ptolemy III Euergetes. Philadelphus means "sister loving" and was adopted after he married a second time to his full sister Arsinoe II. He reigned until his death in 246.

Ptolemy III Euergetes Son of Ptolemy II Philadelphus and Arsinoe I, and born sometime between 285 and 275 B.C.E. He married Berenice II, with whom he had his son and heir, Ptolemy IV Philopater. Euergetes means "beneficent."

Ptolemy IV Philopater Son of Ptolemy III and Berenice II, he was born in 244 B.C.E. His name means "father loving." In 217 he won a battle against Antiochus III at Raphia in Gaza, and two years later opened a grand family mausoleum—the Soma—in Alexandria, probably near the royal palaces. He moved Alexander's body from its original tomb to the new cemetery, and interred it in a subterranean tomb. He died in 204, possibly as a result of burns received during a palace fire.

Ptolemy X Alexander I Philometor Son of Ptolemy VIII and Cleopatra III, born in the year 140–139 B.C.E. He was married twice, first to his sister Cleopatra Selene, and a second time to his stepdaughter Berenice III. Expelled by Alexandria's citizens around 89, he retook the city and is alleged to have melted down Alexander's golden sarcophagus to pay his troops, whereupon he was expelled again and died soon afterward in Cyprus.

Roxanne Bactrian princess, daughter of the Sogdian baron Oxyartes. She became Alexander's wife after his victory at the Sogdian Rock in spring 327 B.C.E. She gave Alexander his only legitimate heir, Alexander IV. After Alexander's death, her fortunes rose and fell, and eventually she and her son were held under house arrest by Cassander, who murdered them both at Amphipolis in 309. Her grave has never been identified.

Ambroise Schilizzi A Greek-born dragoman who worked for the Russian consulate in Alexandria during the mid-nineteenth century, making a living as a travel guide and from collecting antiquities. He infamously claimed to have discovered Alexander's tomb in the depths of the city's Nabi Daniel Mosque. He reported seeing Alexander's mummy in a crystal sarcophagus and wearing a golden crown. Unfortunately his added flourish of scattered papyri gave the lie to his claims, as papyrus does not survive in Alexandria's waterlogged and damp conditions.

Heinrich Schliemann Born in Neubukow in 1822, he had a talent for languages and became a successful businessman before turning to archaeology and developing a knack for sensational discoveries. He excavated in Troy between 1871 and 1873, and uncovered (some say planted) the fabulous Bronze Age golden hoard he called Priam's Treasure. In 1876 he repeated this feat by discovering the so-called death mask of Agamemnon at Mycenae. In 1888 he was in Alexandria hoping to find Alexander's tomb beneath the Nabi Daniel Mosque, but was never granted permission. He left soon afterward and died in 1890.

Stephan Schwartz A self-proclaimed "remote viewer," someone whose psychic talents allow them to see and experience the past as if they were actually present. In 1979 he led an expedition to Alexandria and spent time at the Alabaster Tomb. One of his team members fell into a trance and described seeing what could have been ancient Alexandria and a large ruined tomb. He also suggested that some of the bones he saw in the Monastery of St. Makarios might belong to Alexander.

Septimus Severus (Roman Emperor) Born into a distinguished local family in the North African city of Lepcis Magna (in modern Libya) in 145 C.E. He became emperor in 193 and fought successfully across the empire. During his visit to Alexandria in 199, he became alarmed at the availability of books on occult practices, and removed them from circulation, possibly placing them in Alexander's tomb, which he sealed up. Officially this was to protect Alexander's corpse, though other reasons associating the body with the outbreak of popular magic threatening the official Roman religion might have been involved. Septimus died in York in 211.

Serapis A Greek shortening of the Egyptian Osiris-Apis–the deity into which the sacred Apis bulls transformed after their mummification and interment in the Serapeum temple at Memphis-Saqqara. Ptolemy I reconfigured the cult to his own ends, creating a hybrid Greek-Egyptian deity whose images portrayed a Greek male god with a full beard and long hair, and supporting a miniature corn basket *(kalathos)* on his head, signifying fertility.

Liana Souvaltzi Greek archaeologist little known before 1989, when she began excavating at the well-known Greco-Roman Doric temple in the Siwa oasis in Egypt's western desert. She became convinced that the temple was Alexander's Macedonian-style tomb, and caused an international sensation (and scandal) by publicizing her discoveries to the world's press on several occasions from 1995. Her claims became embroiled in the political unrest in the Balkans, particularly over the status of the former Yugoslav Republic of Macedonia, and issues of Greek nationalism. Her official Egyptian permission to excavate was revoked in 1996, though she continues to visit the site. Her book, *Alexander the Great at the Oasis of Siwa*, was published in 2002.

Strabo Greek geographer, historian, and traveler, born around 63 B.C.E. in Amaseia, Pontus (northern Turkey). His magnum opus was the seventeen-volume *Geography*. In volume 17, he describes his travels in Egypt, at the Serapeum in Saqqara, and gives the best surviving account of Alexandria, where he lived for several years between 24 and 20 B.C.E. He gives glimpses of Alexander's Soma mausoleum, mentions its proximity to the royal palaces, and is the only source for the story that Ptolemy X melted down Alexander's golden sarcophagus and replaced it with one made of glass or crystal. He died around 24 C.E.

Alan John Bayard Wace English archaeologist (1879–1957) who worked at Farouk I University in Alexandria between 1943 and 1952. In 1948 he published an interpretation of the Nectanebo II sarcophagus in the British Museum, London, suggesting it had been used by Ptolemy I to bury Alexander. Part of Wace's thesis has been resurrected by Andrew Chugg.

Zenobia Julia Aurelia Zenobia was queen of Palmyra and reigned between 267 and 272 C.E. She claimed Ptolemaic descent from Cleopatra VII. Her armies invaded Egypt and occupied Alexandria briefly in 269–270. She was defeated by Emperor Aurelian in 272, was paraded in his Roman triumph shackled with golden chains, but allowed to retire to a villa near Tivoli until her death.

Zulqarnein The "Two-horned Lord" whose horns represented physical and spiritual power. Widely, though not universally, identified as Alexander, whom Islam regarded as a prophet (nabi) like Moses, Abraham, and Jesus. This problematic Qur'anic identification of Alexander with Dzoul Karnein may stem from the widespread occurrence of coins used as amulets and which show Alexander's head with the horns of Ammon.

GLOSSARY

Aegae (Vergina) Original Macedonian capital founded during the seventh century B.C.E., strategically sited in the foothills of the Pierian mountains by the Haliacmon River in western Macedonia. It was superseded politically by Pella during the fourth century, but still functioned as a ceremonial city, the center of ancestral funeral rites, and the sacred burial ground of the Macedonian kings. King Philip II, Alexander's father, was murdered in its theater in 336. The stunning royal tombs at the site, now called Vergina, were excavated during the 1970s by Manolis Andronikos, and a new on-site museum opened recently.

Agathos Daimon A great serpent that, according to legend, slithered out of the ground during the building of Alexandria. Alexander had it killed, and a commemorative monument erected on the site. It had its own cult, and Alexandrians worshiped it especially on the anniversary of the city's foundation. Its symbolism was associated with Alexander via his mother's fascination with snake cults, and as the "serpent born" son of Zeus Ammon. Serpent images adorn some of Alexandria's subterranean tombs, such as the catacombs of Kom el-Shuqafa.

Alabaster Tomb Discovered by Evaristo Breccia in the Latin Cemeteries area of eastern Alexandria in 1907, originally it was a pile of disassembled alabaster slabs. Achille Adriani, Breccia's successor as director of the city's Graeco-Roman Museum, reassembled them on the same spot during the 1930s, and today it is a popular candidate for Alexander's tomb. Many archaeological excavations in and around it have failed to confirm this idea, though the tomb is unique. Its Macedonian style dates to early Ptolemaic times, and it probably held a high-ranking (but unknown) Macedonian person. No grave goods were found.

Alexander Romance A collection of legends and stories concerning the life and exploits of Alexander the Great. It is also known as "Pseudo-Callisthenes," as it was originally and erroneously ascribed to Alexander's official historian Callisthenes. The *Alexander Romance* had its origins during Ptolemaic times–possibly in third century B.C.E. Alexandria or Memphis. It became increasingly elaborate over time, especially during the Roman period in the centuries after Christ, when it was influenced by the genre of wonder tales and heavily colored by Christian theology. It has survived in several versions, including Greek, Latin, and Syriac.

Alexander's Sarcophagus The popular name given, at various times, and erroneously, to two quite different sarcophagi. First it was applied to the greenstone sarcophagus of the Egyptian pharaoh Nectanebo II taken from Alexandria's Attarine Mosque by the Frenchman Dominique Vivant Denon, and then transported to the British Museum in 1802. Champollion's 1822 decipherment of Egyptian hieroglyphs finally established its true identity, though several subsequent attempts have been made to invoke its associations with Alexander. The term was applied a second time in 1887 to the sarcophagus of Abdalonymus, king of Sidon, discovered by Osman Hamdi Bey in the royal burial grounds of Sidon in modern Lebanon. This identity was quickly revised, though today is still widely used to describe the tomb now on display in the National Museum in Istanbul.

Alexandria Officially known as Alexandria-by-Egypt, it was founded by Alexander on April 7, 331 B.C.E., at the western edge of the Nile Delta. It became the largest, most successful of the many Alexandrias that Alexander created. Under Ptolemy I Soter, Alexandria became Egypt's new capital, and was the site where Alexander was buried in two successive (and still unlocated) tombs. It was one of the three largest cities of the ancient world well into Roman times, was a center of rioting during the transition to Christianity, and only declined after the Arab conquest of 642 C.E. It was substantially redeveloped from the nineteenth century onward, though the Ptolemaic levels are thought to be well preserved some twelve meters below the modern surface. Hundreds of searches for Alexander's tomb have been conducted throughout the city over the past two hundred years.

Amphipolis City built on a hill overlooking the river Strymon in central eastern Macedonia. It was strategically sited near the gold and silver mines of Mount Pangaeum. Founded by Thracians, it came under Athenian, then Spartan, control, and was finally taken by Philip II in 357 B.C.E. During Alexander's reign it became the center of a large royal mint that mainly issued silver coinage. After Alexander's death, it became infamous as the site where Alexander's wife, Roxanne, and his only legitimate son and heir, Alexander IV, were held under house arrest and then murdered by Cassander.

Antioch City founded in the late fourth century B.C.E. by Seleucus I Nicator, one of the successors after Alexander's death. Situated on the banks of the river Orontes, twenty miles from the sea in northern Syria, it became the capital of Seleucus's empire, rivaling Alexandria, whose grid plan it adopted. Substantially redeveloped during Roman times, but severely damaged by severe earthquakes between 526 and 588. St. Paul gave his first sermon in the city, and the converts were the first to be called Christians. It rapidly became a center for the new faith, with perhaps 100,000 Christians during the fourth century. Ammianus Marcellinus, Libanius, and John Chrysostom were all born in the city. After many dramatic vicissitudes, it finally fell to Egyptian Mameluke Muslims in 1268, and the silting of its port led to permanent decline.

Attarine Mosque Built originally over the ruins of the church of Saint Athanasius in Alexandria (itself founded for the patriarch of Alexandria in 370 C.E.) in early Muslim times. During the seventeenth century, it was one of many holy shrines on the itinerary of Muslim visitors to Alexandria. It was destroyed in 1830, but a new mosque (with the same name) was rebuilt nearby (in its present location) during the late nineteenth century. Consequently maps, drawings, and descriptions of the mosque in Napoleonic times and before, during which the greenstone sarcophagus was seen, described, and sometimes attributed to Alexander, do not relate to the present building.

Babylon A vast city built on the banks of the rivers Tigris and Euphrates in Mesopotamia (modern Iraq), and originally the capital of the sixth-century B.C.E. Neo-Babylonian empire. Surrounded by double walls and featuring eight gates, the most famous of which was the glazed blue-tiled Ishtar Gate. The city god was Marduk, whose stepped temple, the Esagila, towered over the city and was rebuilt on Alexander's command. Alexander probably intended to make Babylon the capital of his new Asian empire due to its geographical position. Alexander died here on June 10, 323 B.C.E.

Bahariya Oasis One of the major oases of the Egyptian western desert, approximately halfway between the Siwa oasis and Memphis in Alexander's time. In 1938, a unique temple to Alexander was discovered at Bahariya by the Egyptian archaeologist Ahmed Fakhry, whose investigations discovered Alexander's name as a hieroglyphic cartouche and images of him making offerings to Ammon. It is unknown whether the temple was built in Alexander's lifetime or afterward. It may have been in use from Ptolemaic times up to the twelfth century C.E. In 1996, the spectacular discovery of the so-called Valley of the Golden Mummies at the site led the Egyptian scholar Zawi Hawass to excavate a small number of an estimated 10,000 burials. The cemetery, which contains Greco-Roman burials, lies adjacent to Alexander's temple, and Hawass believes this is why people chose to be buried there. As Bahariya's occupation spans the transition from pagan to Christian, it would be an ideal place to hide Alexander's remains after the Christian destruction of his Alexandrian tomb.

Behistun Located on the road to Maracanda (later Samarkand) in the Persian province of Media, Behistun is a cliff face adorned with a victory inscription by Darius the Great in 521 B.C.E. Carved five hundred feet up, it is unreadable from ground level, extolling the virtues of the king for the eyes of the Persian gods in three languages, Old Persian, Babylonian, and Elamite. Alexander and his army spent several days admiring the giant propaganda message en route to Ecbatana in the late summer of 324.

Canopic Way The main east–west thoroughfare of Ptolemaic and Roman Alexandria, running 5 kilometers across the city from the western Gate of the Moon to the eastern Canopic Gate, and then on to Canopus. Its identification has been crucially important in the search for Alexander's tomb as it was the main axis of the city's grid plan, and a key point of orientation for locating many of the Ptolemaic city's great buildings. It was identified as road L1 on Mahmoud Bey's nineteenth-century map, and its crossroads with his road R5 (modern Sharia Nabi Daniel) suggested (erroneously) to some that Alexander's mausoleum was nearby, perhaps beneath the Nabi Daniel Mosque. Today its central section is known as Sharia Horriya.

Canopus Ancient Egyptian coastal town located on the westernmost (Canopic) branch of the river Nile in its delta, just east of Alexandria. Its origins are traced back to Homeric myth, but the main archaeological traces belong to Greco–Roman times. During the reign of Ptolemy III Euergetes, in 239 B.C.E., his priests gathered here and bestowed new titles and honors on him and his wife Berenice, the so-called Canopus Decree. During Roman times, Canopus had a reputation for opulence and debauchery, and was destroyed by earthquakes in the fourth century C.E. Today the area is a suburb of Alexandria, Abu Qir (Aboukir).

Chaeronea Site in central Greece where Alexander and his father Philip II defeated the combined armies of Athens, Thebes, and their allies in 338 B.C.E. The victory, in which Alexander led a decisive cavalry charge, effectively made Philip master (Hegemon) of Greece, and ended the period of political autonomy for the Greek city states. Alexander was charged with taking the ashes of the Athenian dead to Athens. Today a giant marble lion marks the spot where the Sacred Theban Band of 105 homosexual warrior couples fell during the battle.

Constantinople Greek city founded in sixth century B.C.E., strategically sited on the Golden Horn at the mouth of the Sea of Marmara, at the crossroads of Europe and Asia. It was refounded as the second imperial capital of the Roman empire by the Christian emperor Constantine I (the Great) on May 11, 330 C.E., and became the capital of the Byzantine empire soon afterward, with the fall of Rome. It developed into the greatest city of the medieval period, and was the spiritual heart of Eastern Orthodox Church. It was decorated with many pagan treasures gathered by Constantine from across the ancient world. Alexandria was part of the Byzantine empire when it was conquered by Muslim Arabs in 642 C.E. Constantinople fell to the Ottomans in 1453.

Contorniate Roman coinlike medallions of bronze whose name derived from the circular incised rim that surrounded the central image. They were decorated on one side with a picture of the emperor, and on the other either with scenes from Roman games, mythology, or heroes such as Alexander the Great. Their purpose is unclear. They may have been entrance tokens to the games, amulets for good luck, or gifts from the emperor or private individuals to the people of Rome. They were issued from the time of Constantine I in 307 C.E. to the end of the reign of Anthemius in 472. Unlike coins, they were cast and not struck.

Copts Copts are Egyptian Christians whose Coptic Orthodox Church separated from the Church of Constantinople in 570 C.E. The Coptic tongue is based on the everyday language of ancient Egypt known as demotic, but was written with letters of the Greek alphabet. It survives today only in religious services. Coptic beliefs and music are also influenced by symbolism from Pharaonic and Greco-Roman times—such as the influence that Isis and her son Horus had on the Virgin Mother and Christ Child. Similarly, the Coptic cross derives from the ancient Egyptian *ankh*, the hieroglyphic sign for life. An understanding of the Coptic language helped Jean-François Champollion decipher hieroglyphs in 1822.

Diocletian's Column An eighty-foot red granite column erected on Alexandria's Serapeum temple by the emperor Diocletian to mark his successful siege of Alexandria in 298 C.E. This siege did much damage to the city's Brucheum district, where Alexander's tomb was situated. Initial speculation that a large statue of Alexander originally stood on the column's summit is groundless, and it is now thought most likely that Diocletian had his own statue placed there. It was given its more popular but erroneous name, Pompey's Pillar, by European travelers seeking antiquities during medieval times. Today it is the oldest object in Alexandria to survive in its original position.

Doric Temple (Siwa) Greco-Roman temple built during the first century C.E., and located at the settlement of Bilad el-Rum in the Siwa oasis. Still standing during the nineteenth century when it was visited and sketched by several European travelers, it has an unusual five-room plan. It was severely damaged during the later years of that century, and today is little more than foundations and scattered blocks. It was investigated by the Egyptian archaeologist Ahmed Fakhry in 1938. Liana Souvaltzi excavated there during the 1990s, and argued that it was the location of a Macedonian style tomb belonging to Alexander. It was the subject of her book, *The Tomb of Alexander the Great at the Oasis of Siwa*, published in 2002. Today, the site is closed to tourists, though special permission to visit is sometimes granted.

Ecbatana Ancient Median city in the Zagros Mountains of Persia (now the city of Hamadan in Iran). It was rebuilt by the Persian kings as a summer retreat, and especially by Artaxerxes (404–359 B.C.E.), who constructed a palace decorated with gold and silver. Alexander and his army spent several months there in autumn 324 B.C.E., celebrating their ten years of Asian campaigns. Hephaestion died there in October, and the heavily damaged Lion of Hamadan stone sculpture is believed by some to have been carved on Alexander's orders to commemorate his friend and lover.

Gedrosian Desert Area of Baluchistan in southern Iran, known also as the Makran. Its coast faces the northern Indian Ocean and the approaches to the Straits of Hormuz. Dry and inhospitable, its lunar landscapes are liable to sudden flash floods, as Alexander discovered when he crossed it in 325 B.C.E. First human settlements date to between 7,000 and 3,000 B.C.E., and it was conquered for Islam in 711 C.E. Its capital is Pura (modern Bampur).

Halicarnassus The capital of the Carian Hecatomnid dynasty strategically sited on a peninsula in southwestern Asia Minor (modern Bodrum in Turkey). It was founded in the tenth century B.C.E. by Greeks who settled on the small offshore island of Zephyria, built over by the Knights of St. John in 1402 C.E., and is today Bodrum Castle. The city was a hybrid of Greek and Carian culture, and the birthplace of Herodotus. Alexander besieged it in 334 B.C.E., and finally broke through the western gate after losing many men. It was here that he saw the famous tomb of King Mausolus (*see* Glossary, Mausoleum).

Hellenistic Period The three-hundred-year period that begins in 323 B.C.E. with the death of Alexander the Great and ends with the establishment of the Roman empire under Octavian/Augustus after 31 B.C.E. The Hellenistic world is composed of the kingdoms created by the successors to Alexander in Greece and Asia, such as Ptolemy in Egypt, Lysimachus in Thrace, Seleucus in Syria, and their descendants. It is marked by gigantism in architecture, scientific advances in Alexandria, elaborate art, and a general air of opulence (some think degeneracy) and ineffectiveness that the Romans despised.

Heptastadion (Alexandria) Literally the Seven Stader–the seven stades long causeway that linked Pharos island in Alexandria to the mainland. It is depicted on Greco-Roman coins and medals, and seems designed to have allowed some waterborne traffic to pass between the city's two seaports. Silt built up against it over the centuries, widening the causeway into a promontory, and it became the focus of the city in late Arab times.

Larnax Small chest designed to contain cremated human remains. Originating in the Greek Bronze Age, most examples are of painted ceramic, but in 1977 Manolis Andronikos found gold ones in the tombs beneath the Great Mound at Vergina, decorated with the so-called Macedonian Star.

Latin Cemeteries (Alexandria) Area originally in eastern Alexandria (now central due to urban expansion) which contains walled cemeteries of the city's nineteenth-century European elite. These include burial grounds and elaborate mausoleums of the Roman Catholic, Jewish, Greek Orthodox, and Coptic faiths, among others. Giuseppe Botti (founder of the city's Graeco-Roman Museum) and the poet Constantine Cavafy are buried in the Latin Cemeteries. The Alabaster Tomb lies in this part of Alexandria.

Lochias Peninsula (Alexandria) Originally a large peninsula forming the eastern jaw protecting Alexandria's main harbor. On this land the Ptolemies built their palaces. Centuries of land subsidence have much reduced the size of the land, now known as the Silsileh promontory, and many Ptolemaic and Roman remains lie beneath the sea.

Macedon/Macedonia Macedon is the term usually applied to the political state (kingdom) ruled by Philip II and then his son Alexander (as well as their predecessors and successors). Macedonia describes the territory that lies between the Balkans in the north and southern Greece in the south. During the late twentieth century, the breakup of Yugoslavia led to the independence of the Former Yugoslav Republic of Macedonia (FYROM) that adopted the name Macedonia. This was vigorously contested by the Greek government, which only recognized its own area of Macedonia in northern Greece. Both sides adopted Alexander the Great and his symbols as emblems of their claims to the name Macedonia.

Magi Name given to the Median priests who were the religious officials of the Persian empire and who administered the rites of the creator god Ahura Mazda.

Mausoleum (Halicarnassus) One of the seven wonders of the ancient world, the mausoleum was the tomb of the Carian dynast Mausolus, whose sister-wife, Artemisia, completed it between 353 and 351 B.C.E., after his death. It was the largest tomb in antiquity, two hundred feet tall, and adorned with statues carved by the renowned artists and sculptors of the time, and standing on blue limestone. Ionic columns, lion sculptures, and friezes showing clashes between humans, centaurs, and Amazons were all part of the original decoration. Its summit was capped by a pyramid on which there was a sculpture of Mausolus driving a four-horse chariot. It stood largely intact until damaged by earthquakes in the thirteenth century C.E. Its tumbled remains were quarried by the Knights of St. John of Malta in 1494 to refortify Bodrum Castle. Still today, segments of the mausoleum can be seen in the castle's walls, though some of the surviving statues (notably Mausolus and Artemisia) and friezes are on display in the British Museum in London.

Memphis-Saqqara Memphis was a huge city on the banks of the Nile, and Saqqara its sacred burial ground up on a limestone ridge west of the city. Memphis was three thousand years old when Alexander arrived in 332 B.C.E., and had been the capital of Egypt (alternating with Thebes) for much of that time. The city was dedicated to the Egyptian creator god Ptah, and was home to the cult of the Apis bull.

After Alexander's conquest it became the center of the imperial satrapy of Egypt, until Ptolemy built a new capital at Alexandria. Saqqara was home to the subterranean temple of the Apis bull cult known as the Serapeum, and it was here that the animals were mummified and interred in huge sarcophagi. The whole area had been a burial ground since 3,000 B.C.E. and was dominated by the stepped pyramid of the pharaoh Djoser (2650 B.C.E.) and temples to Anubis, the jackal-headed god, and Bastet, the cat god. Below ground were countless human burials and mummified animals. Alexander's first tomb was at Memphis-Saqqara, and may be located somewhere near the Serapeum temple. Strabo visited Saqqara around 20 B.C.E., and Auguste Mariette rediscovered and excavated the Serapeum during the mid-nineteenth century, uncovering the Philosophers Circle and the sphinx-lined Serapeum Way.

Mieza Rural site in western Macedonia, near modern Lefkadia, where Alexander and his peers were educated by Aristotle between 343 and 340 B.C.E. Today the remains of a rock shelter with signs of now disappeared architectural elements have been identified as Aristotle's school.

Mustapha Pasha Cemetery (Alexandria) Elaborate subterranean necropolis in eastern Alexandria. Its beautifully preserved high-class tombs are surrounded by columns, courtyards, and doorways, some of which retain their brightly colored mural decoration. There is also evidence for an elaborate water supply associated with cleansing activities that were part of the socialising and banqueting that took place here as part of Alexandrian rituals of respect for the dead. The style of the cemetery dates it to the third century B.C.E.

Nabi Daniel Mosque Possibly founded as early as the fifteenth century, the present mosque dates to the nineteenth century, when it was completely rebuilt during the time of Mohammed Ali (1805–1848). This rebuilding may have been in veneration for the Prophet Daniel and a local holy man Sidi Lokman, who were identified in popular tradition as buried beneath the original mosque; their tombs were preserved beneath the new building. The identification of Prophet Daniel may be an inaccurate folk memory of Sheikh Mohammed Daniel of Mosul, who came to live in Alexandria in the fifteenth century, established a Qur'anic school, and was buried at the same spot which subsequently had the original mosque built over it. In 1850, Ambroise Schilizzi concocted the outrageous story of seeing Alexander's crystal sarcophagus and mummy beneath the mosque, and soon after, Mahmoud Bey el-Falaki was the first to publish the hitherto oral tradition of the site's associations with Alexander. This in turn led to many fruitless investigations in the depths of the mosque, which still today is widely (and totally erroneously) identified as the location of Alexander's tomb.

Natron A naturally occurring salt, composed mainly of sodium bicarbonate and sodium carbonate. It was a dessicant and an antiseptic, and was used in household cleansing as well as a cosmetic and in mummification. Its cleansing qualities were regarded as spiritual as well as physical. Natron was also used in glassmaking, and its abundance south of Alexandria in the Wadi Natrun made the city a center for the glassmaking industry in late Ptolemaic and Roman times.

Nectanebo Sarcophagus Greenstone (breccia) sarcophagus carved for the last native Egyptian pharaoh, Nectanebo II (Nakhthoreb) of the Thirtieth Dynasty, who appears never to have occupied it. It was found in the Attarine Mosque in Alexandria in 1798 by the French savant Dominique Vivant Denon, who removed it against local opposition and with the intention of taking it to Paris. Edward Daniel Clarke found it aboard a French ship and took possession of it. Arriving in London in 1801, it was put on display in the British Museum. Clarke became convinced that its unreadable hieroglyphs recorded that it belonged to Alexander, which was also a popular Arab tradition in Alexandria. Champollion's decipherment of Egyptian hieroglyphs showed it belonged to Nectanebo and not Alexander, but several attempts have been made since to link it again to Alexander. Its unusual drilled holes have been interpreted as indicating that the sarcophagus was used for ritual washing by Muslims, and as an earlier Ptolemaic nymphaeum.

Nymphaeum General name given to a water fountain that was sometimes part of a temple, itself decorated with statues and sculptures. Elaborate hydraulics included supplying the fountain with ceramic water pipes with water spouting from the mouths of mythological figures.

Oxyrhinchus (Papyri project) Oxyrhinchus (modern el-Bahnasa) in Egypt is the location of a vast trove of papyri fragments, preserved due to the environmental conditions. First discovered in 1898 in what was the rubbish dump of the ancient city, the papyri cover a variety of aspects of ancient life, including documents relating to the area's many different religious traditions, especially early Christianity. Everyday life is also represented in fragments of petitions to deities asking for success in love, health, and wealth, as well as tax returns, invoices, spells, and curses. Lost works by Sophocles, Menander, and Sappho have also been found. In 2005 infrared imaging technology was applied to the papyri, enabling previously illegible items to be read and promising significant discoveries in the future.

Papyrus Paper made from the pith of the papyrus plant that grows in abundance in the Nile Delta. It was the most commonly used writing material in the ancient world.

Parian Marble The Parian Marble is a damaged and incomplete set of inscriptions commissioned and set up on the Greek island of Paros by an unknown individual. It covers events that took place between 1581 and 264 B.C.E.; the start and finish dates are stated at the beginning of the inscription. Content is selective, and no mention is made, for example, of such important people as Pericles or the momentous Peloponnesian war. It is also incomplete: of the three known fragments, one is in the Ashmolean Museum, Oxford, a second is now lost, and a third (covering the period 320–298 B.C.E.) is in the Archaeological Museum on Paros. A fourth piece–dealing with the period 297–264 B.C.E.–has never been found, and may refer to the transport of Alexander's remains from Memphis to Alexandria.

Pasargadae Original capital of the Persian empire and its Achaemenid dynasty, founded by Cyrus the Great in 550 B.C.E. Cyrus's tomb stood in a royal park (paradeis), and was tended by the Magi. Alexander possibly visited it twice, the second time in 324, finding it desecrated. He ordered Aristobulous to restore and reseal it.

Pella The city was founded by the Macedonian king Archelaus (reigned 413–399 B.C.E.) as a civic replacement for Aegae, which, however, retained its ceremonial functions. Philip II's conquests and the wealth they generated allowed him to greatly develop Pella into a sophisticated imperial capital for his new Macedonian possessions. The city bene-fited greatly from the wealth that flowed back from Alexander's con-quests and was developed further after his death, the famous pebble mosaics being an example. During Philip's and Alexander's time it was open to the sea, but silting of the Thermaic gulf led to it becoming landlocked.

Persepolis Ceremonial capital of the Persian empire. It was built by King Darius I as a replacement for the original capital at nearby Pasargadae. It was substantially developed by Darius's son, Xerxes. In 330 B.C.E., Alexander set fire to the great hall of the Apadana and the whole city was destroyed.

Pharos The seventh wonder of the ancient world, the world's first lighthouse took its name from the small island of Pharos opposite Alexandria's main harbor, where it was inaugurated by Ptolemy II Philadelphus in 283 B.C.E. Images of it are found on Greco-Roman coins and medallions, mosaics, and arguably on Roman lamps. A miniature is in Alexandria's Graeco-Roman Museum in the form of a terra-cotta lamp, and at Taposiris Magna, twenty miles west of Alexandria, a one-fifth size replica stands as part of a second-century B.C.E. subterranean tomb complex. The original Pharos had three levels, quadrangular at the base, octagonal in the middle, and circular above, though the nature of its reflecting fires is unknown; a bronze mirror is a possibility. Earthquakes and tsunami seriously damaged it, though later, Arab rulers, who greatly admired it, made extensive repairs. It lasted for 1,700 years until totally destroyed by a severe earthquake in 1303 C.E. The Mamluk sultan Qait Bey built his eponymous fortress on the spot during the fifteenth century, and it still stands today.

Philosophers Circle (Saqqara) Discovered by Auguste Mariette at Saqqara in 1851, the Philosophers Circle is a group of eleven Greek-style statues carved from local limestone and set in a semicircle at the end of the Serapeum Way at the point where it enters the approach to the subterranean Serapeum. They represent Homer, Plato, Hesiod, Thales of Miletus, and possibly Demetrius of Phaleron, Ptolemy I Soter's favorite philosopher, among others. Anomalous in a sacred necropolis landscape dedicated to the Egyptian gods and cosmos, the style of the statues dates them to the third century B.C.E. This has suggested to some that they may have been commissioned by Ptolemy (I Soter) to mark the ideological relationship between his new Macedonian kingdom and the Thirtieth Dynasty pharaoh Nectanebo II, and possibly indicate that Alexander's temporary first tomb was somewhere nearby. Today, several of the statues have been removed, and the remaining ones are heavily damaged.

Pompey's Pillar *See* Diocletian's Column.

Rosetta Stone Discovered in 1799 at Rosetta (el-Rashid on the western Nile Delta) by the French soldier Pierre François Xavier Bouchard while rebuilding Fort Rachid to counter British attacks. A gray-black granite slab some three feet high, it weighs three-quarters of a ton. Its surface is covered with the same inscription in three scripts, Greek, Egyptian hieroglyphs, and Egyptian demotic—the common language and script that replaced hieroglyphs. The text celebrates an anniversary of the coronation of Ptolemy V Epiphanes and is dated March 27, 196 B.C.E. Champollion, building on the work of other scholars such as Thomas Young, used the stone's inscriptions to decipher the hieroglyphic code. It was sent to England in 1802 and is on display in the British Museum.

St. Mark's Basilica The first church of St. Mark was built in Venice in 829 C.E. to house the remains widely regarded as those of St. Mark that had been stolen from Alexandria the previous year by the Venetians Buono of Malamocco and Rustico of Torcello. Fire destroyed the building in 976 and a new one was built in 1063. A third and more elaborate basilica was then built and elaborated in subsequent years. Mosaics representing the life of St. Mark were made between 1071 and 1084, and the new building was consecrated in 1094. Today, some believe that St. Mark's remains are possibly the mummified remains of Alexander, though the Italian authorities have so far refused any scientific analyses to be carried out.

Sala Paolina (Rome) Name given to the private rooms of Pope Paul III in the refurbished mausoleum of Emperor Hadrian in Rome (today the Castel Sant' Angelo). Pope Paul admired Alexander and had his rooms decorated with paintings depicting scenes from Alexander's life. Pagan Alexander was thus adopted by the supreme head of the

Roman Catholic Church, and the pagan mausoleum that may have been modeled on Alexander's tomb became the pope's living quarters.

Satrap Greek version of the original Median word for provincial governor.

Second Sophistic Greek cultural movement of the second and third centuries C.E. that saw traveling orators nostalgically imitating the golden age of Greek rhetoric of the fourth and fifth centuries B.C.E. Speakers such as Herodes Atticus spoke vigorously and wittily in theaters across the Roman empire on various topics, including the life and exploits of Alexander.

Sema *See* Soma/Sema.

Serapeum (Alexandria) Built on Alexander's orders on the southwestern edge of Alexandria, the structure was a daughter temple of the Serapeum at Saqqara. Its construction was begun by Ptolemy (I Soter) and extended by Ptolemy III Euergetes, who also had a series of foundation tablets in gold, silver, bronze, and faience inscribed in Greek and hieroglyphs deposited at the temple's corners. Damaged by Jewish unrest in 116 C.E., it was extensively refurbished by the Roman emperor Hadrian, who dedicated a magnificent basalt statue of the Apis bull that was discovered during investigations and is now in the Graeco-Roman Museum in Alexandria. The temple had a huge statue of Serapis made of iron and wood so that by the artful use of magnets it seemed to float in midair. There was also a public access library, a smaller offshoot of Alexandria's great library. The Serapeum was destroyed during the Christian riots of 391 C.E. under the leadership of Bishop Theophilus. Today almost nothing is left on the surface (except the much later Diocletian's Column), but the empty subterranean galleries still evoke some of the Serapeum's mystery.

Serapeum (Saqqara) Large, mainly subterranean, temple and catacombs located on the Saqqara plateau west of Memphis. It was dedicated to the cult of the mummified Apis bulls that were buried in huge sarcophagi in the underground galleries. It was founded during the Eighteenth Dynasty (1550–1295 B.C.E.) in a necropolis area long sacred to Egyptians and elaborated subsequently, notably by the Thirtieth Dynasty pharaohs Nectanebo I and Nectanebo II, who added a large building complex at the approach to the Serapeum's ceremonial entrance (dromos). The Serapeum was approached along the Serapeum Way, a sphinx-lined path that led from the Nile valley up to the plateau.

In Ptolemaic times, the Philosophers Circle of Greek statues was added at the end of this path, between the Nectanebo building and the dromos. This has suggested to some that Alexander's temporary first tomb was nearby. The Serapeum was rediscovered by Auguste Mariette and excavated in 1851, and he also removed the sand to reveal the sphinxes along the path. Today the Serapeum is closed due to structural problems, and the sphinxes once again covered by sand.

Seven Wonders of the Ancient World Based on sheer size and the sense of awe they inspired, the idea of the wonders of the world was probably established by the second century B.C.E., though the Seven Wonders was a Renaissance invention. The list includes the Great Pyramid at Giza in Egypt, the Hanging Gardens of Babylon, the mausoleum at Halicarnassus, the statue of Zeus at Olympia, the temple of Artemis at Ephesus, the Colossus of Rhodes, and, much later, during Renaissance times, the Pharos lighthouse of Alexandria.

Sidon Phoenician coastal town (in modern Lebanon), mentioned by Homer as famous for its glassmakers and purple dye. Seat of the Phoenician royal dynasty, it flourished as part of the Persian empire, and was taken by Alexander after the battle of Issus in 333 B.C.E. Its king, Straton, had supplied Darius with ships, and Alexander replaced him with Abdalonymus, an obscure member of the royal family, in 332. The royal cemetery of Sidon was discovered accidentally in 1887, and several magnificent sarcophagi retrieved by Osman Hamdi Bey. One of these was the so-called Alexander Sarcophagus, thought now to belong to Abdalonymus.

Siwa Large desert oasis settlement in Egypt's western desert. Occupied since prehistoric times, it became home to the sacred oracle of the Libyan-Egyptian god Ammon (Amun). Already famous by Alexander's time, it was consulted by him in 332–331 B.C.E., one result of which was the propaganda story that he was the divine offspring of Ammon, not the mortal son of Philip II. Today, several abandoned medieval mud-built settlements survive, as well as the so-called Oracle Temple that Alexander consulted. In 1995, Siwa was announced as the site of Alexander's tomb by the Greek archaeologist Liana Souvaltzi.

Soma/Sema Soma is the Greek word for body, Sema for tomb. These two names are used interchangeably and confusingly by the ancient writers describing Alexander's second Alexandrian tomb built by Ptolemy IV Philopater in 215 B.C.E. The two terms are applied, variously, to the whole of Philopater's funerary park (marked by its perimeter wall), Alexander's mausoleum within it, Alexander's mummy, and the whole district within which the tombs of Alexander and the Ptolemies were located. Subsequently, scholars have changed Soma to Sema where they thought it appropriate, while others have thought Soma was a colloquial Alexandrian term for the tomb. Mistakes made by those who copied and translated ancient sources have also added to the confusion.

Successors Name given to Alexander's generals (and their offspring) who fought among themselves for parts of his empire after his death in 323 B.C.E. Initially these were Perdiccas, Ptolemy, Antipater, Craterus, Eumenes, Lysimichus, and Antigonus One-Eye, though their assorted sons carried on the fighting and maneuvering for power. Notable amongst these were Cassander in Macedonia, the Ptolemies of Egypt, and the Seleucids of Syria.

Susa Susa, "city of lilies," was the administrative capital of the Persian empire where records were kept in the cuneiform script incised onto sun-dried clay tablets. Located in the region of Elam, Alexander held his mass wedding between Macedonians and Persian women here in 324 B.C.E.

Vergina *See* Aegae.

Vulgate sources Literary sources on Alexander's life originating with the *History of Alexander* written by the Greek historian Cleitarchus, who was not an eyewitness. These sources include the accounts of Diodorus Siculus, Quintus Curtius Rufus, and Justin. They contrast with the so-called Official sources of Arrian, Ptolemy, and Aristoboulos, which derive ultimately from the *Exploits of Alexander* by Callisthenes (Aristotle's nephew), whom Alexander appointed as his historian, and who was an eyewitness to most of the events.

Wadi Natrun Area south of Alexandria rich in deposits of silica and natron, used in mummification, glassmaking, and cosmetics. The ready availability of vast deposits of these minerals helped make the city a center of manufacturing industries based on these natural resources in Ptolemaic and Roman times.

ACKNOWLEDGMENTS

FOR OVER TWENTY YEARS THE IDEA OF ALEXANDER the Great's tomb has been a fascination. It was less an interest in discovering the tomb or its site, than of searching for its traces in the world, tracking its influence on history, and charting the lives and times of the various characters and personalities who have been associated with it for two thousand years. Decades of traveling in Greece, Turkey, and Egypt raised new questions and strengthened this interest. Finally the opportunity for publishing arrived through the intervention of a longtime friend Peter Tallack and Amanda Cook of Basic Books. I am grateful to both for their faith in the topic and in me.

I would like to thank the following, all of whom have influenced my own thinking in one way or another or helped me with source material or practical matters. None, of course, are responsible for what I have made of their published work or the kindnesses they have extended to me. Drora Baharal, Andrew Chugg, Katherine Edgar, Jean-Yves Empereur, Robin Lane Fox, Peter Fraser, Sabine Gevaert, Gunther Grimm, N. G. L. Hammond, Mahdi Hweiti, Jona Lendering (www.livius.org), Museum of Fine Arts Boston, Chip Rosetti, Nermin Sami, Liana Souvaltzi, Neal Spencer, Harry Tzalas, and Eleana Yalouri.

NOTES

INTRODUCTION

1. Samartzidou 1993; Lazardis 1973; Griffith 1979. The most comprehensive account of ancient Macedonia remains the magisterial three-volume *A History of Macedonia*, by N. G. L. Hammond (vol. 1, 1972), N. G. L. Hammond and G. T. Griffith (vol. 2, 1979), and N. G. L. Hammond and F. W. Walbank (vol. 3, 1988). Archaeology has moved on since then, but in other respects these volumes are a mine of scholarly insight. More popular but equally erudite are Hammond 1991 and Borza 1990. Two lavishly illustrated books on Macedonian history and archaeology are Vokotopoulou 1993 and Touratsoglou 1995.

2. Ellis 1976, 66; Griffith 1979, 237–238.

3. Touratsoglou 1995, 335.

4. Lorber 1990; Price 1991.

5. Hammond 1988a, 91.

6. Touratsoglou 1995, 344.

7. Roger 1939; Broneer 1941.

8. Fedak 1990, 24–25. Scholarly debate continues over whether this monument (and others like it) served originally as tombs or cenotaphs. The fragmentary condition of the remains makes this a difficult issue to resolve.

9. Touratsoglou 1995, 340–341.

CHAPTER 1

1. Green 1991, 37.

2. Stoneman 1991; Green 1991, 478–479. The *Alexander Romance* had its origins in the Ptolemaic era, perhaps in Alexandria, during the third century B.C.E. It became increasingly elaborated over time, especially during the centuries after Christ, when it was influenced by the wonder tale genre and heavily colored by Christian theology (Stoneman 1991, 21).

3. Stoneman 1991, 38–40.

4. Dodds 1997. Dodds argues for the shamanistic origins and nature of Greek religion–the "irrational" foundations of what is regarded as the supremely rational Greek civilization. Divination, oracles, sacrifice, fertility festivals, and anthropomorphic deities are just some of the well-documented features of Hellenic spirituality and ritual that, while distinctively Greek, emerge from and partake of older and widespread shamanistic beliefs, which are based on the power of analogy and symbolic reasoning.

5. Heckel 1992, 206–207.

6. Touratsoglou 2000, 198–209.

7. Heckel 1992, 68 n. 47. Olympias also urged Alexander to have intercourse with Kallixeina but to no avail. In later years, Olympias wrote letters to Alexander complaining about Hephaestion's unhealthy influence and advising her son to get married. Alexander allowed Hephaestion to read his mother's correspondence, and on one occasion he replied to Olympias using the royal plural: "Stop quarreling with us. . . . You know that Alexander means more to us than anything" (Green 1991, 465).

8. Heckel 1992, 170.

9. Plutarch 1979; Alexander, p 304.

10. Heckel 1992, 134–135.

11. Green 1991, 37.

12. Griffith 1979, 558.

13. Quoted in Green 1991, 41.

14. Green 1991, 107.

15. Green 1991, 200.

16. Clayton and Price 1989; Hornblower 1982.

17. The head of one of these magnificent horses is on display in the British Museum, London.

18. This painting was originally lodged in Ephesus.

19. Balsdon 1950; Badian 1981, 2003; Bosworth 1996; 1988, 278–290; Cawkwell 2003; Tarn 1948, 2:347–369; Worthington 2003b. The issue of Alexander's deification is fascinating, complex, and endlessly debated by scholars with widely differing views. The focus here is the treatment that Alexander received in death. In regard to kings being deified and accorded godly cults, the situation after Alexander (i.e., during the Hellenistic age) was drastically different from that during his life and before. Consequently Alexander's tomb would represent a new, elaborate, and hybrid experience of ruler cults.

20. The date is known precisely, as it was preceded by an eclipse of the moon a few days previously.

21. Arrian 1971, 344–346.

22. Bosworth 1988, 154.

CHAPTER 2

1. Arrian 1971, 363.
2. Fox 1978, 432.
3. Fox 1980, 383.
4. Arrian 1971, p 371.
5. *Iliad* 23.141.152; Arrian 1971, 372.
6. Diodorus Siculus, 8, 1963, 17.114.4–5.
7. Arrian 1971, 372.
8. Plutarch 1979; Alexander 329.
9. Diodorus Siculus 8, 1963, 17.11.23.
10. Plutarch 1979; Alexander 329.
11. Plutarch; quoted in Stewart 1993, 404 (T134).
12. Plutarch; quoted in Stewart 1993, 405 (T134).
13. Plutarch; quoted in Stewart 1993, 405 (T134); Vitruvius, quoted in Andrew Stewart 1993, 402–403 (T132).
14. Palagia 2002, 169.
15. Diodorus Siculus 8, 1963, 17.115.1–4.
16. Palagia 2002, 170.
17. Palagia 2002, 172.
18. Koldewey 1914; Oates 1986.
19. Arrian 1971, 373.
20. Andronikos 1987, 123–136.
21. Palagia 2002, 174; Karageorghis 1969, 171–199.
22. Diodorus Siculus 9, 1967, 18.4.2.
23. Davies 2000, 197.
24. Plutarch 1979; Alexander, p 329; Arrian 1976, 7.14.7.
25. Bosworth 1988, 171.
26. Diodorus Siculus 8, 1963, 17.117.1–5.
27. Arrian 1971, 393.
28. Green 1991, 476–477.
29. Girling 2003, 29–30.
30. Oldach, Borza, and Benitez 1998, 4.
31. Quintus Curtius Rufus 1988, 256.
32. Marr and Calisher 2003, 1601.
33. Plutarch 1979, 330.
34. Quintus Curtius Rufus 1988, 256.
35. Herodotus 1990, 86–89.
36. Hammond 1988b, 105–106.
37. *Epitoma rerum gestarum Alexandri Magni*; quoted in Stewart 1993, 356 (T47).
38. Green 1991, 477.

CHAPTER 3

1. Quintus Curtius Rufus 1988, 245.

2. Stewart 1993, 222.

3. Stewart 1993, 369, T71; Diodorus Siculus 9, 1967, 18.26.1–28.4, as quoted in Stewart 1993, 370–373, T74. Since no images of this creation have survived on coins, medallions, or other durable materials, we have only this description to go on. A selection of different reconstructions of the hearse based on Diodorus's account can be found in Miller 1986; Müller 1905; Stewart 1993, 217; Heck and Winkles 1851, as reproduced in Chugg 2004b, 40–41.

4. Stewart 1993, 220.

5. Stewart 1993, 223.

6. Pausanias; quoted in Stewart 1993, 375, T80.

7. Diodorus Siculus; quoted in Stewart 1993, 373, T74.

8. Parian Marble; quoted in Stewart 1993, 369, T72.

9. Diodorus Siculus 9, 1967, 18.60–61, 19.15.3–4.

10. Thompson 1988, 12; Diodorus Siculus 9, 1967, 18.34.6–35.

11. At Triparadeisos (Three Parks), the empire was allotted to the main players: Ptolemy kept Egypt; Antigonus One-Eye received Asia; Seleucus, Babylonia; and Lysimachos, Thrace. Antipater became regent and was given custody of the two kings and Roxanne in Macedonia. Diodorus Siculus 9, 1967, 18.39.2; Stewart 1993, 224; Green 1990, 14–15.

12. Fraser 1972, 1:246–276; Stambaugh 1972; Thompson 1988, 191–207, 212–265.

13. Lauer 1976; Ray 1978.

14. Strabo 1917–1932, 17.1.32.

15. Lauer and Picard 1955.

16. Chugg 2004c.

17. Stoneman 1991, 35–41.

CHAPTER 4

1. The original plan may have been to make Pharos the center of the city. It was too small for that, but it did protect the deep-sea harbor that made the site so attractive (Green 2004, 181).

2. Despite the site's association with Alexander, an earlier settlement (perhaps a military garrison or a small fishing village) on the limestone ridge known as Rhacotis was Egyptian; it became part of greater Alexandria as the city took shape (Green 2004, 181).

3. Payne 1991, 175.

4. Fraser 1972, 1:212.

5. Fraser 1972, 1:215; Erskine 2002, 175.

6. Fraser 1972, 1:11–12; Ross Taylor 1927.

7. Fraser 1972, 1:131.

8. Quintus Curtius Rufus 1988, 10.10.20.

9. Diodorus Siculus 9, 1967, 18.18.28.3–5; quoted in Erskine 2002, 172.

10. Pausanias 1918, 1.7.1.

11. The Parian Marble is an enigma. It is damaged and incomplete, and its compiler was notoriously selective. For example, there is no mention of such major historical figures and events as Solon, Pericles, and the Peloponnesian War. The anonymous carver engraved a statement that his marble record finished in 264, not 298. The date of Alexander's reburial in Alexandria may be inscribed on this missing fragment. The definitive source for the marble's translation is in Jacoby 1940–1958.

12. Quintus Curtius Rufus 1988, 6.11.10, quoted in Heckel and Yardley 2004, 16.

13. Hammond 1988c, 164–166.

14. The prospect of Cassander's demise if Alexander IV reached maturity was publicly stated in the so-called Peace of the Dynasts in 311. This treaty ended hostilities between an alliance–consisting of Ptolemy, Cassander, and Lysimachus–and Antigonus One-Eye. The terms included the statement that Cassander was to be "manager of the king's affairs" and "general of Europe" only until Alexander IV came of age. Cassander clearly felt it was the time to act, and did so.

15. Holbl 2001, 21–23.

16. Scholars disagree as to whether or not this event–the Grand Procession of Ptolemy Philadelphus–was part of the Ptolemaia festival or linked to it.

17. Callixeinus's fragmentary account is preserved in another incomplete account written and then anthologized by Athenaeus of Naucratis during the second century C.E.

18. Rice 1981.

19. The golden splendor of royal and wealthy Ptolemaic women can be glimpsed in *Greek Gold from Hellenistic Egypt* by Michael Pfrommer (2001). Necklaces, armbands, bracelets, hairnets, earrings, and intaglio finger rings all reveal the skill and inventiveness of Alexandrian goldsmiths.

20. Philadelphus imported camels into Egypt for the first time in 275–274 to participate in the Ptolemaia and Grand Procession. Later they became part of the native transportation system, often replacing horses that had predominated hitherto (Green 1990, 367).

21. Houlihan 2003.

22. Goldhill 2004, 29–39.

23. Fraser 1972, 1:657–678.

24. Arnold 1999, 128.
25. Fraser 1972, 1:216.
26. Holbl 2001, 94–95.

CHAPTER 5

1. Wolohojian 1969; quoted in Sly 1996, 28.
2. Green 2004, 175.
3. Fraser 1972, 1:10, 2:24 nn. 45–46.
4. Strabo 17.1.8; quoted in Erskine 2002, 164.
5. Fraser 1972, 1:29–31.
6. Fraser 1972, 2:373 n. 285.
7. Clayton and Price 1989; Hornblower 1982.
8. Fraser 1972, 1:81; Zenobius *Proverbia* 3.94.
9. Fraser 1972, 1:225.
10. Zenobius *Proverbia* 3.94.
11. Fraser 1972, 2:32–33 n. 4.
12. Erskine 2002, 166–167. Insider knowledge confused foreign visitors and those who wrote from far away. Scholarly arguments about *soma* and *sema* are ultimately rendered pointless for this reason, and, as many experts agree, because of the spelling errors introduced by those who transcribed and copied them in antiquity. Passing by Alexander's mausoleum was an everyday experience for the city's inhabitants. Philo (30 B.C.E.–50 C.E.) was a prominent Jewish figure and a prolific writer. Privileged and well-educated, Philo linked philosophy with the Hippocratic medical tradition of the day. In one treatise he wrote that the human body *(soma)* was the tomb *(sema)* of the soul, and that we are all nothing but corpse bearers (Sly 1996, 4–5, 163). Philo had a harsh opinion of Hellenistic Alexandria's preoccupation with material wealth and opulent display, an obsession shaped by the nature of the city as a grand funerary park. Philo spent his whole life in Alexandria, in which the Soma was the political and architectural focus of pagan religious cult. If any single object embodied Jewish (and early Christian) loathing of pagan idolatry, Alexander's mausoleum must have been near the top of the list. It is tempting to see Philo's division of body and soul in his treatise as a reaction against Hellenism's obsession with the body over the mind–an obsession focused by the omnipresence of Alexander's innumerable cult images and the dominance of his tomb. In Philo's philosophy, all humanity may have been corpse bearers, but Alexandria's inhabitants bore the extra burden of Alexander's body as well.
13. Zenobius *Proverbia* 1.81; quoted in Erskine 2002, 166.
14. Achilles Tatius 1917.
15. Achilles Tatius 1917, 5.1.
16. Chugg 2004, 81, 238; Fawzi el-Fakharani 1999.

17. Trapp 2004, 114–117.

18. How likely is it that a novelist who sets his story in Alexandria for dramatic effect ignores the most spectacular backdrop any novel could have in favor of describing an open space and right-angled streets? No novelist who visited Alexandria before or after the great siege of the Roman emperor Aurelian could have written such a passage without mentioning Alexander's tomb. Either the Soma had survived the recent violence intact or it had been destroyed. Either way it would have been irresistible to a writer. It is strange that Tatius, said to be a native Alexandrian, adds nothing to his description that was not widely available and widely known at the time. Every detail is standardized, and there are no personal flourishes culled from intimate personal knowledge of the city (Trapp 2004, 114–117).

19. Fraser 1972, 1:523, 779.

20. Fraser 1972, 1:60–61.

21. Fraser 1972, 1:219, 2:369 n. 237.

22. Fraser 1972, 1:15.

23. Fraser 1972, 1:14–15, 23.

24. Fraser 1972, 1:12.

25. Fraser 1972, 1:10, 2:24 nn. 45–46.

26. Green 1990, 663, fig. 20.

27. Bailey 1984; Balil 1962.

28. Chugg 2004, 94–95.

29. Lucan, *Pharsalia*, quoted in Chugg 2004b, 84.

30. Lucan, *Pharsalia*; quoted in Chugg 2004b, 83.

31. Fraser 1972, 1:34.

32. Hornblower 1982; Jeppesen et al. 1981; Jeppesen and Luttrell 1986; Newton 1862; Waywell 1978, 1989.

33. Davies 2000, 52; Bernhard 1956.

34. Davies 2000, 54–55; Fedak 1990, 137–139.

35. Coarelli and Thébert 1988.

36. Davies 2000, 55.

37. Harpath 1978; Hadjinicolaou 1997. Alexander's victories over Darius were symbolically appropriated and cleverly reconfigured by the papacy at the height of Christendom's wars with the Ottoman empire. In an astonishing transformation, pagan Alexander became a heroic role model for Christian popes who saw (and named) themselves after him, as they too waged war against barbarians in the east. Historical and religious accuracy were subverted, and a new religiously inspired ideology created the Alexander it required. Even the Ptolemaic and later Roman practice of striking self-promoting coins and medals bearing images of Alexander was followed by Pope Paul III. In 1546 he commissioned Alessandro Cesati to produce a gold medallion showing his own papal head on one side, and on the reverse Alexander kneeling before the high priest of

Jerusalem. The medallion connected the pope and Alexander on one object, and implied that if Alexander accepted the Judaeo-Christian god then the world should follow suit (Yalouris 1980, fig. 8; Tonsing 2002, 85–86). Michelangelo commented that Cesati's medallion was the epitome of medal making.

38. Davies 2000, 56–60; Coarelli and Thébert 1988, 788–790.

39. Handler 1971, 74.

40. Handler 1971, 68.

41. Making sense of small-scale representations requires a mastery of deciphering skills. A many-columned building is shown with only two or four columns to make room for the cult statue, the key feature of identification at the time, if not today.

42. Handler 1971, 68; Ross Taylor 1930.

43. Handler 1971, 68.

CHAPTER 6

1. Milne 1916.

2. Suetonius Caesar 7; Lucan 1928, 10.19.8.694–697.

3. Spencer 2002, 63.

4. Coarelli and Thébert 1988, 788–789.

5. *Dio's Roman History* 1982, 51.16.45, 47.

6. Suetonius, *Lives of the Caesars,* Augustus, 2.18.

7. Suetonius, *Lives of the Caesars,* Augustus, 2.18.

8. *Dio's Roman History* 1982, 21.16.5.

9. Strabo, 1917–1932, 17.100.793–799.

10. Macfarlane and Martin 2002, 10–13; Nenna 1993, 1998; Shortland 2003, 2004; Hassan 2002, 155; Empereur 2000, 24, fig. 35. Glassmaking first appeared in Egypt between 3000 and 2000 B.C.E., though glass was not produced on a large scale until Ptolemaic and Roman times. Until the Roman era, it retained its magical and sacred qualities, being used for amulets, beads, and jewelry as an exotic man-made precious stone. Until the first century B.C.E., glass objects were made by casting and grinding, but then the superior technique of glassblowing was invented in Syria or Iraq. If Alexander's replacement sarcophagus of 89 B.C.E. was glass, this new technique may have been employed to make it. Alexandria achieved preeminence in glassmaking during Ptolemaic times because natron (mainly used for mummification) and silica were abundant in the Wadi Natrun south of the city.

11. Strabo 1917–1932, 17.C.794; Fraser 1972, 1:15.

12. *Dio's Roman History* 1982, 51.5.3.17.

13. Josephus, *Against Apion* 2.57–58.317.

14. Suetonius, *Lives of the Caesars,* Gaius 52.

15. Quoted in Chugg 2004b, 120.

16. Chugg 2004b, 121, fig. 4.8b.

17. Stevenson et al.; quoted in Chugg 2004b, 124.

18. Lambert 1997.

19. Euphrosyne Doxiadis 1995, 147. Some of these portraits were painted in life and were displayed for years in the home. After death they were cut to fit the face panel of the mummy.

20. Euphrosyne Doxiasis 1995, 12.

21. Tiradrittii 1999, 404–405.

22. *Dio's Roman History* 1982, 76.225.

23. Hornung 2001, 59–60; *Dio's Roman History* 1982, 76.13.

24. Herodian 1969, 4.7.7–8.2; *Dio's Roman History* 1982, 78.7–8, 17.1–2.

25. Herodian 1969, 4.8.7–7.

26. *Epitome de Caesaribus Sexti Aureli Victoris* 21.4; quoted in Stewart 1993, 348. Caracalla's obsession with Alexander led him to commission a set of large gold medallions of himself, Alexander, and Alexander's mother, Olympias. Their purpose was to include Caracalla in Alexander's earthly family, and in the mythical one that identified them with Homeric heroes such as Achilles (Vermeule 1980, 103, items 10–11; Stewart 1993, 50–51; Tonsing 1992, 102). The medallions were found at Aboukir, near Alexandria, at the beginning of the twentieth century.

27. *Dio's Roman History* 1982, 78.7.1–4.

28. Herodian 1969, 4.9.3–5.425.

29. If the Brucheum's walls could be identified archaeologically, then the location of the Soma through its presumably massive foundations might also be identified.

30. Stoneman 1994, 178.

31. Butler 1978, 411.

32. Williams 2000, 80–81.

33. Ammianus Marcellinus, *Res Gestae* 1935–1939, 22.16.15.

CHAPTER 7

1. Fox 1986, 639–641.

2. Fox 1986, 638.

3. Fox 1986, 655.

4. Biddle 1999, 65; Walker 1990, 276.

5. Fox 1986, 671. Golgotha was originally outside Jerusalem's walls but was enclosed within the new walls built by Herod Agrippa between 41 and 44 C.E. The city was destroyed in 70 C.E. when Rome suppressed the Jewish Rebellion; on its ruins arose the Roman Colonia Aelia Capitolina founded by Hadrian in 130 C.E. After Rome suppressed the Bar Kokhba Revolt in 135, new construction

leveled Golgotha, burying the hill of crucifixion under tons of rubble, and a temple of Aphrodite (or perhaps Tyche or Jupiter) was raised on top. This landscaping buried several rock-cut tombs nearby, one of which, according to the Gospels, was the place where Joseph of Arimathea laid Jesus' body to rest in 30 C.E. The Gospels tell the story in different ways but agree that the tomb belonged to a wealthy man but had never been used (Biddle 1998, 54–55). It was surrounded by a garden, had a raised stone-cut bench for the body, and was closed by a movable stone–a typical Jewish tomb of the time. Makarios's diggings were probably guided by a folk memory of Golgotha's location among Jerusalem's Jewish community (Biddle 1999, 64). Some think that the tomb may have been open and accessible for decades, perhaps a century after Christ's death (Biddle 1999, 66).

6. Biddle 1999, xi–xii.

7. Biddle 1999, 1.

8. Fox 1986, 671.

9. Hornung 2001, 68.

10. Ammianus Marcellinus 1935–1939, 22.16.15.

11. Johnson 1978, 99; Baynes 1912.

12. Ammianus Marcellinus 1935–1939, 22.12.6.

13. Marlowe 1971, 275–277.

14. The possibility that Alexander's mausoleum was still standing in 360–361 C.E. is seductive. Ammianus, however, is not always reliable, as scholars have observed (Green 2004, 175). He tells stories that are astoundingly innaccurate, given that he spent time in Alexandria. He claims, for example, that Cleopatra VII had built the Pharos lighthouse and the Heptastadion causeway that linked Pharos island to the mainland. In fact, as historians know today, these famous constructions were already three hundred years old by Cleopatra's time. Ammianus's errors of historical fact highlight a perennial and intriguing issue: How could so many of our sources, living much closer in time to the events than we, make such fundamental mistakes? There must have been many knowledgeable people and more complete written sources that could have been consulted but for whatever reason were not.

15. Ammianus Marcellinus 1935–1939, 26.10.15–19.

16. Sozomenos 1964, 6.2.

17. Chugg 2004b, 159.

18. John Chrysostom, "To the Emperor Theodosius" and "For the Temples," in Libanius 1977.

19. Oration 49, 11–12. In Libanius 1977.

20. Chugg 2004b, 160.

21. Holbl 2001, 310; Hornung 2001, 68.

22. Christides 2000, 167–168; Synaxarium 2005. Theophilus's treasure is erroneously thought to come from Alexander's tomb or be associated with

it–presumably during the time when pagan temples were being looted. Christides (2000, 167) disproves this, noting the inherent irony that pagan gold paid for Christian churches in Alexandria. The further misunderstanding that the relics deposited in these new churches included those of Alexander is also disputed, though unproven.

23. John Chrystostom, Homily 26, 2 Corinthians 2:1.

24. John Chrysostom, Homily 26.12; quoted in Chugg 2004b, 144; Christides 2000, 166–167.

25. John Chrystostom 1889, 2 Corinthians, Homily XXVI.

26. Butler 1978, 374 n. 1.

27. Fulghum 2001, 140.

28. Fulghum 2001, 144–145; Maguire 1997.

29. Saint John Chrysostom 2004. John Chrysostom, *Ad iluminado catechesis* 2.5; quoted in Holt 2003, 3.

30. Scriptore Historiae Augustae, *Tyranni triginta* 14.2–6; quoted in Holt 2003, 3.

31. Vermeule 1980, 116–117, items 34, 36.

32. Fulghum 2001, 145; Alfoldi and Alfoldi 1976.

33. Vermeule 1980, 117, item 37.

34. Finnestad 1998, 236–237.

35. Horning 2001, 71–73.

CHAPTER 8

1. Scholars regard most of these figures as inflated, preferring estimates of four hundred palaces and baths, forty theaters, and perhaps twelve hundred vegetable sellers, though Amr's count of the Jewish population may be more accurate.

2. Butler 1978, 369.

3. Butler 1978, 369.

4. Butler 1978, 371.

5. Butler 1978, 379.

6. El Daly 2005, 32–42. El Daly describes the range of legal and illegal Arab excavations in search of treasure. Some yielded so much gold that treasure hunting was a mainstay of the Islamic Egyptian economy (El Daly 2005, 34). Jewels, gold, silver masks, and glass were among the items sought and found by Arab excavators.

7. Butler 1978, 373.

8. Dzielska 1995, 93.

9. El Daly 2005, 21, 130. El Daly says that medieval Arab sources speak with passionate admiration about Alexander. So many volumes were written about Alexander that El Daly terms the phenomenon "Alexanderomania Arabica." Their

content seems to be a mixture of fantasy and fact in the vein of *The Alexander Romance*.

10. Bruhn 1993; Maguire 1997.

11. Fulghum 2001, 139.

12. Stoneman 1991, 21.

13. Fulghum 2001, 146; Kamil 2002. Copts are Egyptian Christians who maintain their own Coptic Orthodox Church, which declared separation from the Church of Constantinople in 570 C.E. From late Roman times to the thirteenth century, the Coptic language–based on Egyptian Demotic but written in the Greek alphabet–was the main language in Egypt. It is still used today in religious services. Coptic language and beliefs preserve pagan imagery and symbolism from pharaonic and Greco–Roman Egypt that later became (an often unacknowledged) part of mainstream Christianity. The influence of Isis and her son Horus on the Virgin Mother and Christ Child is one important example of such hybrid processes at work; the myth of Osiris' resurrection from the dead is another. The Coptic Museum in Old Cairo contains a rare early Coptic crucifix that depicts a beardless Christ with a Horus hawk and solar disk. The famous pharaonic *ankh*–the hieroglyphic sign for life–was adopted by the Copts as their own distinctive cross.

14. Fraser 1972, 2:36.

15. Wolf 2004, 200.

16. Wolf 2004, 206.

17. Fraser 1972, 2:37 n. 86; Chugg 2004b, xix; Pory 1896, 864–865.

18. Pory 1896, 864–865; quoted in Chugg 2004b, 169.

19. Fraser 1972, 2:37 n. 86.

20. Wolf 2004, 217.

21. Sandys 1617, 112; quoted in Fraser 1972, 2:39.

22. Bacqué-Grammont and Dankoff 2001, 70.8.

23. Chugg 2004b, 170–171.

24. Chugg 2004b, 170–173.

25. Manoncour 1800, 207.

26. Browne 1799, 9–10.

27. Strabo 17.C.793–794.

28. Christides 2000, 170.

29. Wolf 2004, 207; El Daly 2005, 26–27. Classical sources such as Strabo, Josephus, Herodotus, and Plato were, according to El Daly, widely available in their original languages, and in Arabic, Syriac, and possibly Aramaic and Persian as well.

30. Fraser; in Butler 1978, lxxviii.

31. Mostafa El-Abbadi 2004, 175.

32. Mostafa El-Abbadi 2004, 176.

33. Fraser; in Butler 1978, lxxxi.

34. Butler 1978, 492.

CHAPTER 9

1. Coleman 2002, 164.
2. Said 1991.
3. De Bourienne 1891, chap. 3.
4. De Bourienne 1891, chap. 3.
5. Denon 1986, 27–29.
6. "Vedette" 1899, 79.
7. Solé and Valbelle 2002, 3.
8. Solé and Valbelle 2002, 9–10.
9. Solé and Valbelle 2002, 4.
10. Clarke 1805, 30.
11. Clarke 1805, 39.
12. Clarke 1805, 40.
13. Clarke 1805, 40.
14. Clarke 1805; caption for illustration of Attarine Mosque.
15. Clarke 1805, 29.
16. Brierbrier 1999, 111.
17. Heraclides 1806, Letters 1–4.
18. Clarke 1807, i-ii.
19. Neal Spencer, personal communication, January 21, 2003; Alexander 1805.
20. Adkins and Adkins 2000, 71.
21. Dacier 1822.
22. Jenni 1986.
23. St. Clair 1998, 63.
24. St. Clair 1998, 107.

CHAPTER 10

1. Tzalas 1998.
2. El-Fakharani 1964, 179.
3. El-Fakharani 1964, 179.
4. Empereur 1998, 249 n. 3.
5. Jondet 1921, planche 36; I am grateful to Jean-Yves Empereur for this information and for a glimpse of his copy of Mahmoud Bey's rare 1865 map.
6. Fraser 1972, 1:8–9.

7. Fraser 1972, 1:13–14; Hogarth and Benson 1895.

8. Empereur 1998, 56–57.

9. According to Jean Yves Empereur, director of the Centre d'Etudes Alexandrines, much of the original Ptolemaic city lies intact at depths of up to forty feet below the modern street level.

10. Fraser 1972, 2:28–29 n. 68.

11. Empereur 1998, 57. Smaller streets, unsuspected by Mahmoud Bey, have been found, apparently belonging to the fourth century C.E. and pushed through the remains of earlier two hundred-year-old houses.

12. Empereur 1998, 57.

13. Rodziewicz 1995; Empereur 1998, 57.

14. Technology undreamed of by Mahmoud Bey has refined a key orientation of his ancient city. His map shows the Heptastadion causeway entering the street system at an oblique angle that fits awkwardly with the grid. During the 1990s, a team of geophysicists made a remote sensing survey of the area and traced the true direction of the causeway beneath the ground as it entered the city. It is now clear that the Heptastadion was perfectly in tune with the grid system and is aligned to the ancient street called R9 by Mahmoud Bey (Musée du Petit Palais 1998, 89).

15. Peter Fraser (1972, 1:13) has questioned whether Mahmoud Bey's excavations uncovered walls at all, or if so, whether they were the original Ptolemaic ones. Evaristo Breccia, the second director of the Graeco–Roman Museum in Alexandria, also had serious reservations on the same issue (Fraser 1972, 2:26 n. 63). The German scholar Günter Grimm (1996, 57) also believes there is no real proof for Mahmoud Bey's outline of where the city walls were located.

16. Marlowe 1971, 55; Musée du Petit Palais 1998, 52–53.

17. Fraser 1972, 2:38 n. 86.

18. Empereur 1998, 149.

19. Fraser 1972, 2:41 n. 88.

20. Ramonsky told his story in 1933 to Father Andronicus, a monk and history teacher in Alexandria, and it eventuallly found its way to the novelist Lawrence Durrell, who published it in 1966.

21. Fraser 1972, 1:17.

22. Bey and Reinach 1892.

23. Von Graeve 1970.

24. Bell 2005, diary entry for June 6, 1898.

25. Stewart 1993, 294.

26. Palagia 2002, 186.

27. Palagia 2002, 196; Heckel 1992, 69.

28. Palagia 2002, 188.

29. Palagia 2002, 189.

30. Stewart 1993, 297.

31. Stewart 1993, 398.

32. Mariette 1856.

33. Lauer and Picard 1955.

34. Houlihan 2003.

35. Myśliwiec 2000, 186–187.

36. Myśliwiec 2000, 186–187.

37. Myśliwiec 2000, 186–187.

38. Empereur 1997.

CHAPTER 11

1. Adriani 2000, 61; Breccia 1907, 1908; Venit 2002, 8.

2. Adriani 2002, 61; Breccia 1922.

3. Adriani 2002, 61, 63.

4. Adriani 2002, 63.

5. Venit 2002, 9.

6. Venit 2002, 9.

7. Empereur 1998, 152.

8. Schwartz 2001, 2003.

9. Schwartz 2001, 77–79.

10. Schwartz 2001, 72.

11. Gaber et al. 1999.

12. El-Fakharani 1999.

13. Paramarinopoulos et al, 2003, 195.

14. Paramarinopoulos et al, 2003, 207–210.

15. Paramarinopoulos et al. 2003, 210.

16. Empereur 1998, 51.

17. Paramarinopoulos et al. 2003, 210.

18. Empereur 1998, 153.

19. Fraser 1962, 243 n. 2; Fraser 1972, 2:41 n. 87; Venit 2002, 23.

20. Fraser 1962, 243.

21. Grimm 1996, 58.

22. Venit 2002, 22–3.

23. Venit 2002, 44–67.

24. Venit 2002, 22. Whether this north-south cordon of burials from Chatby to Hadra is one long continuous cemetery flanking the entire eastern wall, or perhaps is two or more separate ones that grew to overlap each other is still debated. Hadra seems to have lasted longer, and was still in use between 250 and 180 B.C.E. (Grimm 1996, 58) and may even have lasted into the Christian era (Venit 2002, 22).

25. Venit 2002, 23; Grimm 1996, 58.

26. Grimm 1998, 14–15 (map); Fraser 1972, 1:13.

27. Grimm 1996, 62.

28. Venit 2002, 22. The area east of Chatby also retained vestiges of its earlier importance as a burial ground, as is shown by the splendid Tigrane tomb near the Mustapha Pasha cemetery, with its well-preserved paintings belonging to the time of the Roman emperor Hadrian (117–138 C.E.) (Venit 146, 159)–some three hundred years after the Mustapha Pasha burials.

29. Fraser 1972, 1:31–32; Fraser 1972, 2:102 n. 236; 110 n. 271.

30. Grimm 1996, 71 n. 35.

31. Holt 2001, 10.

32. Keeley 1976, esp. chap. 4; Forster 2004; Durrell 1990.

33. Empereur 1998, 148.

34. Tzalas 2004, 69 n. 13.

35. Tzalas 2004, 69 n. 13.

36. Tzalas 2004, 69 n. 13.

37. Fraser 1962, 244.

38. Fraser 1962, 244.

39. Fraser 1962, 245.

40. Fraser 1962, 247.

41. Fraser 1962, 247.

42. Bianchi 1993.

43. Empereur 1998, 146.

44. Empereur 1998, 146.

45. Empereur 1998, 146.

CHAPTER 12

1. Fakhry 2004, 71–72. Today the native Siwans speak a local dialect of Berber, though the rise of tourism has brought Arabic and English to this place where, a century ago, only one family spoke anything other than the local language. Siwans possess a keen sense of identity (Fakhry 2004, 39–69; Malim 2001), a fact that keeps them separate from, though a part of, modern Egypt.

2. Cartledge 2004, 268–269.

3. Alexander was susceptible to omens and prophecies. He appears to have traveled to Siwa for three reasons: to rival his heroic ancestors Heracles and Perseus, to ask questions of the supposedly infallible oracle (perhaps of his destiny), and to inquire as to the nature of his conception and descent. The issue of his divine paternity rings more true than the others, which may have been added years later. Apparently the chief priest addressed Alexander as the son of a god (though whether Ammon or Zeus is not identified) and reassured him that his father's murder had been fully avenged. In typical oracular fashion, he added that

Alexander would conquer the world–a safe prediction that Alexander was already accomplishing.

4. Fakhry 2004, 150–164.

5. Fakhry 2004, 165–172.

6. Vivian 1990.

7. Vivian 1990, 283.

8. Souvaltzi 1993.

9. Fakhry 2004, 126–127; Tzalas 2004, 69.

10. Caillaud 1923–1927; Rohlfs 1876; von Minutoli 1820; Fakhry 2004, 102–104, 106–107, 110; Bianchi 1993.

11. Fakhry 1944.

12. Grecoreport 2001–2002.

13. Souvaltzi 2002, 42. Liana Souvaltzi's 2002 book, *The Tomb of Alexander the Great at the Siwa Oasis: The History of the Archaeological Excavation and Its Political Background*, is neither a standard archaeology text nor a popular account. It is a potpourri of her experiences, a quasi-diary peppered with ideas, feelings, and prejudices, and illustrated with an interesting choice of color photographs. As a technical document of her excavations it has limited use. But as a personal account of what archaeologists regard as a fraud perpetrated on a global scale it provides fascinating insights.

14. Souvaltzi 2002, 49.

15. Souvaltzi 2002, 134–135.

16. Bianchi 1995.

17. Souvaltzi 2002, 54–55.

18. Bianchi 1995.

19. Souvaltzi 2002, 20.

20. Tzalas 2004, 69.

21. Tzalas 2004, 70.

22. Tzalas 2004, 70.

23. Tzalas 2004, 70.

24. Tzalas 2004, 70.

25. Grecoreport 1995.

26. Grecoreport 1995.

27. Grecoreport 1995.

28. Grecoreport 2001–2002.

29. Bianchi 1995.

30. Souvaltzi 2002, 238–239.

31. Souvaltzi 2002, 239.

32. Grecoreport 2001–2002.

33. Caillaud 1923–1927, 72–74; Fakhry 2004, 126.

34. The site of the Doric temple on the low-lying desert floor is unsuitable for a tomb, due to the high water table. Siwa, although an oasis, has too much water

bubbling up from underground springs which then evaporates into large salty lakes. Presumably this was also the case in late Ptolemaic and Roman times, which explains why the area is dotted with rock-cut tombs on higher ground, and particularly in high cliff-face locations. Placing any burial, let alone a royal one, beneath ground level would invite flooding and destruction of the body, and would not have been contemplated for Alexander.

35. Danforth 2003, 347.

36. Danforth 2003, 351; Alexander Donski 2003.

37. Danforth 2003, 357–358. This provocative issue was largely resolved in 1995, when Greece and FYROM signed an accord that saw the former end its economic blockade in exchange for the latter changing its flag (Danforth 2003, 351).

38. Brown 1998, 83 n. 6.

39. Borza 1990, 303.

40. Green 1989, 154–155.

41. Those who take this view argue that fourth-century B.C.E. history proves their point: Alexander and his father Philip were regarded as non–Greek speaking barbarians who ended the era of autonomous city-states at the Battle of Chaeronea in 338 B.C.E. Even worse, Alexander destroyed Thebes and sold its population into slavery (Green 1989, 154).

42. Green 1989, 153.

43. Danforth 2003, 355.

44. Green 1989, 155.

45. Green 1989, 160–161.

46. Hamilakis and Yalouri 1999, 117.

47. Hamilakis and Yalouri 1999, 117.

48. Papazois 2003.

49. Walbank 1988, 262–263.

50. Papazois 2003.

51. Bartsiokis 2000.

52. Papazois 2003.

53. Palagia 2002, 191–192.

54. Borza 1987.

55. Andronikos 1987, 137–144; Cohen 1997, plate II.

56. Hammond 1982, 127.

CHAPTER 13

1. BBC 2002.

2. Chugg 2002a,b.

3. Wace 1949.

4. Chugg 2004c.

5. Arnold 1999, 337 n. 65.

6. Arnold 1999, 109.

7. Diodorus Siculus 16.51.

8. Arnold 1999, 339 n. 119.

9. Fraser 1972, 1:25; McKenzie 2003, 47; Pliny 1938–1962, *Natural History* 16.9.14; Empereur 1998, 100, 108–109; Petrie and Mackay 1915. Heliopolis was established about 2600 B.C.E. and was an important cult center to the sun god Ra during pharaonic times. During Hellenistic times the Ptolemies used it as a quarry, taking statues, obelisks, and sphinxes to adorn Alexandria's streets and temples, such as the Serapeum. Two obelisks of the pharaoh Thutmose III (1479–1425 B.C.E.) were used to beautify the Caesareum, and later became known as Cleopatra's needles. During the nineteenth century, the Ptolemaic practice of recycling these monuments was continued when one was taken to the United States and erected in New York's Central Park, the other transported to London, where it now stands on the Thames Embankment.

10. Arnold 1999, 93.

11. Thompson 1988, 113.

12. Arnold 1999, 127; and see Kamal 1906.

13. Arnold 1999, 125–127.

14. Arnold 1999, 128.

15. Arnold 1999, 128.

16. Ashton 2003, 213; Ashton, 2001, 20, 84–85. So alike are the royal sculptures of the two Nectanebos (I and II) and the first two Ptolemies (Ptolemy and his son Ptolemy Philadelphus) that even expert scholars have difficulty in distinguishing who is being represented. These similarities are not accidental, and doubtless conceal various political and ideological agendas.

17. Holbl 2001, 88.

18. Bacqué-Grammont and Dankoff 2001, 70.8.

19. Venit 2002, 187.

20. Venit 2002, 187.

21. Venit 2002, 187.

22. Interestingly, the anomalous hole at the rear end appears the least well made from the outside, and from the interior an unusual feature is revealed. It seems that a hole was begun from the inside and then abandoned when the workman realized that he had begun drilling in the wrong position to connect with the wider exterior hole. He started again some inches to the right and connected successfully. Was this hole added later–perhaps to speed up emptying?

23. Another feature supports this view and suggests an orientation for such a display. At the rear end of the sarcophagus, two deep parallel grooves were carved into the flat rim. If, as may have been the case at the time, the original sarcophagus cover was still available to be removed and replaced at will, then these two grooves are deep enough to contain terra-cotta water pipes, and then to lay the cover back

on top, thereby concealing the source of a constant water supply. As the well-made and regularly spaced outer holes adorned both long sides and the curved front end, these three sides may have been on public display with the rear perhaps obscured and used for piping in the water. At the moment, this is all speculation.

24. Fraser 1972, 1:609.

25. Fraser 1972, 1:610–611, 2:860–861 n. 412.

26. Chugg 2004a, 23; 2004b, 252–253, 264, 267.

27. Chugg 2004b, 267.

28. Chugg 2004a, 23.

29. Forlati 1975; Chugg 2004, 267.

30. Chugg 2004b, 266.

CHAPTER 14

1. Grimm 1998, 14–15, 26–27. Recent excavations in this area have uncovered foundations for a monumental late third century B.C.E. building with Doric and Ionic columns, though whether these are remains of the Soma is far from certain (McKenzie 2003, 39).

2. Finnestad 1998, 236–237; Fulghum 2001, 146; Kamil 2002, 71; Oxyrhynchus Papyri 1897–2001; www.papyrology.ox.ac.uk; Budge 1961. The remarkable papyrus finds at Oxyrhynchus (modern Bahnasa), which began in 1898, include scribal documents illustrating the many religions (including early Christianity) that were practiced at the time. Papyri fragments include petitions for success in love, health, worldly wealth, curses, and spells, and they invoke gods from all over the ancient world. Similar pantheistic practices are evident in the Judaeo–Christian–Egyptian amulets found throughout Egypt.

3. Hawass 2000.

4. Payne 1991, 179.

BIBLIOGRAPHY

Adkins, L., and R. Adkins. 2000. *The Keys of Egypt: The Obsession to Decipher Egyptian Hieroglyphs*. London: HarperCollins.

Adriani, Achille. 2000. *La Tomba di Alessandro: Realtà ipotesi e fantasie*. Rome: L'Erma di Bretschneider.

Alexander, W. 1805. *Egyptian Monuments from the Collection Formed by the National Institute Under the Direction of Bonaparte . . . now Deposited in the British Museum*. London: British Museum.

Alföldi, Andreas, and Elizabeth Alföldi. 1976. *Die Kontorniate-Medallions*. 2 vols. Berlin: De Gruyter.

Ammianus Marcellinus. 1935–1939. *Res Gestae*. Translated by J. C. Rolfe. Cambridge: Harvard University Press.

Andronikos, Manolis. 1987. *Vergina: The Royal Tombs and the Ancient City*. Athens: Ekdotike Athenon.

Arnold, Dieter. 1999. *Temples of the Last Pharoahs*. Oxford: Oxford University Press.

Arrian. 1971. *The Campaigns of Alexander*. Translated by Aubrey de Sélincourt. Harmondsworth, U.K.: Penguin.

_____. [1976] 1983. *Anabasis Alexandri and Indica*. Translated by P. A. Brunt. Vols. 1–2. Loeb Classical Library. Cambridge: Harvard University Press.

Ashton, Sally-Ann. 2001. *Ptolemaic Royal Sculpture from Egypt: The Interaction Between Greek and Egyptian Traditions*. British Archaeological Reports. Oxford: Archaeopress.

_____. 2003. "The Ptolemaic Royal Image and the Egyptian Tradition." In *Never Had the Like Occurred: Egypt's View of Its Past*, edited by J. Tait, pp. 213–224. London: UCL Press.

Bacqué-Grammont, J-L, and R. Dankoff. 2001. *D'Alexandrie à Rosette d'après la relation de voyage d'Evliya Çelebi*. Paris: Institut Français d' Études Anatoliennes. Version polygraphiée.

Badian, Ernst. 1981. "The Deification of Alexander the Great." In *Ancient Macedonian Studies in Honor of Charles F. Edson*, edited by H. J. Dell, pp. 27–71. Thessaloniki: Institute for Balkan Studies.

_____. 2000. "Conspiracies." In *Alexander the Great in Fact and Fiction*, edited by A. B. Bosworth and E. J. Baynham, pp. 50–95. Oxford: Oxford University Press.

_____. 2003. "Alexander the Great Between Two Thrones and Heaven: Variations on an Old Theme." In *Alexander the Great: A Reader*, edited by Ian Worthington, pp. 245–262. London: Routledge.

Baharal, Drora. 2003. "Caracalla, Alexander the Great, and Education in Rome." In *Hommages à Carl Deroux, III–Histoire et épigraphie, droit*, edited by Pol Defosse, pp. 29–36. Brussels: Éditions Latomus.

Bailey, D. M. 1984. "Alexandria, Carthage, and Ostia." In *Alessandria e il mondo ellenistico-romano, Studi in onore di Achille Adriani* 2, edited by N. Bonacasa and A. Di Vita, pp. 265–272. Rome: L'erma di Bretschneider.

Balil, A. 1962. "Una nueva representación de la tumba de Alejandro." *Archivo Español de Arqueología* 35: 102–103.

_____. 1984. "Monumentos alejandrinos y paisajes egipcios en Un mosaico romano de Toledo (España)." In *Alessandria e il mondo ellenistico-romano, Studi in onore di Achille Adriani* 3, edited by N. Bonacasa and Di Vita, pp. 433–439. Rome.

Balsdon, J. P. V. D. 1950. "The Divinity of Alexander." *Historia* 1: 363–388.

Bartsiokas, A. 2000. "The Eye Injury of King Philip II and the Skeletal Evidence from the Royal Tomb II At Vergina." *Science,* April 21, pp. 511–514.

Baynes, N. H. 1912. "Julian the Apostate and Alexander the Great." *English Historical Review* 27: 759–760.

BBC. 2002. BBC News World Edition, August 22. www.bbc.co.uk.

Bell,Gertrude. 2005. The Gertrude Bell Archive. www.gerty.ncl.ac.uk/diaries/d750.

Bernhard, M. L. 1956. "Topographie d'Aléxandrie: Le tombeau d'Alexandre et le mausoleum d'Auguste." *Revue Archéologique* 47: 129–156.

Bevan, E. R. 1927. *The House of Ptolemy.* London: Methuen.

Bey, Mahmoud. 1872. *Mémoire sur l'antique Alexandrie, ses Faubourgs et environs découverts.* Copenhagen.

Bianchi, Robert S. 1993. "Hunting Alexander's Tomb." *Archaeology* 46: 54–55.

_____. 1995. "Alexander's Tomb . . . Not." *Archaeology* 48: 58–60.

Biddle, Martin. 1999. *The Tomb of Christ.* Sutton, U.K.: Stroud.

Bierbrier, M. L. 1999. "The Acquisition by the British Museum of Antiquities Discovered During the French Invasion of Egypt." In *Studies in Egyptian Antiquities: A Tribute to T. G. H. James*, edited by W. V. Davies, pp. 111–113, 148–149. British Museum Occasional Paper 123. London: British Museum Press.

Borza, E. N. 1987. "The Royal Macedonian Tombs and the Paraphernalia of Alexander the Great." *Phoenix* 41: 105–121.

_____. 1990. *In the Shadow of Olympus: The Emergence of Macedon.* Princeton: Princeton University Press.

Borza, E. N., and J. Reames-Zimmerman. 2000. "Some New Thoughts on the Death of Alexander the Great." *Ancient World* 31, no. 1: 22–30.

Bosworth, A. B. 1988. *Conquest and Empire: The Reign of Alexander the Great.* Cambridge: Cambridge University Press.

_____. 1996. "Alexander, Euripides, and Dionysus: The Motivation for Apotheosis." In *Transitions to Empire: Essays in Honor of E. Badian*, edited by W. Wallace ands E. M. Harris, pp. 140–166. Norman: University of Oklahoma Press.

_____. 2002. *The Legacy of Alexander: Politics, Warfare, and Propaganda Under the Successors.* Oxford: Oxford University Press.

Bradley, Scott. 2004. *Selected Letters of Libanius From the Age of Constantius to Julian.* Liverpool, U.K.: Liverpool University Press.

Breccia, Evaristo. 1907. *Rapport sur la marche du Service du Musée.* Alexandria: Musée Gréco-Romain.

_____. 1908. "Fouilles et trouvailles: La Nécropole De l'Ibrahmieh." *Rapport sur la marche du Service du Musée Pendant l'Année 1907*, pp. 4–7. Alexandria: Musée Gréco-Romain.

_____. 1922. *Alexandrea ad Aegyptum*. Alexandria: Bergamo.

_____. 1932. *La Musée gréco-romano 1925–1931*. Alexandria: Bergamo.

Broneer, O. 1941. *The Lion Monument at Amphipolis*. Cambridge: Harvard University Press.

Brown, K. S. 1998. "Contests of Heritage and the Politics of Preservation in the Former Yugoslav Republic of Macedonia." In *Archaeology Under Fire: Nationalism, Politics, and Heritage in the Eastern Mediterranean and Middle East*, edited by Lynn Meskell, pp. 68–86. London: Routledge.

Browne, W. G. 1800. *Nouveau voyage dans le Haute et Basse Egypte, La Syrie, le Dar Four, où aucun Européen n'avoit pénétré; Fait depuis les années 1792 jusqu'en 1798*. Paris.

Bruhn, J. A. 1993. *Coins and Costume in Late Antiquity*. Washington, D.C.: Dumbarton Oaks Research Library and Collection.

Budge, E. A. Wallis. 1961. *Amulets and Talismans*. New York: University Books.

Butler, A. J. [1902] 1978. *The Arab Conquest of Egypt and the Last Thirty Years of the Roman Dominion*. 2nd ed. Revised by P. M. Fraser. Oxford: Clarendon.

Caesar, Julius. 1914. *The Civil Wars*. Translated by A. G. Peskett. Loeb Classical Library. Cambridge: Harvard University Press.

Caillaud, Frederic. 1923–1927. *Voyage a Meroë*. Paris: L'Imprimerie Royale.

Cartledge, Paul. 2004. *Alexander the Great: The Hunt for a New Past*. London: Macmillan.

Cawkwell, G. L. 2003. "The Deification of Alexander the Great: A Note." In *Alexander the Great: A Reader*, edited by Ian Worthington, pp. 263–272. London: Routledge.

Christides, Vassilios. 2000. "The Tomb of Alexander the Great in Arabic Sources." In *Hunter of the East: Studies in Honour of C. E. Bosworth*, edited by I. Netton, 1:165–173. Leiden: Brill.

Chrysostom, Saint John. 1889. *Nicene and Post-Nicene Fathers of the Christian Church*. Vol. 9, *Saint Chrysostom, On the Priesthood; Ascetic Treatises; Select Homilies and Letters; Homilies on the Statues*. Vol. 12, *Homilies on the Second Corinthians*. Edited by Philip Schaff. Edinburgh: T & T Clark.

_____. 2004. Instructions to Catechumans: Second Instruction. www.ccel.org/ccel/schaff/npnf109.

Chugg, Andrew. 2002a. "The Sarcophagus of Alexander the Great?" *Greece and Rome* 49, no. 1: 8–26.

_____. 2002b. "The Sarcophagus of Alexander the Great." *Minerva* 13, no. 5: 33–36.

_____. 2004a. "Alexander's Final Resting Place." *History Today* 54, no. 7: 17–23.

_____. 2004b. *The Lost Tomb of Alexander the Great*. London: Periplus.

_____. 2004c. A Candidate for the First Tomb of Alexander the Great. www.alexanderstomb.com.

Clark, Victoria. 2004. *Holy Fire: The Battle for Christ's Tomb*. London: Macmillan.

Clarke, Edward Daniel. 1805. *The Tomb of Alexander: A Dissertation on the Sarcophagus Brought back from Alexandria and now in the British Museum*. Cambridge: Cambridge University Press.

_____. 1807. *A Letter Addressed to the Gentlemen of the British Museum. By the author of the Dissertation on The Alexandrian Sarcophagus (E.D. Clarke)*. Cambridge: R. Watts.

Clayton, P., and M. Price, eds. 1989. *The Seven Wonders of the Ancient World*. London: Routledge.

Coarelli, Filippo, and Yvon Thébert. 1988. "Architecture funéraire et pouvoir: Réflexions sur l'hellénisme numide." *Mélange de l'Ecole française de Rome, Antiquité* 100, no. 2: 761–818.

Cohen, Ada. 1997. *The Alexander Mosaic: Stories of Victory and Defeat.* Cambridge: Cambridge University Press.

Coleman, T. 2001. *Nelson: The Man and the Legend.* London: Bloomsbury.

Danforth, L. M. 2003. "Alexander the Great and the Macedonian conflict." In *Brill's Companion to Alexander the Great,* edited by J. Roisman, pp. 347–364. Leiden: Brill.

Davies, Penelope J. E. 2000. *Death and the Emperor: Roman Imperial Funerary Monuments from Augustus to Marcus Aurelius.* Cambridge: Cambridge University Press.

Denon, Vivant. [1802] 1986. *Travels in Upper and Lower Egypt.* 2 vols. London: Darf.

Dio, Cassius. 1982. *Dio's Roman History.* Edited by G. P. Goold. London: Heinemann.

Diodorus Siculus. *Library of History.* Vol. 7, edited by C. L. Sherman. Loeb Classical Library. Cambridge: Harvard University Press, 1952. Vol. 8 (XVI.66–95.XVII), edited by C. B. Welles. Loeb Classical Library. Cambridge: Harvard University Press, 1963. Vol. 9 (XVIII–XIX.65), edited by R. M. Geer. Loeb Classical Library. Cambridge: Harvard University Press, 1967.

Dodds, E. R. [1951] 1997. *The Greeks and the Irrational.* Berkeley: University of California Press.

Donski, Alexander. 2003. *The Descendants of Alexander the Great of Macedon: The Arguments and Evidence That Today's Macedonians Are Descendants of the Ancient Macedonians.* Sydney: Macedonian Literary Association Grigor Prlichev.

Doxiadis, Euphrosyne. 1995. *The Mysterious Fayum Portraits: Faces from Ancient Egypt.* London: Thames & Hudson.

Durrell, Lawrence. 1966. Letters to the editor. Alexander's Tomb. *Times Literary Supplement,* April 7, p. 295.

———. 2001. *The Alexandria Quartet.* London: Faber & Faber.

Dzielska, Maria. 1995. *Hypatia of Alexandria.* Cambridge: Harvard University Press.

Eddy, S. K. 1961. *The King Is Dead: Studies in the Near Eastern Resistance to Hellenism, 334–31 BC.* Lincoln: University of Nebraska Press.

El-Abbadi, Mostafa. 2004. "The Alexandria Library in History." In *Alexandria, Real and Imagined,* edited by A. Hirst and M. Silk, pp 167–183. Aldershot, U.K.: Ashgate.

El-Daly, Okasha. 2005. *Egyptology: The Missing Millennium, Ancient Egypt in Medieval Arabic Writings.* London: UCL Press.

Ellis, J. R. 1976. *Philip II and Macedonian Imperialism.* London: Thames & Hudson.

Ellis, Walter M. 1994. *Ptolemy of Egypt.* London: Routledge.

Empereur, Jean-Yves, ed. 1997. *ΪΙ ÔÁöΪΙ ÔΪÕ MEÃÁËÏŸ ÁËÂÎÁÄÑÏÕ.* (Hoi Taphoi tou Megalou Alexandrou/The Tombs of Alexander the Great). Athens: ÅÑÌÁÌÁÓ.

———. 1998. *Alexandria Rediscovered.* London: British Museum Press.

———. 2000. *A Short Guide to the Graeco-Roman Museum Alexandria.* Alexandria: Harpocrates.

Engels, Donald. 1978. "A Note on Alexander's Death." *Classical Philology* 73, no. 3: 224–228.

Erskine, Andrew. 2002. "Life After Death: Alexandria and the Body of Alexander." *Greece & Rome* 49, no. 2: 163–179.

Fakharani, Fawzi el. 1964. "An Investigation into the Views Concerning the Location of the Tomb of Alexander the Great." *Bulletin of the Faculty of Arts, Alexandria University* 18: 169–199.

_____. 1999. "The Location of the Royal Ptolemaic Necropolis and the Sema of Alexander." *Proceedings of the International Congress Alexander the Great: From Macedonia to the Oikoumene, Veria 27–31 May.*

Fakhry, Ahmed. 1944. *The Egyptian Deserts: Siwah Oasis, Its History and Antiquities.* Cairo: Service des Antiquités de l'Egypte.

_____. [1990] 2004. *Siwa Oasis.* Cairo: American University in Cairo Press.

Fauvelet de Bourienne, Louis Antoine. 1891. *Memoirs of Napoleon Bonaparte.* New York: Scribner's.

Fedak, Janos. 1990. *Monumental Tombs of the Hellenistic Age.* Toronto: University of Toronto Press.

Finnestad, Ragnild Bjerre. 1998. "Temples of the Ptolemaic and Roman Periods: Ancient Traditions in New Contexts." In *Temples of Ancient Egypt*, edited by Byron Shafer, pp. 185–237. London: I. B. Tauris.

Forlati, Ferdinando. 1975. *La Basilica Di San Marco Attraverso I Suoi Restauri.* Trieste: Edizioni Lint.

Forster, E. M. [1922] 2004. *Alexandria: A History and a Guide and Pharos and Pharillon.* Edited by Miriam Allott. Cairo: American University in Cairo Press.

Fraser, Peter M. 1962. "Some Alexandrian Forgeries." *Proceedings of the British Academy* 47: 243–250.

Fredericksmeyer, Ernest A. 1966. "The Ancestral Rites of Alexander the Great." *Classical Philology* 61, no. 3: 179–182.

_____. 1972. *Ptolemaic Alexandria.* 3 vols. Oxford: Clarendon.

Fulghum, Mary Margaret. 2001. "Coins Used as Amulets in Late Antiquity." In *Between Magic and Religion: Interdisciplinary Studies in Ancient Mediterranean Religion and Society*, edited by S. R. Asirvatham, C. O. Pache, and J. Watrous, pp. 139–147. Lanham, MD: Rowman & Littlefield.

Gaber, S., A. A. El-Fiky, A. S. Shagar, and M. Mohamaden. 1999. "Electrical Resistivity Exploration of the Royal Ptolemaic Necropolis in the Royal Quarter of Ancient Alexandria, Egypt." *Archaeological Prospection* 6: 1–10.

Girling, Richard. 2003. "Death of a Tyrant." *Sunday Times Magazine,* October 12, pp. 22–31.

Goldhill, Simon. 2004. *Love, Sex, and Tragedy: How the Ancient World Shapes Our Lives.* London: John Murray.

Grafton, Milne, J. 1916. "Greek and Roman Tourists in Alexandria." *Journal of Egyptian Archaeology* 3: 76–80.

Grecoreport. 2001–2002. Alexander the Great's Tomb at the Oasis of Ammon Ra. www.grecoreport.com/grekili_2001–2002.htm.

_____. 2002. Review of Liana Souvaltzi's book *The Tomb of Alexander the Great at the Siwa Oasis.* www.grecoreport.com/the_tomb_of_alexander_the_great_at_the_siwa_oasis.htm.

Green, Peter. 1989. "The Macedonian Connection." In *Classical Bearings: Interpreting Ancient History and Culture*, pp. 151–164. London: Thames & Hudson.

_____. 1990. *Alexander to Actium: The Hellenistic Age.* London: Thames & Hudson.

_____. 1991. *Alexander of Macedon 356–323 B.C.: A Historical Biography.* Berkeley: University of California Press.

_____. 2004. "Alexander's Alexandria." In *From Ikaria to the Stars: Classical Mythification, Ancient and Modern*, 172–196. Austin: University of Texas Press.

Greenwalt, W. S. 1988. "Argaeus, Ptolemy II, and Alexander's Corpse." *Ancient History Bulletin* 2, no. 2: 39–41.

Griffith, G. T. 1979. "The First Adventures Abroad." In *A History of Macedonia.* Vol. 2, *550–336 B.C.*, edited by N. G. L. Hammond and G. T. Griffith, pp. 216–258. Oxford: Clarendon.

Grimm, Günter. 1996. "City Planning?" In *Alexandria and Alexandrianism: Papers Delivered at a Symposium Organized by the J. Paul Getty Museum and The Getty Center for the History of Art and Humantities*, edited by K. Hamma, pp. 55–74. Malibu, CA: J. Paul Getty Museum.

———. 1998. *Alexandria: Die erste Königsstadt der hellenististischen Welt.* Mainz am Rhein: Verlag Philipp von Zabern.

———. 2004. "Alexanders letzte Ruhestätte." *Städel Jahr-buch* 19:374–385.

Haas, Christopher. 1997. *Alexandria in Late Antiquity: Topography and Social Conflict.* Baltimore, MD: Johns Hopkins University Press.

Hadjinicolaou, Nicos. 1997. "The Dispute About Alexander and His Glorification in the Visual Arts." In *Alexander the Great in European Art*, edited by Nicos Hadjininicolaou. Thessaloniki: Organization for the Cultural Capital of Europe. www.macedonian-heritage.gr.

Hamdy Bey, O., and T. Reinach. 1892. *Une nécropole royale à Sidon.* Paris: Leroux.

Hamilakis, Yannis, and Eleana Yalouri. 1999. "Sacralising the Past." *Archaeological Dialogues* 6, no. 2: 115–166.

Hammond, N. G. L. 1972. *A History of Macedonia.* Vol. 1, *Historical Geography and Prehistory.* Oxford: Clarendon.

———. 1982. "The Evidence for the Identity of the Royal Tombs at Vergina." In *Philip II, Alexander the Great, and the Macedonian Heritage*, edited by W. Lindsay Adams and Eugene N. Borza, pp. 111–127. Lanham, MD: University Press of America.

———. 1988a. "Alexander and the Macedonians." In *A History of Macedonia.* Vol. 3, *336–167 B.C.*, edited by N. G. L. Hammond and F. W. Walbank, pp. 86–94. Oxford: Clarendon.

———. 1988b. "The Legacy of Alexander and the Outbreak of Civil War Among the Macedonians." In *A History of Macedonia.* Vol. 3, *336–167 B.C.*, edited by N. G. L. Hammond and F. W. Walbank, pp. 95–122. Oxford: Clarendon.

———. 1988c. "The Ambition of Antigonus, the End of the Temenid House, and Claims to Kingship." In *A History of Macedonia.* Vol. 3, *336–167 B.C.*, edited by N. G. L. Hammond and F. W. Walbank, pp. 151–179. Oxford: Clarendon.

———. 1991. *The Miracle That Was Macedonia.* London: Sidgwick & Jackson.

Hammond, N. G. L., and G. T. Griffith. 1979. *A History of Macedonia.* Vol. 2, *550–336 B.C.* Oxford: Clarendon.

Hammond, N. G. L., and F. W. Walbank. 1988. *A History of Macedonia.* Vol. 3, *336–167 B.C.* Oxford: Clarendon.

Handler, Susan. 1971. "Architecture on the Roman Coins of Alexandria." *American Journal of Archaeology* 75, no. 1: 57–74.

Harptah, Richard. 1978. *Papst Paul III. Als Alexander der Grosse: Das Freskenprogramm der Sala Paolina in der Englesberg.* Berlin: De Gruyter.

Hassan, Fekri, ed. 2002. *Alexandria, Graeco-Roman Museum, A Thematic Guide.* Cairo: National Centre for Documentation of Cultural and Natural Heritage (CULTNAT) and The Supreme Council of Antiquities (S.C.A.).

Hawass, Zahi. 2000. *Valley of the Golden Mummies: The Greatest Egyptian Discovery Since Tutankhamun.* London: Virgin Books.

Heckel, Waldemar. 1992. *The Marshals of Alexander's Empire.* London: Routledge.

Heckel, Waldemar, and J. C. Yardley. 2004. *Alexander the Great: Historical Sources in Translation*. Oxford: Blackwell.

Heraclides. 1806. *The Tomb of Alexander Reviewed*. London.

Herodian. 1969. *History of the Empire*. Translated by C. R. Whittaker. Loeb Classical Library. Cambridge: Harvard University Press.

Herodotus. 1990. *The Persian Wars*. I. Books 1–2. Translated by A. D. Godley. Loeb Classical Library. Cambridge: Harvard University Press.

Hogarth, D. G., and E. F. Benson. 1895. "Report on Prospects of Research in Alexandria." *Egypt Exploration Fund*, pp. 1–33.

Hölbl, Günther. 2001. *A History of the Ptolemaic Empire*. London: Routledge.

Holt, Frank L. 2001. "Dead Kings Are Hard to Find." *Saudi Aramco World* 52, no. 3: 10–11.

———. 2003. *Alexander the Great and the Mystery of the Elephant Medallions*. Berkeley: University of California Press.

Homer. 1950. *The Iliad*. Translated by E. V. Rieu. Harmondsworth, U.K.: Penguin.

Hornblower, Simon. 1982. *Mausolus*. Oxford: Clarendon.

Hornung, Erik. 2001. *The Secret Lore of Egypt: Its Impact on the West*. Ithaca, NY: Cornell University Press.

Houlihan, Patrick F. 2003. "The Peacock." *Ancient Egypt Magazine* 4, no. 3. www.ancient egyptmagazine.com.

Jacoby, Felix. 1923–1930, 1940–1958. *Die Fragmente der griechischen Historiker*. Berlin.

Jenni, H. 1986. *Das Dekorationsprogramma des Sarkophages Nektanebos' II*. Geneva: Éditions de Belles-Lettres.

Jeppesen, K., F. Hojlund, and K. Aaris-Sorensen. 1981. *The Mausolleion at Halikarnassos*. Vol. 1, *The Sacrificial Deposits*. Aarhus.

Jeppesen, K., and A. Luttrell. 1986. *The Mausolleion at Halikarnassos*. Vol. 2, *The Written Sources and Their Archaeological Background*. Aarhus: Jutland Archaeological Society.

Johnson, Paul. 1978. *A History of Christianity*. Harmondsworth, U.K.: Penguin.

Jondet, M. Gaston. 1921. *Mémoires presentes a la Societe Sultanieh de Geographie et publies sous les auspices de a Hautesse Ahmed Fouad, Sultan d'Egypte*. Vol. 2, *Atlas Historique de la ville et des portes d'Alexandrie*. Cairo: Imprimerie de L'Institut Francais.

Josephus. 1926. *The Life Against Apion*. Translated by H. St. J. Thackeray. Loeb Classical Library. Cambridge: Harvard University Press.

Kamal, Ahmed Bey. 1906. "Sébennytos et son temple." *Annales du Service des Antiquités de l'Égypte* (Cairo) 7: 87–94.

Kamil, Jill. 2002. *Christianity in the Land of the Pharaohs: The Coptic Orthodox Church*. Cairo: American University in Cairo Press.

Karageorghis, V. 1969. *Salamis in Cyprus*. London: Thames & Hudson.

Keeley, Edmund. 1976. *Cavafy's Alexandria*. Princeton: Princeton University Press.

Koldewey, Robert. 1914. *The Excavations at Babylon*. London: Macmillan.

Laistner, M. L. W. [1951] 1968. *Christianity and Pagan Culture in the Later Roman Empire*. Ithaca, NY: Cornell University Press.

Lambert, Royston. 1997. *Beloved and God: Story of Hadrian and Antinous*. London: Weidenfeld & Nicolson.

Lane Fox, Robin. 1978. *Alexander the Great*. London: Futura.

———. 1980. *The Search for Alexander*. London: Allen Lane.

———. 1986. *Pagans and Christians in the Mediterranean World from the Second Century AD to the Conversion of Constantine*. London: Penguin.

Lauer, Jean-Philippe. 1976. *Saqqara: The Royal Cemetery of Memphis: Excavations and Discoveries Since 1850*. London: Thames & Hudson.

Lauer, Jean-Philippe, and Charles Pierre Picard. 1955. *Les statues Ptolémaiques du Sarapieion de Memphis*. Paris: Institut d'Art et d'Archéologie de l'Université de Paris.

Lazardis, D. 1973. "The Organization of the City-State of Amphipolis." *Ekistics* 35: 35–39.

Lettre à M. Dacier, secrétaire perpétuel de l'Académie royale des inscriptions et belles-lettres relative à l'alphabet des hiéroglyphs phonétiques employés par les Égyptiens pour inscrire sur leurs monuments les titres, les noms, et les surnoms des souverains grecs et romains. 1822. Paris.

Libanius. 1977. *Libanius: Selected Works*. Vol. 2, *Selected Orations*. Translated by A. F. Norman. Loeb Classical Library. Cambridge: Harvard University Press.

Lorber, Catherine C. 1990. *Amphipolis: The Coinage in Silver and Gold*. Los Angeles: Numismatic Fine Arts International.

Lucan. 1928. *Pharsalia*. Translated by J. D. Duff. Loeb Classical Library. Cambridge: Harvard University Press.

Macfarlane, Alan, and Gerry Martin. 2002. *The Glass Bathyscaphe: How Glass Changed the World*. London: Profile.

Maguire, H. 1977. "Magic and Money in the Early Middle Ages." *Speculum* 72: 1037–1054.

Malim, Fathi. 2001. *Oasis, Siwa: From the Inside, Traditions, Customs, and Magic*. Al Katan.

Mariette, Auguste. 1856. *Choix de monuments et dessins Découverts ou exécutés pendant le déblaiement du Sérapéum de Memphis*. Paris.

Marlowe, J. 1971. *The Golden Age of Alexandria: From Its Foundation by Alexander the Great in 331 BC to its Capture by the Arabs in 642 AD*. London: Victor Gollancz.

Marr, John S., and Charles H. Calisher. 2003. "Alexander the Great and West Nile Encephalitis." *Emerging Infectious Diseases* 9, no. 12: 1599–1603.

McKechnie, Paul. 1995. "Diodorus Siculus and Hephaestion's Pyre." *Classical Quarterly* 45: 418–432.

McKenzie, Judith. 2003. "Glimpsing Alexandria from Archaeological Evidence." *Journal of Roman Archaeology* 16: 35–63.

Miller, S. G. 1986. "Alexander's Funeral Cart." *Ancient Macedonia* 4: 401–412.

———. 1993. *The Tomb of Lyson and Kallikles: A Painted Macedonian Tomb*. Mainz am Rhein: Verlag Philipp von Zabern.

Mørkholm, O. 1991. *Early Hellenistic Coinage*. Cambridge: Cambridge University Press.

Müller, Kurt F. 1905. *Der Leichenwagen Alexanders des Grosses*. Leipzig.

Musée du Petit Palais. 1998. *La Gloire d'Alexandrie*. Paris: Musée du Petit Palais.

Myśliwiec, Karol. 2000. "The Tombs of Alexander." In *The Twilight of Ancient Egypt: First Millennium B.C.E.*, edited by K. Mysliwiec, pp. 185–187. Ithaca, NY: Cornell University Press.

Nena, Marie-Dominique. 1993. "Éléments de incrustation en verre des nécropoles alexandrines." *Annales du 12 congrès de l'Association internationale pour l'histoire du verre*. Vienna, 1991.

———. 1998. "Le rôle d'Alexandrie et de l'Égypte dans les arts verriers à l'époque Hellenistique." In *La Gloire d'Alexandrie*, pp. 152–154. Paris: Musée du Petit Palais.

Newton, Charles Thomas. 1862. *A History of Discoveries at Halicarnassus, Cnidus, and Branchidae*. London.

Oates, J. 1986. *Babylon*. London: Thames & Hudson.

Oldach, D. W., Eugene N. Borza, and R. M. Benitez. 1998. "A Mysterious Death." *New England Journal of Medicine* 38:1764–1769.

Oxyrhynchus Papyri. 1898–2001. *The Graeco-Roman Memoirs of the Egypt Exploration Society.* 67 volumes to date. www.papyrology.ox.ac.uk. www.ees.ac.uk.

Palagia, O. 2002. "Hephaestion's Pyre and the Royal Hunt of Alexander." In *Alexander the Great in Fact and Fiction*, edited by A. B. Bosworth and E. J. Baynham, pp. 167–206. Oxford: Oxford University Press.

Papamarinopoulos, St.P., A. Liosis, L. Polymenakos, P. Stephanopoulos, and K. Limnaeou-Papakosta. 2003. "In Search of the Royal Ptolemaic Cemetery in Central Alexandria, Egypt: The First Contact." *Archaeological Prospection* 10: 193–211.

Papazois, Triantafyllos D. 2003. The Royal Tomb II at Vergina Reveals Alexander the Great. http://tdpapazois.gr.

Pausanias. 1918. *Description of Greece.* Vol. 1. Translated by W. H. S. Jones. Loeb Classical Library. Cambridge: Harvard University Press.

Payne, Martha. 1991. "Alexander the Great: Myth, the Polis, and Afterward." In *Myth and the Polis*, edited by Dora C. Pozzi and John M. Wickersham, pp. 164–181. Ithaca, NY: Cornell University Press.

Pearson, Birger, and James Goehring, eds. 1986. *The Roots of Egyptian Christianity.* Philadelphia: Fortress.

Petrie, W. M. F., and E. Mackay. 1915. *Heliopolis, Kafr Ammar, and Shurafa.* London: School of Archaeology in Egypt, University College London.

Pfrommer, Michael. 2001. *Greek Gold from Hellenistic Egypt.* Los Angeles: Getty Publications.

Pliny. 1938–1962. *Natural History.* Vols. 1–10. Translated by H. Rackham. Loeb Classical Library. Cambridge: Harvard University Press.

Plutarch. 1979. "Alexander." In *The Age of Alexander*, pp. 252–334. Harmondsworth, U.K.: Penguin.

Pory, J. 1896. *The History and Description of Africa and of the notable things therein contained written by Al Wezaz Al-Fasi, a Moor, baptised as Giovanni Leone, but better known as Leo Africanus done into English in the year 1600, by John Pory.* Edited by Robert Brown. 3 vols. London: Hakluyt.

Prag, John, and Richard Neave. 1999. *Making Faces: Using Forensic and Archaeological Evidence.* London: British Museum Press.

Price, M. J. 1991. *The Coinage in the Name of Alexander the Great and Philip Arrhidaeus.* London: British Museum.

Quintus Curtius Rufus. 1988. *The History of Alexander.* London: Penguin.

Ray, J. D. 1978. "The World of North Saqqara." *World Archaeology* 10: 149–157.

Reames-Zimmerman, Jeanne. 2001. "The Mourning of Alexander the Great." *Syllecta Classica* 12: 98–145.

Reames-Zimmerman, Jeanne. 2004. *Alexander's Tomb (and Hephaistion's).* www.livejournal.com/community/megalexandros/1185.html.

Rice, Ellen E. 1981. *The Grand Procession of Ptolemy Philadelphus.* Oxford: Oxford University Press.

Rodziewicz, M. 1995. "Ptolemaic Street Directions in Basilea." In *Alessandria e il Mondo Ellenistico-Romano, Congrès Alexandrie*, pp. 227–235. Rome, 1992.

Roger, J. 1939. "Le Monument au Lion d'Amphipolis." *Bulletin de correspondence hellénique* 63: 4–42.

Rohlfs, Gerhard. 1876. *Drei Monate in der libyschen Wüste.* Berlin.

Rowlandson, Jane, and Andrew Harker. 2004. "Roman Alexandria from the Perspective of the Papyri." In *Alexandria: Real and Imagined*, edited by A. Hirst and M. Silk, pp. 79–111. Aldershot, U.K.: Ashgate.

Said, E. W. 1991. *Orientalism: Western Conceptions of the Orient*. London: Penguin.

Samartzidou, S. 1993. "Amphipolis." In *Greek Civilization, Macedonia, Kingdom of Alexander the Great*, edited by Julia Vokotopoulou, pp. 57–59. Athens: Kapon Editions.

Sandys, George. 1617. *Relation of a Journey Begun A.D. 1610*. London: W. Barrett.

Sauer, E. Berhard. 2003. *Archaeology of Religious Hatred in the Roman and Early Medieval World*. Stroud: Tempus.

Schwartz, Stephan A. 2001. *The Alexandria Project: The Engineering of Psi*. Vol. 2. Lincoln, NE: Authors Guild Backinprint.com edition. iUniverse.com.

_____. 2003. *Remote Viewing: The Road to Limitless Self*. New York: HarperCollins.

Shayegan, Rahim. 2005. "The Cult of Alexander the Great Under the Late Severans and Its Impact upon the Political Ideology of the Late Arsacids (Parthians) and the Early Sasanians." In *Philostratus's Heroikos: Religion and Cultural Identity in the Third Century C.E.* Edited by Ellen Bradshaw Aitken and Jennifer K. Mclean. Leiden: Brill.

Shortland, A. J. 2004. "Evaporites of the Wadi Natrun: Seasonal and Annual variation and Its Implication for Ancient Exploitation." *Archaeometry* 46, no. 4: 497–516.

Sly, Dorothy I. 1996. *Philo's Alexandria*. London: Routledge.

Solé, Robert, and Dominique Valbelle. 2002. *The Rosetta Stone: The Story of the Decoding of Hieroglyphics*. London: Profile Books.

Sonnini de Manoncour, Charles S. 1800. *Voyage dans la Haute et Basse Egypte*. Paris: Buisson.

Souvaltzi, Liana. 1993. "Discovering a Macedonian Tomb in Siwa Oasis." In *Sesto Congresso Internazionale di Egittologia: Atti*, edited by Silvio Curto et al., 2:511–514.

_____. 2002. *The Tomb of Alexander the Great at the Siwa Oasis: The History of the Archaeological Excavation and Its Political Background*. Athens: Editions Georgiadis.

Sozomenus. 1964. "Ecclesiastical History." In *Patrologia Graeca*. Vol. 67. Edited by J-P Migne. Paris: Garnier.

Spencer, Diana. 2002. *The Roman Alexander: Reading a Cultural Myth*. Exeter: Exeter University Press.

St. Clair, W. 1998. *Lord Elgin and The Marbles: The Controversial History of the Parthenon Sculptures*. Oxford: Oxford University Press.

Stambaugh, John E. 1972. *Sarapis Under the Early Ptolemies*. Leiden: Brill.

Stevenson, S. W., C. Roach Smith, and F. W. Madden. 1889. *Dictionary of Roman Coins*. London: George Bell.

Stewart, Andrew. 1993. *Faces of Power: Alexander's Image and Hellenistic Politics*. Berkeley: University of California Press.

Stoneman, Richard, trans. 1991. *The Greek Alexander Romance*. Harmondsworth, U.K.: Penguin.

Stoneman, R., ed. and trans. 1994a. *Legends of Alexander the Great*. London:Everyman.

Stoneman, R. 1994b. *Palmyra and Its Empire: Zenobia's Revolt Against Rome*. Ann Arbor: University of Michigan Press.

_____. 1995. "Naked Philosophers: The Brahmans in the Alexander Historians and the Alexander Romance." *Journal of Hellenic Studies* 105: 88–114.

Strabo. 1917–1932. *Geography*. Vols. 1–8. Translated by H. S. Jones. Loeb Classical Library. Cambridge: Harvard University Press.

Suetonius. 1913–1914. *Lives of the Caesars*. Translated by J. C. Rolfe. Loeb Classical Library. Cambridge: Harvard University Press.

_____ [1957] 1979. *The Twelve Caesars*. Translated by R. Graves and M. Grant. London: Penguin.

Synaxarium. 2005. Synaxarium (Lives of Saints): The Departure of the Honorable Father Saint Theophilus 23rd Pope of Alexandria. www.copticchurch.net.

Tarn, W. W. 1948. *Alexander the Great*. Cambridge: Cambridge University Press.

Tatius, Achilles. 1917. *Clitophon and Leucippe*. Translated by S. Gaselee. Cambridge: Harvard University Press, Loeb.

Taylor, Lily Ross. 1927. "The Cult of Alexander at Alexandria." *Classical Philology* 22, no. 2: 162–169.

_____. 1930. "Alexander and the Serpent of Alexandria." *Classical Philology* 25, no. 4: 375–378.

Thompson, Dorothy J. 1988. *Memphis Under the Ptolemies*. Princeton: Princeton University Press.

Thompson, Jonathan, and Nicholas Pyke. 2004. "Does the Tomb of St Mark in Venice Really Contain the Bones of Alexander the Great?" *Independent*, June 16.

Tiradritti, Francesco. 1999. *The Treasures of the Egyptian Museum*. Cairo: American University of Cairo Press.

Tonsing, Ernst F. 2002. "From Prince to Demi-God: The Formation and Evolution of Alexander's Portrait." In *Alexander's Revenge: Hellenistic Culture Through the Centuries*, edited by Jon M. Asgeirsson and Nancy van Deusen, pp. 85–109. Reykjavik: University of Iceland Press.

Touratsoglou, Ioannis. 1995. *Macedonia: History-Monuments-Museums*. Athens: Ekdotike Athenon.

Trapp, M. B. 2004. "Images of Alexandria in the Writings of the Second Sophistic." In *Alexandria, Real and Imagined*, edited by A. Hirst and M. Silk, pp. 113–132. Aldershot, U.K.: Ashgate.

Tzalas, Harry E. 1993. "The Tomb of Alexander the Great: The History and the Legend in the Greco-Roman and Arab Times." *Graeco-Arabica* 5: 329–354.

_____. 1998. The Tomb of Alexander the Great: The History and the Legend in Greco-Roman and Arab Times. www.greece.org/Alexandria/tomb2.

_____. 2004. "Fantastic Discoveries in Archaeology: The Case of the Tomb of Alexander the Great." In *Europe, Hellas, and Egypt: Complementary antipodes During Late Antiquity*, edited by Amanda-Alice Maravelia, pp. 67–88. British Archaeological Reports S1218. Oxford: Archaeopress.

Vedette [W. H. Fitchett]. 1899. *Deeds That Won the Empire: Historic Battle Scenes*. London: Smith, Elder.

Venit, Marjorie Susan. 2002. *Monumental Tombs of Ancient Alexandria: The Theater of the Dead*. Cambridge: Cambridge University Press.

Vermeule, Cornelius. 1980. "The Catalogue." In *The Search for Alexander: An Exhibition*, edited by Katerina Rhomiopoulou, Ariel Herrmann, and Cornelius Vermeule, pp. 95–151. Boston: New York Graphic Society.

Vivian, Cassandra. 1990. *Islands of the Blest: A Guide to the Oases and Western Desert of Egypt*. Monessen, PA: Trade Routes Enterprises.

Vokotopoulou, Julia, ed. 1993. *Greek Civilization, Macedonia, Kingdom of Alexander the Great*. Athens: Kapon Editions.

Von Graeve, Volkmar. 1970. *Der Alexandersarkophag und seine Werkstatt.* Istanbuler Forschungen 28. Berlin: Gebr. Mann Verlag.

Von Minutoli, Heinrich. 1824. *Reise zum Tempel des Jupiter Ammon.* Berlin.

Wace, A. J. B. 1948. "The Sarcophagus of Alexander the Great." *Farouk I University, Bulletin of the Faculty of Arts* 4: 1–11. Alexandria.

Walbank, F. W. 1988. "Antigonus Gonatas: The Early Years (276–261 B.C.)." In *A History of Macedonia.* Vol. 3, *336–167 B.C.*, edited by N. G. L. Hammond and F. W. Walbank, pp. 259–289. Oxford: Clarendon.

Walker, P. W. L. 1990. *Holy City, Holy Places? Christian Attitudes to Jerusalem and the Holy Land in the Fourth Century.* Oxford: Clarendon.

Waywell, G. B. 1978. *The Free-Standing Sculptures of the Mausoleum at Halicarnassus.* London: British Museum Press.

———. 1989. The Mausoleum at Halicarnassus. In *The Seven Wonders of the Ancient World*, edited by Peter Clayton and Martin Price, pp 100–123. London: Routledge.

Williams, Stephen. 2000. *Diocletian and the Roman Recovery.* London: Routledge.

Wolf, Anne. 2004. "Merchants, Pilgrims, Naturalists: Alexandria Through European Eyes from the Fourteenth to Sixteenth Century." In *Alexandria: Real and Imagined,* edited by A. Hirst and M. Silk, pp 199–225. Aldershot, U.K.: Ashgate.

Wolohojian, A. M. 1969. *The Romance of Alexander the Great by Pseudo-Callisthenes: Translated from the Armenian Version.* New York: Columbia University Press.

Worthington, Ian, ed. 2003. "Alexander and Deification." In *Alexander the Great: A Reader,* edited by Ian Worthington, pp. 236–241. London: Routledge.

Yalouris, Nicholas. 1980. "Alexander and His Heritage." In *The Search for Alexander: An Exhibition,* edited by Katerina Rhomiopoulou, Ariel Herrmann, and Cornelius Vermeule, pp. 1–20. Boston: New York Graphic Society.

Zenobius. 1839. *Proverbia.* Edited by E. L. von Leutsch and F. G. Schneidewin. Corpus Paroemiographorum Graecorum 1. Göttingen.

Zogheb, Alexandre Max de. 1910. *Études sur l'ancienne Alexandrie.* Paris.

INDEX